THE GREAT BRITISH
BAKING SHOW

A Bake for
ALL SEASONS

THE GREAT BRITISH
BAKING SHOW

A Bake for
ALL SEASONS

sphere

CONTENTS

Foreword by Paul & Prue 6

Introduction 11

Meet the Bakers 14

A Baker's Kitchen 18

A Baker's Larder 23

CHAPTER ONE
SPRING 30

CHAPTER TWO
SUMMER 86

CHAPTER THREE
AUTUMN 154

CHAPTER FOUR
WINTER 212

Conversion Tables & Cook's Notes 268

Baking Tips & Techniques 270

Inspire me... 272

Index 281

Acknowledgements 288

A NOTE FROM PAUL

In many ways, the last year, as we've come in and out of lockdowns, has given us a slower pace of life. For those of us who were asked to work from home, or were furloughed, there was more time to bake and to cook in general. This meant more time to think about what we're eating, how far our produce has travelled to reach us, and whether or not we're eating it at the 'right' time of year. Talking to friends and family, I've noticed a frequently repeated theme of how the last year has taught us to appreciate more of what we have available immediately around us and how to use fresh, local ingredients to show off their best. All that makes a *Great British Bake Off* homage to seasonal baking a timely addition to the world of cook books.

My favourite time of year will always be Christmas. The months of November to January are a time when, if I'm baking, I love to bake sponge puddings with custard and of course mince pies, using traditional ingredients that are evocative of the cosiness of the season. That said, summer runs a close second – a time when it's a joy to be able to sit outside on a warm, sunny morning to indulge in a freshly made strawberry Danish.

This year, our fabulous bakers have again offered up some of their favourite family recipes, each with a seasonal lilt, and each offering a window into the bakers' private worlds. It's a privilege to get to know the bakers over their time in the tent and to see first-hand how much they appreciate flavour and texture in their bakes – and how intuitive they are about seasonality and the importance of buying fresh, local produce. These instincts are reflected throughout the recipes in this book – whether from Prue or me, the team behind *Bake Off*, or the bakers themselves. Whatever the time of year, choose something timely, bake it with love and enjoy it with friends – whether that's in the garden in summer, beside a roaring fire in winter, or anywhere in between.

A NOTE FROM PRUE

Seasonal produce has always been at the heart of my approach to cooking. If you use really fresh seasonal ingredients, you'll really taste the difference. And if your food hasn't had to travel half way across the world, it will not only put less strain on the environment, but it's also bound to taste better.

Each season brings its own culinary joys – warming pies in winter, spicy plum and ginger cakes in autumn and the bright colours of a delicious rhubarb tart in spring. But for me, summer trumps them all. The sheer abundance of fresh summer fruit and veg is an inspiration for the keen cook or baker. The recipes in the summer section of the book are perfect for a jubilant summer picnic or garden party with friends and family. After so long living under Covid restrictions, don't we all need just such a celebration?

One of the few benefits of this horrific pandemic has been the boost it has given to baking. People who have never baked

anything before have got stuck in and had the satisfaction of producing really good cakes, biscuits, pies and puddings. And keen cooks and bakers have upped their game to make *Bake Off*-worthy creations.

This year we spent six weeks of summer in the *Bake Off* tent, and it was wonderful to get to know the bakers as the weeks went by. Every year I learn so much from them, and every year I come home with a clutch of recipes. They are all so creative and talented, so open to new ideas and so knowledgeable about what is happening in the baking world. They always come up with new approaches to baking, original and delicious flavour combinations, and exciting ingredients I've barely heard of.

The recipes in this book celebrate the talent of the bakers, my own enthusiasm and Paul's too, and favourite bakes of the wider *Bake Off* team. This is a book packed full of deliciousness to take you through the whole year. Happy baking.

INTRODUCTION

Welcome to *The Great British Bake Off: A Bake for all Seasons*, a collection of sweet and savoury bakes from Paul, Prue and the team behind the show – as well as, of course, from our wonderful 2021 bakers themselves.

————

Modern life enables us – mostly – to use any ingredients in our cooking at any time in any place. Supermarkets provide us with strawberries in winter or blood oranges in spring. The joy of seeing the first of the year's asparagus appear in May has been lost over time – bunches of those delicious, aromatic green spears now appear all year round on supermarket shelves.

Of course, there is much to recommend the freedom of being able to bake and eat whatever we fancy whenever we fancy it, but any chef will tell you that a tomato only really tastes as glorious as a tomato can taste if you eat it in summer, picked from vines that have grown in soil best suited to the plant and kissed by the warmth of the warmest sun. Furthermore, seasonal produce – grown, harvested and eaten as Nature intended – generally has a far smaller carbon footprint than equivalent produce that may have ripened under artificial lamps or been flown thousands of miles in order to land on our plates at the 'wrong' time of year.

In 2020, demand for baking ingredients was up 3,400 per cent. Faced with a directive to minimise our trips outdoors, and with more time on our hands, we turned to making for ourselves staples – bread, cakes, biscuits – that we so casually drop into our shopping trolley in a 'normal' week. We began to realise – or perhaps, to remember – the great pleasure in starting from scratch. As a happy consequence, we began to select for our cooking and baking produce that was readily and easily available. As we avoided busier, out-of-town supermarkets with their long queues, we stayed closer to home, shopping at our local greengrocer and farmers' markets with their displays of cheerful, bountiful fruits and vegetables that were inevitably far more in line with what the season had to offer there and then than we might find at the supermarket. At the same time, long weekend walks not only provided escape, but also brought into sharp focus the abundance of food in our countryside (elderflowers, blackberries, wild garlic and more) and the layby signs inviting us to take armfuls of apples and leave a donation in the honesty box. We became unexpected foragers and we felt inspired to make sure the glut of windfalls didn't go to waste – there are jams and pickles to be made!

It's in this spirit of Nature's bounty that, a year on, the team from *The Great British Bake Off* has created *A Bake for All Seasons*.

This book both celebrates our bakers of 2021 and, more mindful than ever of the responsibility we all share for our environment, honours abundance as Nature intended.

Of course, seasonality is not just about what's on the trees or in the earth – time, celebrations and mood mark the seasons as much as an orange in winter or a gooseberry in summer. Celebrations such as Easter and Purim herald springtime, along with the sense of growth and new beginnings; summer talks of sunshine and holidays, picnics and fêtes, not to mention berries in abundance; autumn brings us the harvest, yes, but also Thanksgiving, which reminds us all, wherever we live, to be grateful for everything we have – a sense of belonging, togetherness and home, especially as the evenings draw in. And so to winter with its host of festivities – Christmas, of course, but also both western and eastern New Year celebrations, and – in spirit and mood – a sense of hunkering down with warm fires, cosy blankets and convivial cheer.

We've tried to capture all these elements of the seasons in this book – ingredients, but also the changing physical and emotional landscape of the year, bringing us back in touch with the natural rhythms of both land and mood.

USING THIS BOOK
Throughout the book you'll find coloured GF and Vg symbols on some recipes. These flag the gluten-free and vegan bakes (our vegan wedding cake on page 123 is to die for). Even if you aren't specifically looking for a free-from idea, we really encourage you to try these recipes – they have been developed with every tastebud and diet in mind, and are so full of flavour and texture, we think none of your guests will be able to tell the difference.

Remember, too, that there are lots of fruits and vegetables that are easily swapped when their season ends. The Strawberry & Clotted Cream Cake (see Summer, page 120), for example, would be equally delicious topped with blackberries in autumn; the Vegetable Samosas (see Autumn, page 181) can quickly become a springtime treat simply by substituting the squash and sweet potato for new potatoes and the spring greens or Brussels sprouts for the first, sweetest peas, fresh from their pods. Feel free to experiment with what you see appearing locally around you – these seasonal recipes are just the beginning.

Finally, we recognise that sometimes baking is about more than responding to the time of year. Who hasn't felt the call of a Beef & Potato Pies (see page 241) having been swept by a biting, wintry wind on an apparently springtime walk, or wanted an indulgent Mini Hummingbird Cake (see page 68) with a friend on an autumn afternoon huddled around the kitchen table? At the end of the book, then, as well as a standard index, we've provided a thematic index to group together the recipes according to their type. We hope this will inspire you to use the book creatively and intuitively and in as many fun and fulfilling ways as possible.

SEASONAL HARVESTS

This table provides a guide to vegetables and fruits in the recipes that are native to or widely grown in the UK, and gives the broad months of the year when they are at their best.

If you're growing your own, where in the UK you live, the direction your garden faces, and even small fluctuations in daylight hours, sunshine and rainfall can shift the perfect time to harvest.

Key to colours: ● Spring / ● Summer / ● Autumn / ● Winter

	JAN	FEB	MARCH	APRIL	MAY	JUNE	JULY	AUG	SEPT	OCT	NOV	DEC
Almonds								A	S	O		
Apples, Braeburn									S	O	N	
Apples, Bramley								A	S			
Apricots					M	J	J	A	S			
Asparagus					M	J	J	A	S			
Basil					M	J	J	A	S	O		
Beetroot	J					J	J	A	S	O	N	D
Blackberries								A	S	O		
Blackcurrants						J	J					
Blueberries								A	S	O		
Broccoli, purple spr		F	M	A	M	J	J	A	S	O		
Brussels sprouts	J	F	M							O	N	D
Carrots					M	J	J	A	S	O		
Cauliflower	J	F	M		M	J	J	A	S	O	N	D
Cherries						J	J	A				
Cherry blossom				A	M							
Chestnuts	J								S	O	N	D
Chives					M	J	J	A	S			
Cranberries										O	N	D
Elderflowers					M	J						
Fennel						J	J	A	S	O		
Figs							J	A	S	O		
French beans							J	A	S			
Gooseberries						J	J	A	S			
Grapes								A	S	O		
Hazelnuts									S	O		
Kale	J	F	M						S	O	N	D

	JAN	FEB	MARCH	APRIL	MAY	JUNE	JULY	AUG	SEPT	OCT	NOV	DEC
Lemons							J	A	S	O	N	D
Limes					M	J	J			O		
Mint					M	J	J	A	S	O		
Olives									S	O		
Oranges, blood	J	F	M	A								D
Oranges, navel	J	F	M	A	M						N	D
Oregano						J	J	A	S			
Parsnips	J	F	M								N	D
Pea shoots			M	A	M	J	J	A	S	O		
Peaches							J	A	S			
Pears						J		A	S	O	N	D
Peas					M	J	J	A	S	O	N	
Plums								A	S	O		
Potatoes (new)				A	M	J	J					
Pumpkins										O	N	D
Quinces										O	N	D
Raspberries						J	J	A	S	O		
Rhubarb (forced)	J	F	M	A								
Rhubarb (unforced)				A	M	J	J					
Runner beans						J	J	A	S			
Spinach			M	A	M	J	J	A	S			
Spring onions				A	M	J	J	A	S			
Strawberries					M	J	J	A	S			
Sweet potatoes								A	S	O		
Tomatoes						J	J	A	S	O		
Walnuts									S	O	N	
Wild garlic			M	A	M							

AMANDA, 56
London
Met Police Detective

CHIGS, 40
Leicestershire
Sales Manager

CRYSTELLE, 26
London
Client Relationship Manager

Raised in London with Greek-Cypriot heritage, Amanda studied graphic design at college and worked in advertising before moving to the Metropolitan Police to train as a detective. As a child she baked with her mum, and she learned specifically about Greek baking from her paternal Auntie Julie. She put her knowledge to good use, baking favourite dishes for her father. Her style is generous and creative with Greek and Middle Eastern influences. She loves painting directly on to her cakes, often giving them a pretty, feminine aesthetic that's inspired by her two daughters. Whatever the season, Amanda loves to start her day with an outdoor swim – the colder, the better!

Despite a lifelong love of food, Chigs is relatively new to baking, only seriously embarking on his baking journey at the start of lockdown in 2020. Through the careful study of online videos, he managed to teach himself how to produce complex bakes and intricate chocolate work. When it comes to baking, he has no fear of being thrown in at the deep end – which is a pretty accurate reflection of his life! A thrill-seeker, he relishes high-octane activities such as bouldering, skydiving and trekking. He has already smashed the Three Peaks Challenge in Yorkshire and now has his sights set on conquering Kilimanjaro. When he's not baking or climbing, you'll find him spending time with his nephews, whom he adores.

Quadrilingual Crystelle is a baker who brings her wonderfully diverse heritage – born in northwest London to Kenyan-born, Portuguese-Goan parents – to the flavours in her baking. The youngest of three daughters (and definitely the naughty one!), she was also the chief taster as she helped her mother prepare their family meals. When she travels with friends, it's her job to make a list of the best restaurants and bakeries in the cities they visit. She began baking seriously only three years ago and loves blending spices from the places she's visited into her bakes – a fougasse infused with turmeric, curry powder and spring onion is a favourite. Crystelle is also an enthusiastic singer, having kept herself busy over lockdown with an online choir.

FREYA, 19
North Yorkshire
Student

GEORGE, 34
London
Shared Lives Co-ordinator

GIUSEPPE, 45
Bristol
Chief Engineer

Freya has been dreaming of entering *Bake Off* since the first series, when she was nine and saw the tent in Bakewell. Studying for a psychology degree, Freya lives at home with her parents so that she can continue to care for her horse, Winnie, while she's at university. Her passion for horses and baking are the result of spending lots of time, as she was growing up, with her grandma. Five years ago, Freya began making plant-based versions of classic bakes for her dad – now it's her goal to bake so that no one can tell the results are vegan. She likes to be 'unexpected' with her baking, and enjoys creating intricate designs… and usually makes a lot of mess in the process!

Londoner George grew up in a close-knit Greek-Cypriot family where food was always a big part of family life. Now married to his childhood sweetheart (they met when George was just 16), he has three children and a house full of animals, including a dancing Japanese Spitz, called Eli. His mum taught him to bake (a legacy he's now passing on to his own children), and he loves all the Greek classics. His flavours often include home-grown herbs and he likes to give his bakes a touch of class with a shabby-chic, vintage vibe. He has a keen eye for detail, looking for perfection in the finished presentation. When George isn't baking, gardening or looking after his miniature zoo, he'll be in the great outdoors with his family, on bike rides and walks.

Originally from Italy, Giuseppe now lives in the UK with his wife and their three young (and noisy!) sons. His love for baking comes from his father, a professional chef who did all the cooking at home as Giuseppe was growing up, including making a cake every Sunday. Inspired by this Italian heritage, Giuseppe loves using Italian flavours in his bakes, while also bringing his engineer's precision to the results. A self-confessed food snob, he is determined to feed his children homemade confectionery, rather than anything that's been mass-produced. When he's not baking, Giuseppe loves indulging his passion for design and architecture, and with his wife has renovated their family home. He also loves gardening.

JAIRZENO, 51
London
Finance

For Trinidadian-born Jairzeno 'baking is like breathing'! He started baking in 2014, after becoming disillusioned with delicious-looking bakes that just didn't deliver on flavour – and now, in his own baking, he obsesses over flavour combinations (guava and chocolate is a firm favourite), using lots of Caribbean spices, and aiming for the perfect pâtisserie finish. Jairzeno moved to the UK from Trinidad & Tobago 15 years ago and now lives in London. He has completed multiple half marathons across Europe, and ran the London Marathon in 2012. When he's not baking or running, he and his partner can be found cooking up a storm in their kitchen, or on walks, looking for shapes in nature to inspire Jairzeno's next bake.

JÜRGEN, 56
Sussex
IT Professional

Originally from the Black Forest in Germany, Jürgen moved to the UK in 2005 and now lives with his wife and son overlooking the sea. Unable to find traditional German bread in his adopted home, Jürgen decided to bake his own – and his passion for baking has grown ever since. He is particularly well-known for his Jewish challah bread, and for the celebration cakes that he loves to bake for friends and family. He approaches baking like the physicist he is – making calculations that help to ensure the utmost precision and perfect results. Jürgen is also an accomplished jazz trombonist – a talent that he is proud to have passed on to his son.

LIZZIE, 28
Lancashire
Car Production Operative

Lizzie and her partner live with their dog, Prudence, in an annexe in Lizzie's parents' garden. A baker who prefers simple presentation and believes in flavour and quantity over precision, Lizzie may look on the outside like she's frantic and messy, but she is usually calm and collected within. Her baking comfort zone is cake, but she loves experimenting with flavour and is generally prepared to give anything a go... as long as it doesn't involve putting cheese in bread, which she thinks can only spell disaster. When she's not baking, Lizzie can be found on the dance floor, doing the samba in a suitably jazzy costume; or investigating the lives of serial killers – a fascination she developed during her study for her criminology degree.

MAGGIE, 70
Dorset
Retired Nurse & Midwife

Having grown up surrounded by family who constantly cooked and baked, Maggie finds that baking comes naturally to her. She has an impressive collection of classic recipe books and loves recreating traditional bakes while at the same time experimenting with flavour. Her favourite thing to bake is bread – it never occurs to her to buy a loaf (or a cake). A retired midwife, Maggie believes the excitement of delivering a baby can only be excellent preparation for taking part in *Bake Off*! She loves canoeing, kayaking and sailing (a passion inherited from her father), and regularly takes off in her campervan, heading for adventure. When she's not baking or thrill-seeking, Maggie loves spending time with her great nieces and great nephews.

ROCHICA, 27
Birmingham
HR Advisor

With a big Jamaican family on both sides, Rochica bakes in a way that reflects her Caribbean heritage: with flavour, passion and love. She is always especially proud when her nan and aunties tell her she has baked a cake that reminds them of the treats they grew up with. A dancer from the age of two, Rochica developed an interest in baking while she recovered from an injury that left her unable to walk, let alone dance, for months. Although she has started dancing again, she still finds plenty of time and reasons to bake – her nephew expects biscuits when she collects him from nursery, and she particularly loved the challenge of baking a birthday cake to live up to her niece's vivid imagination.

TOM, 28
Kent
Software Developer

Although he proudly remembers his place as the only boy in his primary school baking club, Tom discovered his true passion for baking a mere four years ago, when he made his dad a sticky toffee pudding cake. Now he bakes several times a week, rustling up everything from pies and quiches to bread. His mum describes him as the 'midnight baker' – before Tom moved out of the family home, his mum would often wake up in the morning to a sweet treat… and a pile of washing up! Tom likes to take the foundations of a recipe and then make the details his own, creating bakes that are fun and often follow a theme. Away from his stand mixer, Tom works for the family software company and loves singing and amateur dramatics. He is also a keen runner.

A BAKER'S KITCHEN

You don't need a lot to be able to bake. With an oven, scales, a bowl and a baking sheet you can bake bread, biscuits, scones... add a couple of cake tins and a wooden spoon and you can whip up a cake. So, although the following list seems long, please don't feel overwhelmed – build up your kitchen gradually, as you build up your skills.

_____

BAKING BEANS

An essential to keep the base of a pastry case flat and the side upright while you blind bake (that is, bake it without its filling). Ceramic baking beans intended for this purpose are handy and reusable, but uncooked dried beans, lentils or rice will work well multiple times, too. Just make sure you store them in a labelled jar afterwards as, once baked, they won't be suitable for eating.

BAKING PAPER AND LINERS

These help prevent sticking. Choose non-stick baking paper (sometimes called parchment). Greaseproof is less sturdy and has a waxy coating that doesn't stand up as well to the heat of the oven. Reusable silicone liners are more expensive, but are easy to use, can be cut to fit your tins and trays (or buy them ready-cut) and can be wiped clean. With proper care they can last for life.

BAKING SHEETS AND TRAYS

A baking sheet is flat with only one raised edge for gripping, making it good for bakes (such as biscuits and pavlovas) that you might want to slide to another surface. A baking tray has a rim or shallow edge all the way around. Aim to have at least one heavy-duty baking sheet, and two or three trays or lightweight sheets.

BAKING TINS

Always use the baking tin that's specified in the recipe as the quantities and baking time have been calculated accordingly. (See the 'You Will Need' lists at the end of each set of ingredients.) A really solid, good-quality tin will withstand repeated baking without scorching or losing its shape. Clean and dry your tins thoroughly after you've used them. Occasionally, a recipe will call for a specialist tin or mould, but in general the following will see you through nicely:

Loaf tins are essential for neat, brick-shaped breads and cakes. They're available in a variety of sizes, but the most-used sizes are 450g (measuring about 19 x 12.5 x 7.5cm and also sold as 1lb loaf tins) and 900g (measuring about 26 x 12.5 x 7.5cm, and also sold as 2lb loaf tins). Heavy-duty loaf tins won't dent or warp and will give you a better crust than equivalent silicone versions.

Muffin or cupcake tins are what you need for small bakes. They are usually 6- or 12-hole. Non-stick and silicone versions will produce equally good results (although metal is best for the Cruffins on page 147), so choose what suits you best.

Pudding moulds (mini ones) are a bit of a luxury, but handy for making individual dessert bakes, such as individual chocolate fondants and sponge puddings.

Sandwich (or sponge) tins are essential. Aim to own two 20cm-diameter sandwich tins, each 4–5cm deep. A third tin is useful for baking American-style layer cakes.

Springform (or springclip) tins are deep metal tins with a spring release. Use them for cakes, tortes, pies, cheesecakes and pull-apart bread rolls because they won't damage the side of a fragile bake as you remove it.

Swiss roll tins are rectangular (usually 20 x 30cm or 23 x 33cm) and about 2cm deep.

Tart and tartlet tins, available with fluted and straight sides, give the most professional results when made from sturdy metal, such as anodised aluminium. Choose non-stick, loose-bottomed versions for the best results.

Traybake tins are square or rectangular and about 4cm deep, and are used for brownies, shortbread and all traybakes. Buy loose-bottomed tins to help free your bakes easily.

BOWLS

For versatility, sturdiness and durability, heatproof glass and stainless steel bowls are good choices for mixing and whisking, and glass or ceramic are best for melting ingredients over hot water, although plastic bowls are cheaper. (Note, too, that ceramic bowls look pretty but can be heavy.) A very large bowl with a snap-on lid is useful for mixing and rising bread doughs. Incidentally, make your bowls non-slip by resting them on a damp cloth as you mix.

CAKE-DECORATING TURNTABLE

Although not essential, a cake-decorating turntable makes easy work of smoothing out buttercreams or ganache around the sides of a cake. It's especially handy if you're going for a semi-naked effect (such as in the Pear & Walnut Cake on page 161) or perhaps an ombre.

COOLING/WIRE RACKS

A large wire rack with legs allows air to circulate around and underneath a bake as it cools, avoiding any sogginess. A clean wire grill-pan rack makes a good improvisation, if necessary.

DOUGH SCRAPER

One of the cheapest and most useful pieces of equipment, the dough scraper helps to scoop, scrape and divide bread dough, and makes easy work of cleaning bowls and worktops.

ELECTRIC STAND MIXERS, PROCESSORS AND WHISKS

Lots of the recipes in the book call for a helping hand from an electric gadget, such as a stand mixer. Although these can make life easier, if you're new to baking, don't feel you have to rush out and buy one. Most of the recipes in the book can be made with muscle power – just remember to keep going (with a hand whisk, a wooden spoon, or your bare hands), until you reach the consistency described in the method.

A large-capacity stand mixer is a good investment if you do a lot of baking. Use the whisk attachment for meringues, buttercreams and light sponge mixtures; the paddle or beater attachment for heavier mixtures, such as richer cakes, choux pastry, and savarin-type enriched doughs; and the dough hook for mixing, then kneading bread doughs. A spare bowl will help with multi-element sponges.

An electric hand whisk is a good, versatile choice if you want to make whisked mixtures, creamed sponges, meringues, buttercreams or batter, or mixtures whisked over heat.

A hand-held stick blender (often with a whisk attachment, too) is good for smoothing out fruit sauces and crème pâtissière.

A food processor makes light work of blending fat and flour to make pastry. Use the 'pulse' button to avoid any overworking. It's also good for finely chopping nuts and herbs (try a mini version for small quantities).

HAND OR BALLOON WHISK
A wire hand whisk can be balloon-shaped or flat; a hand-held rotary whisk consists of a pair of beaters in a metal frame. Any

of these is essential, even if you have an electric version.

KNIVES
The better the knife, the better your knife skills. Stainless steel knives are easy to keep clean, but need to be sharpened regularly; carbon-steel knives are more expensive, but easier to keep sharp. Gather a medium knife, about 20cm long; a small knife (useful for pastry work, trimming edges, and making decorations); and a good-quality serrated bread knife (for sawing through crusts).

LAME
A lame is useful for scoring bread – it's like a double-sided razor blade on a handle.

MEASURING EQUIPMENT
Baking is a science and, for perfect results, precision is essential. The following pieces of measuring equipment are must-haves for guaranteed success.

Digital scales are particularly useful. As well as weighing tiny ingredients and switching easily between units, you can 'zero' ingredients you've already weighed, then add further ingredients to the same bowl, weighing each as you go.

Measuring jugs, even if you have digital scales, are a must. Pick a heat-resistant and microwave-safe jug that starts at 50ml (ideally) or 100ml, and goes up to 2 litres.

Measuring spoons do a far better job than everyday spoons (teaspoons, dessert spoons, tablespoons), which will give inconsistent results. Spoon measures in this book are level, not heaped or rounded, unless specified.

METAL SPOON
A large, long metal spoon is invaluable for folding wet ingredients into dry.

OVEN THERMOMETER
Built-in oven thermostats can be inconsistent between brands and will become less efficient with age, so an oven thermometer is a good way to make sure your oven reaches the right temperature before you bake, as well as to identify the hot and cool spots to avoid uneven bakes. If you don't have a thermometer, get to know your oven, then increase or decrease the temperature or baking time accordingly to get the right results.

PALETTE KNIFE
An offset palette knife (with a kink near the handle) is useful for spreading icings and delicate mixtures where you need a smooth, precise result. A straight palette knife is good for lifting and moving bakes from one surface to another.

PASTRY BRUSH
Opt for a heat- and dishwasher-proof, medium pastry brush. It's a must-have you'll use not only for glazing pastry and bread, but for tasks such as brushing down sugar crystals from the side of a pan as you make caramel.

PASTRY CUTTERS
Pick a double-sided (plain on one side, fluted on the other) nest of metal cutters.

A pizza wheel-cutter is handy for cutting straight lines. Shaped cutters are infinite and lovely, too.

PIPING BAGS AND NOZZLES
The recipes in this book use both reusable and paper piping bags in various sizes. Piping nozzles, made from metal or plastic, range from wide, round tips for piping choux pastry and meringue, to star-shaped for icings, to small writing tips for delicate work. Set the nozzle in the bag, stand it in a jug, tall glass or a mug for support, then fill. Twist the top before you pipe to stop the contents of the bag escaping the wrong way.

PROVING BAGS
Although not strictly necessary (covering with oiled cling film will do), proving bags (ideally two) are reusable, which makes them kinder to the environment. Slide your dough inside on a baking tray and inflate the bag a little to stop the dough sticking to it as it rises.

ROLLING PIN
A fairly heavy wooden pin about 6–7cm in diameter and without handles will make the easiest work of rolling out pastry.

RUBBER SPATULA
A strong and flexible spatula is useful for mixing, folding and scraping with ease.

SIEVE
Every baker needs a sieve – to combine flour with raising agents; remove lumps from icing and sugars; and for straining and puréeing. Go for a large metal sieve that will sit over your largest mixing bowl

for sifting tasks, and a smaller, tea-strainer-sized one for dusting.

SUGAR THERMOMETER/ COOKING THERMOMETER

Essential for sugar work (and deep-frying), a sugar thermometer will ensure your sugar reaches the correct temperature if, for example, you're making caramel or nougat, or tempering chocolate – among other baking tasks. Pick one that's easy to read and can clip on to the side of the pan. A thermometer with a probe will help you to measure the internal temperatures of your bakes for doneness, too.

TIMER

A digital kitchen timer with seconds as well as minutes (and a loud bell) is essential baking equipment – don't rely on just your oven timer. Set the timer for a minute or two less than the suggested time in your recipe (especially if you're uncertain of your oven) – you can always increase the time your bake is in the oven if it's not quite done yet.

WOODEN SPOON

Cheap, heat-resistant, and safe on non-stick pans, a wooden spoon mixes, beats, creams and stirs – the essentials of good baking. (You can even use the handle to shape brandy snaps and tuiles.) Store your savoury and sweet spoons separately, as wood can absorb strong flavours.

ZESTER

A long-handled zester is the best and quickest way to remove the zest from citrus fruits (use unwaxed citrus fruits for zesting). Pick one that's sturdy and easy to hold.

A BAKER'S LARDER

Most of the bakes throughout this book use ingredients that are easy to find and store. Keep the following in your store cupboard and, whether you need to whip up something for a cake sale, find an activity for the kids for the afternoon, or create a dinner-party showstopper, you'll be ready to start baking. As a rule of thumb: the best-quality ingredients tend to give the best results.

———

BAKING POWDER, BICARBONATE OF SODA AND CREAM OF TARTAR

Chemical raising agents, all these ingredients increase the lightness and volume of cakes and small bakes, and some types of biscuit and pastry. Always use the amount given in the recipe – but check the date stamps before you start, as raising agents will lose their potency over time. If you've run out of baking powder, you can easily make your own: for 1 teaspoon of baking powder combine ½ teaspoon of cream of tartar with ¼ teaspoon of bicarbonate of soda. If you are making a gluten-free bake, bear in mind that baking powder should be gluten-free, but some manufacturers add filling agents that may contain gluten. Always check the label.

BUTTER AND OTHER FATS

Most of the recipes in this book use unsalted butter, as it has a delicate flavour, adds a good, even colour (perhaps because it contains less whey than salted), and allows you to season your bake to taste yourself, as relevant. Store butter tightly wrapped in the fridge, well away from strong flavours. When relevant, a recipe will tell you whether to use butter chilled (from the fridge) or softened at room temperature (in that case, don't be tempted to soften it in the microwave – you're looking for a texture that yields easily when pressed with a finger, but holds the shape, not melted). Cubed butter enables you to add small amounts at a time and makes the butter easier to combine with the other ingredients.

Lard, from pigs, gives a short, flaky texture to traditional hot-water-crust pastry so that it bakes to a crisp, golden finish. White solid vegetable fat is a good alternative.

Dairy-free spreads, made from vegetable and sunflower oils, make good substitutes in most recipes that require softened or room-temperature butter, but always check the label to make sure it's good for baking beforehand. Some are made specifically for baking and you can use them straight from the fridge. They give good results, but may lack that buttery flavour. Avoid spreads designed for use on bread/crackers – they contain too much water and not enough fat to make good baking ingredients.

Solid coconut oil is a good option for dairy-free and vegan recipes, but isn't a like-for-like butter substitute.

Suet, from cows in its non-vegetarian form, gives a light, soft pastry rather than a very crisp or flaky one. Suet is more solid than butter or lard and melts much more slowly, forming tiny pockets in the dough as it cooks. Most supermarkets now sell vegetarian suet, too.

Oil often pops up in bakes these days. Vegetable oil is a good all-rounder, but in baking, sunflower oil gives the best results as it's especially light and mildly flavoured.

CHOCOLATE

Chocolate is a must in baking – from shards and shavings to ganache and buttercream, it features in many of the recipes in this book.

Dark chocolate, with around 54% cocoa solids, is the kind most used in these recipes as it gives a good balance of flavour. Some recipes recommend 70% dark, which is a little less sweet. Chocolate with a higher percentage (75% and above) may be too bitter and dry for general baking.

Milk chocolate has a much milder and sweeter flavour – choose a good-quality favourite, and expect the best results from milk chocolate with good amounts of cocoa solids.

White chocolate doesn't contain any cocoa solids, just cocoa butter. Look out for brands with 30% or more cocoa butter as a measure of quality. White chocolate sets less firmly than dark or milk chocolate owing to the higher fat content, and melts at a lower temperature, so take care as it easily scorches and becomes unusable.

COCOA POWDER

A dark, unsweetened powder made from pure cocoa beans after they have been dried and had all the cocoa butter removed. Cocoa powder is very bitter, strongly flavoured and gives a powerful hit. Never substitute cocoa powder with drinking chocolate, which contains milk powder and sugar, as well as cocoa powder itself.

CREAM

For best results, chill cream thoroughly before whipping (in really hot weather, chill the bowl and whisk before you start, too).

Buttermilk, sometimes labelled 'cultured buttermilk', is low-fat or non-fat milk plus a bacterial culture to give it an acidic tang. It is often used along with bicarbonate of soda to add lightness as well as flavour to scones and cakes.

Crème fraîche is a soured cream with a creamy, tangy flavour. It won't whip, but you can use it for fillings, toppings and serving.

Double cream contains at least 48% butterfat. It whips well and has a richer flavour than whipping cream. The extra-rich type of double cream available is designed for spooning, rather than for whipping or for making ganache.

Lactose-free and soya-based dairy-free creams can give varied results, and are usually unsuitable for whipping.

Single cream contains 18% butterfat and is good for adding to sauces and fillings, for adding richness to rubbed-in mixtures, or for pouring over desserts and pastries.

Soured cream has only 18% butterfat. It is made by introducing a bacterial culture to cream, giving a naturally sour tang.

Whipping cream usually contains at least 36% butterfat and is designed to whip well without being overly rich.

DRIED FRUIT

Store dried fruit out of direct sunlight and tightly sealed in containers. Vine fruit, such as raisins, sultanas and currants, have a long shelf-life, but will always be best bought when you need them. Soft-dried apricots, as well as dried figs, cranberries, blueberries, sour cherries, and dates, can replace vine fruits in many recipes. They add sweetness and moisture, which is useful if you want to reduce refined sugar.

EGGS

When it comes to eggs, size really does matter. Unless otherwise stated, all the recipes in this book use medium eggs. If the eggs are too small, a sponge may not rise properly and look thin or dry; too big and a pastry or bread dough may be too wet or soft to handle.

For baking, use eggs at room temperature, which means taking them out of the fridge

30–60 minutes before you start cooking. If you forget, pop them into a bowl of lukewarm water for a couple of minutes.

Spare egg whites will keep for 3–4 days in a sealed container or jar in the fridge, or for up to a month in the freezer (defrost overnight in the fridge before using; yolks can't be frozen).

EXTRACTS AND FLAVOURINGS

Avoid synthetic flavourings as much as you can – they often have an aftertaste that will spoil your hard work. Here's a guide to the best to use.

Almond extract may be pricey, but most recipes need only a few drops. Avoid anything marked 'flavouring'.

Ground spices are best when you use them fresh, but if you're storing them, do so in screw-topped jars, rather than open packets, to prolong their flavour.

Vanilla is usually the most expensive flavouring used in baking, although you need to use only small amounts of the real thing. Vanilla extract – labelled 'pure' or 'natural' – costs more than vanilla essence, which might contain artificial flavourings. Vanilla paste is made from the seeds of the pods and has a thicker texture and more concentrated flavour. Best of all, though, are vanilla pods, which you can split to scrape out the tiny seeds to flavour custards, crème pâtissière and fillings. Don't throw away the pods: rinse and dry them carefully, then put them in a jar of caster sugar to make vanilla sugar.

FLOUR

Whether made from wheat or other grains, flour has to be the most valued ingredient in the baker's larder. Avoid poor-quality, out-of-date or stale flour, as this will affect the result and taste of the final bake. Always buy the best and freshest flour you can afford.

Cornflour is a finely milled white powder added to biscuits to give a delicate crumb, and used to thicken custard and crème pâtissière.

Gluten-free flours are wheat-free mixtures of several ingredients, including rice, potato, tapioca, maize, chickpea, broad bean, white sorghum or buckwheat – depending on the brand. Ready-mixed gluten-free flours sometimes suggest adding xanthan gum (a powder sold in small tubs) to improve the texture and crumb of your bake – check the packet and, if your flour mixture doesn't already include it, add 1 teaspoon of xanthan gum per 150g gluten-free flour. Some gluten-free flours need a little more liquid than wheat flour doughs, so you can't substitute them exactly, but it is well worth experimenting.

Plain flour is a type of wheat flour used for making pastry, pancakes and rich fruit cakes, for example, and has no added raising agents.

Rye flour has a deep, dark flavour that works well in breads, particularly sourdoughs. It's low in gluten, which makes it harder to knead than wheat flours, and the dough rises less well. Available as wholegrain and a finer 'light' rye, which has had some of the bran sifted out, it is useful for crackers and adding to wheat flour for savoury pastry recipes.

Self-raising flour has added baking powder and is most often used in sponge-cake recipes to give a light, risen texture. If you run out of self-raising flour you can easily make your own: add 4 teaspoons of baking powder to every 225g plain flour, sifting them together a couple of times. Sponge self-raising flour is more expensive than regular self-raising, but is slightly 'softer' and silkier, as it is more finely milled.

Semolina flour is a slightly gritty, pale yellow flour made from durum wheat, and is often used for pasta and Italian-style breads (as well as semolina pudding).

Speciality wheat flours are created from wheat varieties that are specifically grown to make flour for baking ciabatta, pizza bases, and baguettes.

Spelt flour comes from the same family as wheat, but has a slightly different genetic make-up and a richer and more nutty flavour – it is good for most recipes that call for flour, except very delicate biscuits and sponges.

Stoneground flour means that the grain (wheat, rye, spelt and so on) is milled between large stones instead of steel rollers, giving a coarser texture and fuller flavour.

Strong bread flour is made from wheat with a higher ratio of protein to starch than the cake and pastry flours. This increased ratio is crucial to bread-making: as you knead the dough, the protein develops into strands of gluten that stretch as the gases produced by the yeast expand, enabling the dough to rise. Strong bread flour has about 12–16% protein, which is ideal for most breads. Extra-strong or Canadian strong flour has even more (15–17%) – good for bagels or larger loaves.

Wholemeal or wholegrain flours are made from the complete wheat kernel, making them far more nutritious than white flours (which are made using 75% of the cleaned wheat kernel, and have most of the wheat bran and wheatgerm removed). The small specks of bran in these flours mean that they give a dough that rises less well than one made with all white flour. Wholemeal plain flour has been milled to make it lighter and more suitable for making pastry and cakes.

NUTS
Buy nuts in small quantities to use up quickly (always before the use-by date) – the high oil content means that once opened, nuts can quickly turn rancid. If you're storing them, do so in an airtight container in a cool, dark place. Most nuts benefit from being lightly toasted before use, to impart a richer, nuttier flavour to the finished bake.

Almonds are incredibly versatile – ground, chopped, flaked (toasted and untoasted) and whole (blanched or unblanched). To blanch (remove the skins) yourself, put the nuts in a small pan, add water to cover and bring to the boil. Remove the pan from the heat and drain, then slip the nuts out of their casings. Dry on kitchen paper.

Hazelnuts are usually ready-blanched (without their brown papery skins) or ground.

Pistachios are easy to find shelled and unsalted, but they usually come with their papery skins attached. To reveal the deep-green colour of the nuts, carefully tip them into a pan of boiling water. Remove from the heat, leave for 1 minute, then drain. Transfer the nuts to a clean, dry tea towel and rub gently to loosen the skins, then peel if necessary. Ready-ground pistachios are also available these days.

Walnuts and **pecans**, usually halved or chopped, are interchangeable in most baking recipes as they share a similar texture and appearance (walnuts are slightly more bitter). Gently toasting walnuts and pecans in a medium-heat oven gives them a much deeper, richer flavour.

SUGAR
Different sugars combine and interact with other ingredients in different ways, affecting the end results of the bake. Always use the sugar the recipe specifies. Sugar doesn't have a shelf-life and will keep indefinitely in an airtight container in a cool, dark place.

Caster sugar comes as both refined white and unrefined golden. White provides sweetness with a neutral colour and flavour that is, for example, perfect for white meringues or very pale sponges. Unrefined golden caster sugar has a slight caramel, rich flavour. Use it when having a warmer colour in your final bake is not an issue.

The fine grains of caster sugar break down easily during beating or creaming with butter for sponges, melt quickly for lemon curd, and disappear in pastry mixtures.

Fondant icing sugar sets hard, so it's good for decorating as it doesn't smudge. It contains glucose syrup to give a smooth, glossy finish.

Granulated sugar, available as white or golden, has bigger grains that take longer to dissolve. Keep it for making sugar syrups and drizzles, and for sprinkling on top of bakes to give a satisfying crunch.

Icing sugar is also available as refined (white) and unrefined (golden). Again, the unrefined version has a pale caramel colour and flavour. Use white icing sugar for icings, fillings and frostings that need to be very pale or that are to be coloured with food colouring. Sift icing sugar before use to remove any lumps so that your icing is perfectly smooth.

Jam sugar contains added pectin to help jam set, making it good for making jams that use fruits without high natural levels of pectin – raspberries, strawberries, apricots and ripe cherries, among them.

Muscovado sugars come as light muscovado and dark muscovado. These add a stronger, warmer caramel or molasses flavour and darker colour to bakes, but they can make them more moist and heavy. They are good in rich fruity cakes, gingerbreads, parkins, and spice cakes. Press out any lumps with the back of a spoon before using.

SYRUP AND TREACLE

Golden syrup and thick black treacle add a rich, toffee-ish flavour, as well as sweetness, to bakes. They can be difficult to measure if you're spooning out of a tin, so warm the measuring spoon in a mug of just-boiled water before scooping, or stand the syrup or treacle tin in a bowl of boiled water for a few minutes to loosen the stickiness. Easier is to use a squeezy bottle – many brands of golden syrup now come readily available this way (similarly, for honey). Maple syrup has a lighter texture than golden syrup, but a distinctive flavour that works particularly well with nuts, and, of course, over pancakes.

YEAST

Yeast is a living organism that makes bread doughs rise. It needs moisture, gentle warmth and flour (or sugar) to stimulate its growth and the production of carbon dioxide, which expands the dough. The recipes in this book use fast-action dried yeast, available in 7g sachets or in tubs as easy blend or instant dried yeast. Always weigh your yeast, unless it's the exact amount in a sachet, and add the yeast powder to the flour, never to the liquid. If you add it with the salt, do so on opposite sides of the bowl, as salt (and too much sugar) retards its growth. (And hot water kills it.) If you use too much yeast in a bake, the dough will be lively, but the baked loaf may have a strong aftertaste and will go stale more quickly. If you use too little, the dough will take longer to rise and prove, but it will have a deeper flavour and will most likely keep better.

SPRING

RECIPES

PRIMROSE & LEMON CAKE

SEMLOR

RHUBARB & CUSTARD TART

ASPARAGUS, HAM & CHEESE DANISH PASTRIES

PRUE'S PRINZREGENTENTORTE

BRUNCH PIKELETS

RUBY GRAPEFRUIT BUNDT

MINI ROLLS

CHERRY BLOSSOM SHORTBREADS

CRYSTELLE'S CHAI & JAGGERY CAKE

PIZZA BIANCA DI PRIMAVERA

MINI HUMMINGBIRD CAKES

SUPER-SEEDED SODA BREAD

PASSIONFRUIT SOUFFLÉS

CHIGS'S MANGO & COCONUT UPSIDE DOWN CAKE

SPICED LAMB & SPINACH FILO PIE

JAIRZENO'S CHOCOLATE MINT CAKE

WILD GARLIC FLATBREADS

HAMANTASCHEN

PRIMROSE & LEMON CAKE

Yellow primroses are such a welcome sign that spring has arrived. These delicate, edible blooms have a subtle floral aroma that pairs perfectly with the tangy sharpness of lemon. If you can't source wild primroses, you can use edible, yellow primula, which often have a stronger flavour. Make the syrup and curd in advance, if you like, and keep it in the fridge for up to a week.

For the sponge
280g ground almonds
240g gluten-free
    self-raising flour, sifted
450g unsalted butter,
    softened
450g golden caster sugar
8 eggs
100ml lemon curd yogurt
finely grated zest of
    1 unwaxed lemon
pinch of salt
primrose & lemon syrup,
    for brushing (below)

For the primrose
& lemon syrup
2 large handfuls of
    primrose flowers
½ unwaxed lemon,
    cut into wedges
100g caster sugar

For the primrose
& lemon curd
3 large eggs
300g caster sugar
100ml primrose &
    lemon syrup (above)
100g unsalted butter,
    cubed

Continues overleaf

1. Heat the oven to 180°C/160°C fan/Gas 4.

2. Make the sponge. Mix together the ground almonds and flour.

3. Beat the butter and sugar in a stand mixer fitted with the beater, on medium speed for 10 minutes, until pale and creamy, scraping down the inside of the bowl from time to time.

4. Add the eggs, one at a time, beating well between each addition. If the mixture starts to curdle, add a spoonful of the flour mixture. Stir in the yogurt. Fold in the ground almond and flour mixture, and the lemon zest and salt.

5. Divide the mixture equally between the lined tins and spread it level. Bake on the middle shelves for 30–35 minutes, until risen and a skewer inserted into the centres comes out clean.

6. Meanwhile, make the primrose and lemon syrup. Put the primroses, lemon wedges, sugar and 250ml of water in a small pan and bring the liquid to the boil. Reduce the heat to low and simmer for 30 minutes, until the syrup starts to thicken. Strain the syrup through a sieve into a jug and set aside until ready to use.

7. Make the primrose and lemon curd. Whisk the eggs and sugar in a heatproof bowl set over a pan of barely simmering water until thick and mousse-like, and the mixture leaves a ribbon trail when you lift the whisk.

8. Whisk in the primrose syrup and the cubes of butter, one at a time, and keep stirring until the mixture thickens and coats the back of a spoon. Leave it to cool and chill.

Continues overleaf

For the lemon buttercream
225g unsalted butter, softened
420g icing sugar, sifted
finely grated zest of ¼ unwaxed lemon
3 tbsp whole milk

To decorate
edible spring flowers, such as primroses, pansies, bellis or violas
thyme sprigs
blueberries (optional)
lemon balm or mint sprigs
5 pistachios, finely chopped
icing sugar, for dusting

You will need
20cm sandwich tins x 4, greased, then lined (base and sides) with baking paper
wooden skewer or cocktail stick
medium piping bag fitted with a large plain nozzle

9. Using a wooden skewer or cocktail stick, prick holes all over the top of each warm sponge and carefully brush over the remaining primrose & lemon syrup. Leave the sponges to cool completely in the tins, then turn them out.

10. Make the lemon buttercream. Beat the butter in a stand mixer fitted with the beater, on low speed for 5 minutes, until pale and creamy. Add the icing sugar, a little at a time, then add the lemon zest and milk, also a little at a time, until you have a smooth, fluffy buttercream. Spoon the buttercream into the medium piping bag fitted with a large plain nozzle and twist the end to seal.

11. To assemble, pipe dots of buttercream onto a cake board and place one sponge on top. Pipe buttercream on top of the sponge and spread it evenly to the edges. Pipe a ring of buttercream around the edge of the sponge and fill the middle with the curd. Place the second sponge on top. Repeat with another layer of sponge, layering with buttercream and curd, and finishing with the final layer of sponge.

12. Pipe a generous layer of the remaining buttercream on top and make a swirl pattern with a large, offset spatula. Decorate the cake with spring flowers, thyme, blueberries (if available), lemon balm or mint, and pistachios. Dust with icing sugar to serve.

SEMLOR

These sweet Swedish buns are traditionally baked and eaten during the Christian festival of Lent. They are delicate, flavoured with cardamom, filled with almond paste and topped with a swirl of lightly spiced whipped cream. Almond paste (mandelmassa) is not to be confused with marzipan – it has a higher percentage of almonds to sugar. The paste is easily available online, but you could use marzipan instead – just add a few drops of almond extract to boost the flavour.

For the buns
475g strong white
   bread flour
50g caster sugar
7g fast-action dried yeast
1 tsp ground cardamom
½ tsp salt
250ml whole or
   semi-skimmed milk
75g unsalted butter,
   cubed
1 large egg, beaten,
   plus 1 egg, beaten,
   to glaze
sunflower oil,
   for greasing bowl

For the filling
200g almond paste
100ml whole milk
500ml double cream
1 tsp vanilla paste
½ tsp ground cardamom
2 tbsp icing sugar, sifted,
   plus extra for dusting

You will need
2 baking trays, lined
   with baking paper
large piping bag fitted
   with a large open
   star nozzle

1. Make the buns. Tip the flour into the bowl of a stand mixer fitted with the dough hook. Add the sugar, yeast, cardamom and salt and mix to combine.

2. Heat the milk and butter either in a suitable jug in the microwave or in a small pan over a low heat until the milk is warm and the butter is very soft and almost melted.

3. Pour the milk and butter and the beaten egg into the mixing bowl with the dry ingredients and mix on low speed until combined, scraping down the inside of the bowl from time to time. Increase the speed to medium and knead the dough for a further 5 minutes, until silky smooth and the dough cleanly leaves the side of the bowl.

4. Scoop the dough onto the work surface and lightly oil the mixing bowl. Shape the dough into a ball, return it to the oiled bowl, cover it and leave it at room temperature for about 1 hour, until doubled in size.

5. Lightly flour the work surface, turn out the dough and knead it for 20 seconds to knock out any large air pockets. Divide the dough into 12 equal portions (roughly 75g each), then roll and shape each portion into a neat, smooth ball. Arrange the balls on the lined baking trays, leaving space between each bun. Cover loosely and leave the balls to prove for a further 45 minutes to 1 hour, until doubled in size.

6. Heat the oven to 200°C/180°C fan/Gas 6.

7. Brush the buns with beaten egg and bake them for 12–14 minutes, until golden brown and the undersides sound hollow when tapped. Leave them to cool on a wire rack.

Continues overleaf

8. Cut an inverted cone-shaped hole into the top of each bun. Trim off the pointy end of each cut cone and crumble this into a bowl. Scoop out 2 teaspoons of filling from each bun, crumbling the filling into the bowl. You will now have a bowl of crumbs and 12 bun 'hats'.

9. Make the filling. Crumble the almond paste into the bowl of crumbs. Add the milk and beat the mixture to a smooth paste, then divide it equally between the hollows in the buns.

10. In a large bowl, whip the cream with the vanilla, cardamom and icing sugar until it just holds firm peaks. Spoon the cream into the large piping bag fitted with a large open star nozzle and pipe a generous swirl of cream into each bun.

11. Trim the bun 'hats' into neat squares and place one on top of each cream-filled bun. Dust with icing sugar and serve immediately.

RHUBARB & CUSTARD TART

This is the super-simplest of rhubarb tarts. You can use any rhubarb, but we've chosen 'forced', which is covered as it grows. This technique hastens the ripening time to give bright pink stems ready for the spring season. Topped with seasonal flowers, what tart could be prettier?

For the pastry
250g plain flour
pinch of salt
150g unsalted butter,
    cubed and chilled
40g icing sugar, sifted,
    plus extra for dusting
2 egg yolks, plus 1 white
1½ tbsp ice-cold water
juice of ¼ lemon

For the baked rhubarb
600g tenderstem
    rhubarb, trimmed and
    cut into 11–13cm lengths
juice of 1 blood orange
2 tbsp caster sugar
½ vanilla pod, split
    lengthways and seeds
    scraped out, or
    1 tsp vanilla paste
seasonal flowers, such
    as violas, to decorate

For the custard
300ml whole milk
1 vanilla pod, split,
    or 1 tsp vanilla paste
4 egg yolks
75g caster sugar
1 tbsp cornflour
1 tbsp custard powder
2 platinum-grade
    gelatine leaves
100ml double cream

You will need
36 x 13cm rectangular
    fluted tart tin
baking beans or rice

1. Make the pastry. Sift together the flour and salt in a large mixing bowl. Rub in the butter until the mixture resembles breadcrumbs. Add the icing sugar and mix to combine. Make a well in the centre and add the egg yolks, cold water and lemon juice. Using a table knife, cut through the mixture to combine the ingredients and bring the dough together. Very lightly knead it into a ball, then flatten it into a disc. Wrap it, then chill it for 2 hours.

2. Lightly flour the work surface and roll out the pastry to a rectangle, about 3mm thick and big enough to fit the tart tin. Carefully and neatly line the tart tin, pressing the pastry into the corners. Trim the excess, prick the base with a fork, and chill for 30 minutes.

3. Heat the oven to 180°C/160°C fan/Gas 4. Place a baking sheet on the middle shelf to heat up at the same time.

4. Line the pastry case with baking paper and fill it with baking beans or rice. Bake the case on the hot baking sheet for 20–25 minutes, until the edges start to turn crisp and golden. Remove the paper and beans or rice and bake for a further 4–5 minutes, until the base of the tart case is cooked. Lightly beat the egg white and thinly brush it over the base of the tart case. Return the shell to the oven for 1 minute – the egg white will form a seal between the pastry and the filling. Remove it from the oven and leave it to cool.

5. While the oven is still on, arrange the rhubarb in a single layer in a glass or ceramic (non-reactive) ovenproof dish. Add the blood orange juice, sugar and vanilla and mix to combine. Cover the dish with foil and bake it on the middle shelf for about 20 minutes, until tender. Remove the rhubarb from the oven and leave it to cool in the dish.

6. Make the custard. Warm the milk with the split vanilla pod or paste in a small pan over a low heat.

Continues overleaf

7. Remove the pan from the heat just before the milk boils and leave the milk to infuse for 15 minutes. In a medium bowl, whisk together the egg yolks, sugar, cornflour and custard powder. Soak the gelatine leaves in cold water in another bowl.

8. Remove the vanilla pod (if using) from the pan, re-heat the milk to just below boiling, then pour the hot milk onto the egg mixture, whisking continuously until smooth and thoroughly combined. Return the custard to the pan and cook, stirring continuously, over a low–medium heat for 1–2 minutes, until the custard is just boiling and it starts to thicken. If you can taste the cornflour in the custard, continue to cook for a further 20 seconds, until the flavour has gone and the custard is glossy, thickened and smooth.

9. Drain the gelatine, squeezing out any excess, then add it to the custard and whisk to combine. Add the double cream and mix again until smooth. Pour the custard into the cooled pastry case, spread it level and leave it to cool (about 1 hour).

10. Arrange the cooled, baked rhubarb in rows on top of the custard and spoon over any roasting juices. Dust the top with icing sugar and decorate with seasonal flowers to serve.

ASPARAGUS, HAM & CHEESE DANISH PASTRIES

British asparagus spears are at their finest from late spring, and this recipe is a wonderful way to make the most of them. These savoury Danish pastries are filled with cheese sauce, smoked ham and tender asparagus spears. At a glance, the pastries look challenging, but it's time and detail rather than complicated effort – rounds of rolling, folding and chilling will give perfect results.

For the Danish pastry dough
500g strong white
    bread flour
2 tbsp caster sugar
10g fast-action
    dried yeast
2 tsp salt
250ml whole milk,
    plus extra for brushing
1 egg, lightly beaten
250g unsalted butter

For the topping
25g unsalted butter
25g plain flour
250ml whole milk
1 rounded tsp
    Dijon mustard
150g mature cheddar or
    gruyère cheese, grated
1 egg, beaten with 1 tbsp
    whole milk, to glaze
18 thin asparagus spears,
    trimmed and halved
1 tbsp snipped chives
125g thinly sliced ham
salt and freshly ground
    black pepper

You will need
2 baking sheets, lined
    with baking paper

1. Make the Danish pastry dough. Combine the flour, sugar, yeast and salt in the bowl of a stand mixer fitted with the dough hook. Warm the milk until lukewarm and pour this into the bowl along with the beaten egg. Mix on low–medium speed to combine, adding 1–2 tablespoons of water, if needed, to bring the dough together. Continue mixing for 2–3 minutes, until the dough is smooth.

2. Turn out the dough onto your work surface, shape it into a ball and return it to the bowl. Cover and leave it to rise at room temperature for about 1½ hours, until doubled in size.

3. Meanwhile, cut the butter into 1cm-thick slices and arrange them side-by-side on a sheet of baking paper. Cover the slices with another sheet of baking paper and, using a rolling pin, flatten the butter into a neat 17–18cm square. Transfer the butter square to the fridge to chill for 30 minutes.

4. Turn out the dough onto a lightly floured work surface. Punch the dough to expel any large pockets of air and roll it out into a neat 27–28cm square. Take your time over this and if the dough is not very elastic, roll it a little, leave it to rest briefly and roll again.

5. With the dough positioned squarely in front of you, place the chilled butter square at an angle on top, so that the butter corners point north, south, east and west. Fold the exposed dough over the butter so that the corners meet in the middle and completely encase the butter.

Continues overleaf

6. Lightly flour the work surface and gently roll the dough, starting at the middle and working away from you and then towards you, into a neat rectangle three times as long as it is wide.

7. Fold the top third of the rectangle down to cover the middle third and the bottom third up to cover this, as if you were folding a business letter. Rotate the dough 90 degrees clockwise, wrap it in baking paper and chill it for 30 minutes.

8. Lightly flour the work surface and roll out the dough again to a neat rectangle three times as long as it is wide. Take your time over this and roll, then rest and roll again if needed.

9. Turn the rectangle so that one of the long sides is nearest you and fold each side in to meet in the middle, so that the edges are just touching. Fold the dough at the middle, so that the left-hand side goes over, on top of the right, giving you a four-layer thick rectangle – this is called a book fold. Wrap the dough in baking paper and chill it for 30 minutes.

10. Lightly flour the work surface and roll out the dough again into a rectangle three times as long as it is wide. Fold the top third down to the middle and the bottom third up over this as in Step 7. Wrap and chill again for 1–2 hours while you prepare the topping.

11. In a small pan, melt the butter over a low heat. Stir in the flour and cook, stirring continuously, for 1 minute, until the mixture smells biscuity.

12. Gradually add the milk, stirring continuously until smooth. Bring the mixture to the boil, reduce the heat to a gentle simmer and cook the sauce for 3–4 minutes, until it is thick and glossy.

13. Remove the pan from the heat, add the mustard and season well with salt and pepper. Spoon the sauce into a bowl and leave it to cool. Then, add 100g of the grated cheese. Cover and chill the sauce until you're ready to assemble.

14. Lightly flour the work surface and cut the dough in half. Roll each piece into a rectangle roughly 38 x 26cm. Slide each one onto a lined baking sheet and chill them for 15 minutes.

15. Trim the edges of the dough to neaten and cut each rectangle into six 12cm squares to make 12 in total.

16. To make the kite shapes, fold one square in half to make a triangle. With the long side of the triangle nearest you, use a sharp knife to cut a straight line through the dough 8mm in from the bottom right-hand corner to the top corner, stopping 1cm in from the top corner. Repeat on the left side, making sure that the cut stops 1cm in from the top corner of the triangle.

17. Open out the triangle into a square and lightly brush the top with milk (or water). Take the left-hand corner of the square and fold it to the inside right-hand corner, making sure that the sides line up neatly.

18. Pick up the right-hand corner and fold it over and neatly onto the left-hand edge. Gently press the edges together to seal. You should now have a diamond shape with a square middle, borders and twists top and bottom. Place the pastry kite onto the lined baking tray and repeat with the remaining squares to make 12 diamond shapes in total.

19. Spoon the cold cheese sauce into the middle of each square, cover the pastries (ideally with oiled cling film) and leave them to prove in the fridge for at least 4 hours, but preferably overnight, until the pastries have risen to nearly double their height.

20. Heat the oven to 200°C/180°C fan/Gas 6.

21. Carefully brush the edges of the Danishes with egg wash to glaze. Arrange the halved asparagus spears on top of the cheese sauce (three per pastry) and sprinkle with the chives. Divide the ham between the pastries and scatter with the remaining 50g of grated cheese. Bake for about 20 minutes, until crisp, golden brown and well risen. Serve hot, warm or at room temperature.

PRUE'S PRINZREGENTENTORTE

Created to celebrate Prince Regent Luitpold, born in March 1821 and who reigned from 1886-1912, this traditional Bavarian cake is made up of eight layers of sponge, symbolising the eight administrative districts of Bavaria that existed at the time.

For the sponge
10 large eggs, separated
¼ tsp salt
180g caster sugar
3 x 8g packets of
    vanilla sugar
175g plain flour
1 tsp bicarbonate of soda
65g unsalted butter,
    melted

For the chocolate cream filling
600ml whole milk
3 large egg yolks
60g cornflour
40g cocoa powder
150g 54% dark
    chocolate, chopped
375g unsalted butter,
    softened
200g icing sugar, sifted

For the chocolate crown decorations (optional)
150g 54% dark
    chocolate, chopped
edible gold powder

Continues overleaf

1. Make the sponge. Heat the oven to 190°C/170°C fan/Gas 5 and evenly space three shelves in the oven. Using the base of a 25cm round cake tin or dinner plate as a guide, draw a 25cm-diameter circle on eight sheets of baking paper (the same size as your baking sheets). Turn the sheets of baking paper over so the pencil or pen is underneath and use three of them to line the three baking sheets.

2. Whisk the egg whites and salt in a stand mixer fitted with the whisk until firm but not dry, then gradually whisk in half (90g) of the caster sugar and all the vanilla sugar until you have a firm meringue. Spoon the meringue into a clean bowl and set aside.

3. In the same mixer bowl (no need to wash it), whisk the egg yolks with the remaining 90g of caster sugar until thick, pale and mousse-like, and the mixture leaves a ribbon trail when you lift the whisk.

4. Remove the bowl from the stand mixer and gently fold the egg whites into the yolk mixture, using a large metal spoon. Sift the flour and bicarbonate of soda over the egg mixture and fold them in, being careful not to knock the air out of the mixture. Finally, pour the melted butter down the inside of the bowl and fold it in.

5. Divide the mixture into eight portions and spoon one portion onto one of the lined baking sheets in the centre of the circle. Using a palette knife, spread the mixture thinly and neatly up to the edge of the circle. Repeat with two more quantities to make three circles of cake mixture. Bake for 6-8 minutes, until the sponge is golden and springy to the touch. Remove the sponges from the oven and transfer to wire racks to cool.

Continues overleaf

For the chocolate ganache
200g 54% dark chocolate, chopped
300ml double cream
25g unsalted butter, softened

You will need
25cm round cake tin or dinner plate
3 large baking sheets
23cm springform tin, greased, then lined (base and sides) with baking paper
crown template (about 2cm in diameter), downloaded and printed x 12 times on a sheet of A4 paper (optional)
cooking thermometer
small piping bag fitted with a small writing nozzle
A4 sheet of acetate
large piping bag fitted with a medium closed star nozzle

6. Continue baking in batches until you have eight sponges. Once they are cool, peel off the baking paper and, using the base of the 23cm cake tin as a guide, trim each sponge into a neat 23cm circle.

7. Make the chocolate cream filling. Pour 500ml of the milk into a pan and bring it to just below boiling point. In a large bowl, whisk the egg yolks, cornflour, cocoa powder and remaining 100ml of milk together.

8. Pour the hot milk over the egg mixture, whisking continuously, then pour the mixture back into the pan and whisk it over a gentle heat until the mixture thickens (about 3–5 minutes). Pour the custard into a shallow dish, cover the surface with cling film to prevent a skin forming and leave to cool.

9. Once cool, melt the chocolate in a heatproof bowl set over a pan of barely simmering water, stirring until smooth, then remove the chocolate from the heat and leave it to cool.

10. In a large mixing bowl, beat the butter and icing sugar together until pale and fluffy. Slowly whisk in the cooled custard until thoroughly combined, then add the cooled melted chocolate and whisk until combined.

11. To assemble, place one of the cooled sponges in the base of the lined cake tin. Spoon about one quarter of the chocolate cream filling into a bowl and set aside. Spoon about one seventh of the remaining filling over the top of the sponge in the tin and spread it out evenly. Place the next sponge on top and repeat, layering with the sponges and chocolate cream filling until you have eight sponges and seven layers of chocolate filling. Do not spread any chocolate filling on the top sponge. Chill the cake for 30 minutes.

12. Make the chocolate crown decorations, if using. To temper the chocolate, melt 100g of the chocolate in a heatproof bowl set over a pan of barely simmering water until it reaches 44°C on the cooking thermometer. Remove the bowl from the heat and add the remaining 50g chocolate, stirring until the chocolate melts and cools to 32°C.

13. Spoon the chocolate into the small piping bag fitted with a small writing nozzle. Lay your acetate over your crown template and pipe 12 chocolate crown shapes, then set them aside to set.

14. Once the chocolate crowns have set, rub them with gold powder, so that they look gilded. Carefully peel away the crowns to reveal shiny tempered chocolate on the back.

15. Remove the cake from the fridge and turn it out of the tin onto a flat plate or board. With a palette knife and using half of the reserved chocolate cream, spread a thin layer of chocolate cream around the side of the cake to crumb coat, then chill the cake for 20 minutes, until the chocolate cream is firm. Spoon the remaining chocolate cream into the piping bag fitted with a medium closed star nozzle.

16. Make the chocolate ganache. Place the chocolate in a heatproof bowl. Warm the cream in a pan to just below boiling point, then pour it over the chocolate. Leave it to stand for 3 minutes, then stir the chocolate into the cream to form a smooth ganache. Stir in the butter and leave the ganache to cool to a coating consistency (about 32°C).

17. Remove the cake from the fridge and place it on a wire rack. Pour the chocolate ganache over the cake, evenly covering the top and side, then leave the ganache to set for 10–15 minutes.

18. Pipe 12 rosettes around the top edge of the cake, and top each rosette with a gilded chocolate crown, if using. When the ganache is beginning to harden, use a knife to score the top of the ganache to mark out 12 equal portions, ready for slicing.

BRUNCH PIKELETS

Pikelets are a cross between crumpets and drop scones. You can make them in advance and warm them up in a moderate oven or lightly toast them to serve. Here, as a seasonal brunch dish, we've topped them with smoked salmon, snipped fresh chives and pea shoots, but they are good with jam, too!

125g plain flour
125g strong white
   bread flour
4g fast-action
   dried yeast
1 tsp caster sugar
½ tsp salt
225ml whole milk
125ml buttermilk
20g unsalted butter,
   melted
1 tsp sunflower oil

To serve
1 tsp white wine vinegar
4–6 eggs
30g unsalted butter
1 tsp espelette pepper
   or dried chilli flakes
125g smoked salmon
1 tbsp snipped chives
   (and chive flowers,
   if available)
handful of pea shoots
4–6 lemon wedges

1. Tip both flours, and the yeast, sugar and salt into a mixing bowl, stir to combine and make a well in the centre.

2. Warm the milk until lukewarm, pour it into the dry ingredients with the buttermilk and whisk for 1–2 minutes, until completely smooth. Scrape down the inside of the bowl with a rubber spatula, cover and leave at room temperature for 1–1½ hours, until doubled in size and the surface of the batter is covered in active bubbles.

3. Heat a heavy-based frying pan or flat (not ridged) griddle pan over a low–medium heat. Brush it with the melted butter and oil, then use kitchen paper to blot off any excess fat from the pan.

4. Using a large spoon, gently fold the batter over a couple of times to knock out any large air bubbles. Drop a rounded tablespoon of the mixture into the pan and let it spread to 8cm in diameter. You should be able to cook 3–4 pikelets at a time in a large pan. Cook the pikelets over a low heat, without turning, for 3–4 minutes, until no wet batter remains on the top and the underside is golden.

5. Flip the pikelets over and cook the other side for a further 1–2 minutes, until golden. Remove them from the pan and leave them to cool on a wire rack while you use the remaining batter to make 12 in total.

6. To serve, bring a medium pan of salted water to a gentle simmer and add the vinegar. Break the eggs, one at a time, into a ramekin or tea cup and carefully drop them into the simmering water. Poach the eggs for 2 minutes, or until cooked to your liking, then remove them from the pan using a slotted spoon and drain them on kitchen paper.

7. Meanwhile, melt the butter and add the espelette pepper. Warm the pikelets in a moderate oven or under a hot grill, if needed, and arrange them on plates. Top them with the smoked salmon and poached eggs, then drizzle over the espelette butter and scatter with chives and pea shoots. Serve with a lemon wedge on the side.

RUBY GRAPEFRUIT BUNDT

The ripest and most flavourful pink grapefruit are usually available between November and April, making this beautiful citrus bundt, with its delicate pink icing, a fitting centrepiece for a springtime coffee date with friends. If you have time, make the sponge and drizzle it with the syrup the day before icing and serving.

For the candied peel and grapefruit syrup
1 ruby grapefruit
6 tbsp caster sugar

For the sponge
175g unsalted butter, softened
250g golden caster sugar
3 large eggs, beaten
1 tsp vanilla paste
juice and finely grated zest of 2 ruby grapefruits
200g plain flour, sifted
150g ground almonds
2 tsp baking powder
pinch of salt
3 tbsp full-fat Greek yogurt

To decorate
150g icing sugar, sifted
2 tbsp ruby grapefruit juice (reserved from above)
pink food-colouring gel (optional)

You will need
baking tray, lined with baking paper
1.75-litre bundt cake tin, greased and dusted with flour

1. Make the candied peel. Using a vegetable peeler, remove the skin from the grapefruit and cut it into very thin shreds (reserve the grapefruit to make the syrup later). Tip these into a bowl with 2–3 tablespoons of caster sugar. Mix, then spread the peel out on the lined baking tray. Leave it for at least 4 hours, until dry and crisp.

2. When you're ready to bake, heat the oven to 170°C/150°C fan/ Gas 3 and make the sponge. Beat the butter and sugar in a stand mixer fitted with the beater, on medium speed for 3–5 minutes, until pale and creamy, scraping down the inside of the bowl from time to time. Add the eggs, a little at a time, beating well between each addition. Add the vanilla and beat again to combine.

3. Beat in 6 tablespoons of the grapefruit juice and all the zest to combine – the mixture may curdle but don't worry (reserve any remaining juice). Tip in the flour, ground almonds, baking powder and salt. Add the yogurt and beat for another 20–30 seconds to combine.

4. Spoon the mixture into the prepared tin and spread it level with a spoon. Bake just below the middle shelf for about 45 minutes, until golden brown, well risen and a skewer inserted into the centre comes out clean. Leave the sponge in the tin for 2 minutes, then turn it out onto a wire rack to cool for 15 minutes, until warm.

5. Make the grapefruit syrup. Squeeze the juice from the peeled grapefruit and mix it with the remaining 3–4 tablespoons of caster sugar to dissolve. Using a wooden skewer, poke holes over the top of the warm bundt, then brush it with the syrup and leave it to cool.

6. To decorate, whisk together the icing sugar and the 2 tablespoons of reserved grapefruit juice to make a thick but pourable icing (make up the liquid with water, if necessary), adding more icing sugar or juice/ water as necessary and a tiny dot of pink food colouring, if using. Spoon the icing over the bundt, letting it drizzle down the side. Leave the icing to set, then scatter with the candied peel to finish.

MINI ROLLS

These mini-rolls are orange-flavoured joconde sponge filled with an orange blossom ricotta and mascarpone filling. Set aside an uninterrupted hour or two to make them – they're not difficult, but you'll need to bake, fill and roll in one sitting.

For the filling
500g ricotta cheese
75g icing sugar, sifted
250g mascarpone cheese
1 tsp orange blossom
    water, or to taste
1 tsp vanilla paste

For the sponge
200g icing sugar, sifted
200g ground almonds
6 eggs
finely grated zest of
    1 large unwaxed orange
¼ tsp orange food-
    colouring gel
½ tsp orange extract
6 egg whites
¼ tsp cream of tartar
pinch of salt
30g caster sugar
30g plain flour, sifted

To decorate
200g white chocolate,
    chopped
100g roasted almonds,
    finely chopped

You will need
cooking thermometer
2 large baking trays
    (each about 40 x 30cm),
    lined with baking paper
2 sheets of baking paper
    (each about 40 x 30cm)
small piping bag
    fitted with a small
    writing nozzle

1. Start the filling. Place the ricotta in a sieve over a bowl to drain off any excess liquid. Leave it to stand while you make the sponge.

2. Heat the oven to 200°C /180°C fan/Gas 6.

3. Make the sponge. Place the icing sugar, ground almonds, 4 eggs and the orange zest in a large glass or stainless steel bowl. Set the bowl over a pan of barely simmering water and whisk with an electric hand whisk until doubled in volume and the mixture leaves a ribbon trail when you lift the whisk.

4. Add the remaining 2 eggs to the bowl and continue whisking until the temperature reaches 50°C on the cooking thermometer. Remove the bowl from the pan and whisk in the orange food-colouring gel and orange extract.

5. Whisk the egg whites in a stand mixer fitted with the whisk, on medium speed until they form soft peaks.

6. Add the cream of tartar and salt, then, 1 teaspoon at a time, add the sugar, whisking well between each addition until the meringue is silky smooth and forms firm peaks.

7. Using a large metal spoon, fold one third of the meringue into the sponge mixture, then fold in the remaining meringue along with the flour. Divide the mixture equally between the lined baking trays, spreading it out smoothly and evenly to the edges. Bake for 9 minutes, until golden and just firm to the touch.

8. Meanwhile, continue to make the filling. Place the drained ricotta in a bowl with the icing sugar, mascarpone, orange blossom water and vanilla, then beat until smooth.

9. Place the two 40 x 30cm sheets of baking paper on the work surface and as soon as the sponges come out of the oven, turn them out onto the paper.

Continues overleaf

10. Peel off the top layers of baking paper. Leave the sponges to cool for 5 minutes, then spread the filling equally and evenly over the top of each sponge. If necessary, turn the sponges so that you have a short end closest to you. Then, cut each sponge vertically in half to make four long pieces.

11. Using the baking paper to help you, one by one, roll up each sponge from a long, outside edge to give four long rolls in total. Leave the rolled-up sponges wrapped in the baking paper for 30 minutes, until set.

12. Unwrap the rolls from the baking paper and trim the ends of each roll so that all are of equal length. Then, cleaning the knife between cuts, slice each roll into three equal pieces to give 12 mini rolls in total.

13. To decorate, melt half the white chocolate in a heatproof bowl set over a pan of barely simmering water. Meanwhile, put the roasted almonds in a bowl.

14. Once the chocolate has melted, remove it from the heat and dip in one end of each roll, then dip the same end into the roasted almonds to coat. Leave to set.

15. Melt the remaining white chocolate in a separate heatproof bowl set over a pan of barely simmering water. Spoon the melted chocolate into the small piping bag fitted with a small writing nozzle. Pipe fine lines of chocolate back and forth across each roll to decorate. Leave to set before serving.

CHERRY BLOSSOM SHORTBREADS

These delicate iced biscuits are a celebration of the beautiful cherry blossom that bursts into bloom on our trees during spring. Sugar paste is perfect for making delicate floral decorations for cakes and biscuits, as it is easy to roll thinly, then press and shape into soft petals.

200g unsalted butter, softened
50g icing sugar, sifted
50g caster sugar
1 egg yolk
1 tsp cherry extract
225g plain flour, sifted
50g ground almonds
pinch of salt

To decorate
500g icing sugar
2 egg whites
brown, pink and teal blue food-colouring pastes
50g pink sugar paste
50g white sugar paste

You will need
6cm square cutter
2 baking sheets, lined with baking paper
4 small piping bags, each fitted with a small writing nozzle
5mm and 1cm flower cutters

1. Beat the butter and both sugars in a stand mixer fitted with the beater, on medium speed for about 3–5 minutes, until pale and creamy, scraping down the inside of the bowl from time to time. Add the egg yolk and cherry extract and mix again to combine.

2. Add the flour, ground almonds and salt and mix again to bring the mixture together. Turn the mixture out of the bowl and gather it together into a neat ball using your hands. Flatten it into a disc, then cover it and chill it for 1 hour, until firm.

3. Roll out the dough on a lightly floured work surface to about 2–3mm thick. Using the square cutter, stamp out the shortbreads and arrange them on the lined baking sheets. Gather the dough scraps together and re-roll and stamp out more squares until all the dough is used and you have about 20 shortbreads. Chill the shortbreads for 20 minutes. Meanwhile, heat the oven to 170°C/150°C fan/Gas 3.

4. Bake the biscuits for about 12 minutes, until firm and lightly browned at the edges. Leave them on the baking sheets to cool and further firm up.

5. To prepare the icing, sift the icing sugar into the bowl of a stand mixer fitted with the whisk. Add the egg whites and 2 tablespoons of water. Whisk for about 2 minutes, until smooth and thick.

6. Spoon 1 tablespoon of the icing into a small bowl, cover and set aside. Spoon 2 tablespoons of the icing into another bowl and tint this brown using the brown food-colouring paste. Cover it and set it aside. Spoon another 2 tablespoons of icing into a third bowl and tint this pink; cover and set aside. Colour the remaining icing teal blue and spoon 2 tablespoons of it into a piping bag fitted with a small writing nozzle. Cover the remaining blue icing.

Continues overleaf

7. Pipe a neat, continuous outline of blue icing around the edge of each shortbread and leave it to dry for 30 minutes.

8. Add a drop more water to the blue icing in the bowl until it's loose enough to just run smoothly off a spoon. Spoon 1 teaspoon of the icing into the middle of each biscuit and, using a teaspoon or small palette knife, tease the icing into the square to fill the outline. Repeat to ice the remaining shortbreads and leave the icing to harden and dry for about 2 hours.

9. Meanwhile, make the cherry blossom flowers. Roll out the pink sugar paste between two sheets of baking paper, to about 1mm thick. Then, do the same for the white sugar paste. Using the flower cutters, stamp out as many flowers as possible in each colour. You will need four or five flowers for each shortbread.

10. Lightly press each flower between your fingers and lay it on a piece of slightly scrunched foil so that each flower is 'ruffled', then leave the flowers to dry for about 2 hours.

11. Spoon the brown icing into a second piping bag fitted with a small writing nozzle and pipe a branch shape trailing across each iced shortbread. Arrange four or five cherry blossoms on each branch.

12. Spoon the white and pink icings each into a remaining piping bag fitted with a small writing nozzle and pipe little dots in the middle of each cherry blossom and more dots around the flowers. Leave the iced biscuits for about 2 hours for the icing to set before serving.

BAKER'S RECIPE

CRYSTELLE'S CHAI & JAGGERY CAKE

My mum is an expert in making chai. When I began working from home at the start of lockdown in spring 2020, she served me chai every day – so this cake is my thank you to her. The jaggery filling uses ingredients true to my Goan heritage and gifted to me by my Nana. In all, this is the cake version of me!

For the sponge
350g unsalted butter, softened
250g caster sugar
150g light brown soft sugar
3 large eggs
2 egg whites (save the yolks for the filling)
1 tbsp vanilla paste
400g plain flour
40g cornflour
1 tsp salt
2 tsp baking powder
¾ tsp bicarbonate of soda
2 tsp ground ginger
2 tsp ground cinnamon
1 tsp ground cardamom
½ tsp ground cloves
2 chai tea bags
350ml buttermilk, at room temperature

For the coconut & jaggery filling
50g desiccated coconut
300ml coconut cream
150g jaggery
6 large egg yolks
2 tsp cornflour

Continues overleaf

1. Heat the oven to 180°C/160°C fan/Gas 4.

2. Make the sponge. Beat the butter with both sugars in a stand mixer fitted with the beater, on medium speed for about 3–5 minutes, until pale and creamy, scraping down the inside of the bowl from time to time.

3. In a jug, beat together the whole eggs and egg whites. A little at a time, add the eggs to the sponge mixture, beating well between each addition. Add the vanilla and beat again to combine.

4. Sift the flour, cornflour, salt, baking powder, bicarbonate of soda, ginger, cinnamon, cardamom, cloves and the contents of the chai tea bags into the bowl (discard the bags) and lightly fold them in using a rubber spatula. Add the buttermilk and mix to combine.

5. Divide the mixture equally between the lined tins and spread it level in both. Bake the sponges on the middle shelves for about 25 minutes, until risen, golden and a skewer inserted into the centre of each comes out clean. Leave the sponges to cool in the tins for 2–3 minutes, then turn them out onto wire racks to cool completely.

6. While the oven is hot, scatter the desiccated coconut onto a baking tray and toast it for 2–3 minutes, until pale golden. Leave the toasted coconut to cool until needed.

7. Meanwhile, prepare the rest of the coconut and jaggery filling. Combine the coconut cream and jaggery in a small pan and warm it briefly over a medium heat, stirring until the jaggery melts. It shouldn't boil – just heat it until warm.

Continues overleaf

For the buttercream
350g caster sugar
6 large egg whites
¾ tsp salt
500g unsalted
    butter, softened
2 tbsp vanilla paste

To decorate
1 tbsp cinnamon
    pearl sugar
50g toasted
    coconut flakes
bronze edible sprinkles

You will need
18cm round cake tins x 4,
    greased, then base-lined
    with baking paper
sugar thermometer
large piping bag
    fitted with a large
    plain nozzle
medium piping bag
    fitted with a medium
    closed star nozzle

8. In a bowl, beat the egg yolks with the cornflour until smooth. Gradually, add two thirds of the warm coconut-cream mixture, whisking continuously until smooth. Return the mixture to the pan and cook, stirring continuously, over a low–medium heat for about 4 minutes, until thickened and the cornflour is cooked out. Stir in the toasted desiccated coconut and transfer the filling to a bowl. Cover the surface of the filling with cling film to prevent a skin forming and leave to cool to room temperature, then chill until ready to use.

9. Make the buttercream. Tip the sugar into a pan and pour in 225ml of water. Set the pan over a low heat, swirling the pan from time to time to dissolve the sugar (do not stir). Bring the syrup to the boil and cook it until the mixture reaches 115°C on a sugar thermometer and becomes syrupy (about 5 minutes).

10. At this point, whisk the egg whites and salt in a stand mixer fitted with the whisk, on medium speed until the egg whites form soft peaks. Slowly and steadily pour the hot syrup into the bowl while whisking on low speed. Continue whisking for about 15 minutes, until the meringue has cooled and holds firm peaks. Add the butter, a little at a time, whisking continuously until smooth and creamy. Add the vanilla and mix to combine. Spoon about one quarter of the buttercream into the piping bag fitted with a large plain nozzle.

11. To assemble, lay three of the sponges on the work surface and pipe a ring of buttercream around the outside edge of the top of each. Fill the middle of the buttercream border with the coconut jaggery filling, about one third per layer. Layer up the sponges on a serving plate and top with the fourth sponge layer.

12. With a palette knife and using about 4 tablespoons of the remaining buttercream in the bowl, spread a thin layer of buttercream over the top and side of the cake, to crumb coat. Chill for 30 minutes, until firm. Spread half the remaining buttercream over the top and side of the cake, using the back of a spoon or the palette knife to create a spiral swirl over the top.

13. Spoon the remaining buttercream into the medium piping bag fitted with a medium closed star nozzle. Pipe rosettes in assorted sizes to form a crescent shape on the top of the cake. To decorate, scatter the crescent with cinnamon pearl sugar, toasted coconut flakes and bronze edible sprinkles.

PIZZA BIANCA DI PRIMAVERA

This pizza bianca has lashings of creamy mascarpone, buffalo mozzarella and gorgonzola (in place of the tomato sauce found on its cousin, the pizza rossa) and is topped with spring veggies – new potatoes and purple sprouting broccoli or curly kale. Prepare the dough 24–48 hours before you plan to bake.

For the pizza dough
250g strong white
    bread flour
250g '00' flour
1 tsp caster sugar
1 tsp salt
2g fast-action dried yeast
300ml lukewarm water
2 tbsp extra-virgin
    olive oil, plus extra
    for greasing

For the toppings
400g new potatoes
2 onions, sliced
2 tbsp extra-virgin
    olive oil, plus extra
    for drizzling
2 garlic cloves, crushed
1 tbsp chopped rosemary
250g mascarpone cheese
100g trimmed kale leaves
200g purple sprouting
    broccoli, trimmed
125g buffalo mozzarella,
    torn into small pieces
125g gorgonzola dolce,
    crumbled
50g parmesan,
    finely grated
1 tsp dried chilli flakes
salt and freshly ground
    black pepper

You will need
large baking tray or
    plastic food box, oiled
1–2 pizza stones or heavy
    baking sheets

1. Make the pizza dough the day before, or up to 48 hours in advance. Combine both flours, and the sugar, salt and yeast in the bowl of a stand mixer fitted with the dough hook. Add the water and 2 tablespoons of olive oil and knead on low speed to combine. Increase the speed to medium and continue to knead for a further 5–6 minutes, until the dough is silky smooth and elastic.

2. Shape the dough into a ball, return it to the lightly oiled bowl, cover and leave at room temperature for 1 hour, until doubled in size.

3. Weigh the dough and cut it into four equal-sized portions, then shape each portion into a neat, tight ball. Place the balls, spaced well apart, on the oiled baking tray or in the plastic box. Dust them with flour, then cover them and chill them for 24–48 hours.

4. Make the pizza toppings. Cook the potatoes in boiling salted water until tender, then drain them, leave them to cool, and cut them into 3mm-thick slices. Fry the onions in 2 tablespoons of olive oil over a medium heat for about 10 minutes, stirring often, until softened and starting to caramelise at the edges. Add half the garlic and cook for a further 1 minute. Remove from the heat, add the rosemary and season well with salt and pepper.

5. Mix the mascarpone with the remaining garlic and season well with salt and pepper.

6. Lightly flour the work surface and gently pat the pizza dough balls into 15cm rounds. Place each pizza base on a sheet of baking paper, lightly dust each with flour, then cover them and leave them for 30 minutes to rest. Meanwhile, heat the oven to 230°C/210°C fan/ Gas 8 or as hot as your oven can go. Heat the pizza stone(s) or baking sheet(s) in the oven at the same time.

Continues overleaf

7. Top and bake one pizza at a time – unless you have 2 pizza stones or baking sheets. Take a pizza base, and still on the baking paper and using floured hands, gently pull and stretch it into a circle about 25cm in diameter, with the edge thicker than the middle to make a crust.

8. Scatter one quarter of the cooked onions over the middle, then, using a teaspoon, dollop over one quarter of the seasoned mascarpone. Scatter over a quarter of the kale, purple sprouting broccoli and sliced potatoes, followed by the buffalo mozzarella, gorgonzola and parmesan. Season with chilli flakes and pepper, then drizzle over a little olive oil.

9. Quickly and carefully slide the pizza, still on the baking paper, onto the hot pizza stone or baking sheet (or stones/sheets if you're baking two pizzas at a time) and bake for 8–10 minutes, until the crust is crisp and brown and the topping is bubbling.

10. Cut the pizza into wedges and eat it while piping hot. While one pizza is baking, prepare the next until you have topped and baked them all.

MINI HUMMINGBIRD CAKES

A perfect treat for Mother's Day, these mini hummingbird cakes are easy to make, even for little hands. Make sure you use a super-ripe and juicy-sweet pineapple and overripe bananas that are freckled with brown spots, to get the right level of sweetness in the finished cakes.

40g pecan nuts
125g peeled,
    cored pineapple,
    finely chopped
1 ripe banana, mashed
25g desiccated coconut
175g plain flour
½ tsp baking powder
½ tsp bicarbonate of soda
½ tsp ground cinnamon
¼ tsp ground allspice
pinch of salt
125g golden caster sugar
100g sunflower oil
2 eggs, lightly beaten
1 tsp vanilla paste

To decorate
50g coconut flakes
1 tbsp golden caster sugar
1cm slice of pineapple,
    peeled, cored and cut
    into 12 small wedges

For the frosting
300g full-fat cream cheese
3 tbsp coconut nectar
    or maple syrup
¼ tsp ground cinnamon

You will need
12-hole mini Victoria
    sponge tray, greased,
    then base-lined with
    baking paper discs;
    or a greased and
    floured muffin tray

1. Heat the oven to 180°C/160°C fan/Gas 4.

2. Spread the pecans onto a baking sheet and bake for 3 minutes, until toasted. Chop them into small pieces and tip them into a bowl. Add the pineapple, banana and desiccated coconut.

3. Sift the flour, baking powder, bicarbonate of soda, cinnamon, allspice and salt into a large mixing bowl. Add the sugar and mix well to combine, then make a well in the centre.

4. Combine the oil, eggs and vanilla in a jug, pour this into the well in the dry ingredients and beat the mixture until almost smooth. Add the pineapple and banana mixture and stir to combine.

5. Divide the mixture equally between the holes in the prepared sponge or muffin tray. Bake the cakes on the middle shelf for about 18 minutes, until risen, golden brown and a skewer inserted into the centre of each comes out clean. Remove the cakes from the oven, leave them to cool in the tray for 2–3 minutes, then carefully transfer them to a wire rack, top upwards, and leave them to cool completely.

6. Begin the decoration. While the oven is hot, scatter the coconut flakes onto a baking tray and toast them for 1–2 minutes, until crisp, and golden at the edges. Leave to cool.

7. Heat the sugar in a non-stick frying pan over a medium heat until it melts and starts to turn golden. Add the pineapple pieces and cook them, turning frequently, until caramelised. Remove the coated pineapple from the pan and leave it to cool.

8. Make the frosting. Beat the cream cheese with the coconut nectar or maple syrup and the cinnamon until smooth and thickened.

9. Cut each cake in half horizontally and trim to level the tops if needed. Spread a layer of frosting over the bottom half of each cake, then top with the second layer and a swirl of frosting. Decorate each with a few toasted coconut flakes and a piece of pineapple.

SUPER-SEEDED SODA BREAD

In a homage to St Patrick's Day (March 17), we simply had to include an Irish soda bread. Possibly the easiest bread to make, soda bread requires no kneading or proving – you just bake it immediately after mixing. Turn it into doorstep sandwiches filled with a good, strong Irish cheddar to complete the theme.

225g plain flour
225g plain
    wholemeal flour
1 tsp bicarbonate of soda
1 tsp salt
100g mixed seeds
    (pumpkin, sunflower,
    linseed, sesame and
    poppy), plus extra
    to garnish
50g oat, rye or wheat
    flakes, plus extra
    to garnish
350–400ml buttermilk,
    plus 2 tbsp to glaze
1 tbsp runny honey

You will need
baking sheet, lined
    with baking paper

1. Heat the oven to 200°C/180°C fan/Gas 6.

2. Sift both types of flour with the bicarbonate of soda and salt into a large mixing bowl. Tip in the bran left in the sieve, then add the seeds and oat, rye or wheat flakes and mix to combine.

3. In a jug, mix together the buttermilk and honey and add this to the dry ingredients. Mix everything together using a rubber spatula. The dough should be only just combined – there's no need to knead.

4. Lightly flour the work surface, turn out the dough and shape it into a 20cm-diameter ball. Carefully lift the ball onto the lined baking sheet, flatten the top of the loaf slightly and, using a long-bladed knife, cut a deep cross almost all the way through the loaf. Brush with buttermilk and scatter with extra seeds and oat, rye or wheat flakes.

5. Bake the loaf for 40 minutes, until golden brown, well risen and it sounds hollow when tapped underneath.

6. Remove the loaf from the oven and transfer it to a wire rack to cool. Serve it on the day of baking, slathered with salted butter or turned into sandwiches.

PASSIONFRUIT SOUFFLÉS

Passionfruit vary enormously in size and juiciness, so use passionfruit pulp or purée in a carton for the soufflés and save the fresh fruit to decorate. Served with vanilla ice cream, these delicate soufflés are a light dessert for a springtime gathering.

300g passionfruit purée
150g caster sugar
1 tbsp cornflour
2 egg yolks
½ tsp vanilla paste
4 egg whites
pinch of cream of tartar
pinch of salt
icing sugar, for dusting
2 passionfruits, cut in half
    and pulp scooped out

You will need
150ml ramekins x 6,
    greased, then dusted
    with caster sugar

1. Mix together the passionfruit purée and 50g of the caster sugar in a small pan and bring the mixture to the boil over a low–medium heat. Reduce the heat and simmer for 20 minutes, until thickened and reduced by about half – you need 150g. Remove from the heat.

2. In a small bowl, mix the cornflour with 1 tablespoon of water to a smooth paste. Pour 3 tablespoons of the reduced passionfruit purée into the bowl, stirring continuously until smooth. Return the mixture to the pan and return to the boil, stirring until thickened and the taste of cornflour has gone – this will take about 30 seconds. Pour the mixture into a bowl and leave it to cool for 20 minutes.

3. Heat the oven to 190°C/170°C fan/Gas 5.

4. In a large mixing bowl, whisk the egg yolks, 50g of the caster sugar, and the vanilla until thick and mousse-like and the mixture holds a ribbon trail when you lift the whisk. Add the remaining cooled passionfruit purée and whisk until thickened.

5. In another bowl, whisk the egg whites, cream of tartar and salt to soft, floppy peaks. Gradually add the remaining 50g of caster sugar, whisking continuously to firm, smooth, glossy peaks. Using a large metal spoon, fold 1 large tablespoon of the egg white into the egg-yolk mixture to lighten, then fold in the remaining egg whites.

6. Divide the soufflé mixture equally between the prepared ramekins, slightly overfilling them and ensuring there are no large air pockets. Using a palette knife, smooth the top of the soufflés so the mixture is level with the top of each ramekin. Run your thumb around the top inside edge of each and arrange the ramekins on a baking tray.

7. Bake the soufflés on the middle shelf for 10–11 minutes, until well risen and golden on top, and with a very slight wobble. Using a fish slice, carefully and quickly transfer the ramekins to small plates. Dust the soufflés with icing sugar and serve them immediately with the passionfruit pulp spooned on top.

BAKER'S RECIPE

CHIGS'S MANGO & COCONUT UPSIDE DOWN CAKE

This cake always puts a smile on my mum's face – it is her perfect pick-me-up, which makes it a favourite for me. Try a slice with a cup of Indian tea.

For the caramel
100g caster sugar
50g unsalted butter
2 mangoes, peeled, stoned and finely sliced

For the sponge
200g block of creamed coconut
100g unsalted butter, softened
200g caster sugar
3 large eggs
6 tbsp just-boiled water
200g self-raising flour, sifted
½ tsp baking powder
60g desiccated coconut
finely grated zest of 1 unwaxed lime
1 tsp ground cardamom
½ tsp salt
vanilla custard, to serve (optional)

You will need
23cm springform tin, greased, then base-lined with baking paper

1. Make the caramel. Place the sugar in a medium heavy-based pan over a medium heat and cook until the sugar dissolves – do not stir, just swirl and shake the pan gently. Increase the heat to high and let the sugar caramelise around the edges, shaking the pan occasionally until the sugar turns golden brown. Add the butter and swirl the pan until it melts, then use a spoon to stir until combined and no longer oily. Pour the caramel into the lined tin and tip the tin to coat the base evenly in the caramel. Leave to set hard (a few minutes).

2. Arrange the mango slices on top of the caramel. (If you have any mango left, finely chop it and add to the sponge mixture.)

3. Make the sponge. Place 10g of the white coconut oil at the end of the block into a bowl. Cut off 65g of the hard creamed coconut and chop it finely. Add this to the oil and microwave it in short bursts on full power until the mixture is soft enough to mash with a fork.

4. Tip the mashed coconut, the butter and the caster sugar into the bowl of a stand mixer fitted with the beater, and beat on medium speed for about 3–5 minutes, until pale and creamy, scraping down the inside of the bowl from time to time. One at a time, add the eggs, beating well between each addition.

5. Finely chop the rest of the block of creamed coconut. Place it in a bowl with any residual coconut oil and the just-boiled water and mix to make a paste. Add the paste to the mixing bowl, along with the flour, baking powder, desiccated coconut, lime zest, ground cardamom and salt and mix on medium speed for 1 minute, until just combined.

6. Spoon the sponge mixture over the mango in the tin and spread it level. Bake the cake on the middle shelf for 40–45 minutes, until golden and a skewer inserted into the centre comes out clean. Leave the cake to cool in the tin for 5 minutes, then turn it out onto a serving plate. Serve with vanilla custard, if you wish.

SPICED LAMB & SPINACH FILO PIE

You can prepare the filling for this aromatic spring lamb pie in advance (at least a day is good) and it will be all the better for it – the spices will have time to mellow and further season the meat.

2 tbsp olive oil
1kg boned leg of lamb, trimmed of excess fat and cut into 3cm chunks
2 onions, sliced
3 garlic cloves, crushed
1 tsp ground cumin
1 tsp ground coriander
½ tsp cayenne pepper
½–1 tsp dried chilli flakes
1 tbsp tomato purée
1 x 400g tin of chopped tomatoes
400ml chicken, vegetable or light lamb stock
finely grated zest of ½ unwaxed lemon
1 tsp dried mint
1 cinnamon stick
1 bay leaf
2 tbsp pomegranate molasses or runny honey
200g tinned chickpeas, drained weight
200g spinach
100g dried apricots, quartered
2 tbsp chopped coriander
8 sheets of filo pastry
50g unsalted butter, melted
1–2 tsp za'atar
salt and freshly ground black pepper

1. Heat 1 tablespoon of olive oil in a large frying pan and brown the lamb in batches over a high heat, until browned, taking care not to overcrowd the pan. Tip the browned meat into a lidded casserole.

2. Heat the oven to 150°C/130°C fan/Gas 2.

3. Add the remaining olive oil and the onions to the frying pan and cook over a low–medium heat for about 10 minutes, until the onions are tender and starting to caramelise. Add the garlic and cook for a further 1 minute.

4. Add the cumin, coriander, cayenne pepper and chilli flakes to the onions, mix well and cook for 1 minute. Stir in the tomato purée and cook for another 1 minute before adding the chopped tomatoes and stock. Bring the liquid to the boil, simmer for 30 seconds, then pour the mixture into the casserole with the lamb.

5. Add the lemon zest, dried mint, cinnamon stick, bay leaf, pomegranate molasses or honey and season well with salt and pepper. Bring slowly to the boil, cover and transfer to the oven to cook for 2–2½ hours, until the lamb is tender and the sauce thickened. Add the chickpeas, cook for a further 20 minutes, then remove from the oven and cool while you prepare the spinach.

6. Cook the spinach in a large frying pan over a medium heat until wilted. Tip into a colander to drain off any excess water, then leave to cool before squeezing to further dry out.

7. Remove the cinnamon stick and bay leaf from the lamb, add the spinach, apricots and coriander, then spoon the filling into a large ovenproof or pie dish.

8. Increase the oven temperature to 180°C/160°C fan/Gas 4.

9. Brush each sheet of filo pastry with melted butter. Scrunch up the buttered filo and place it on top of the lamb mixture. Scatter with the za'atar and bake the pie on the middle shelf for about 40 minutes, until the pastry is golden and crisp and the filling is heated through.

JAIRZENO'S CHOCOLATE MINT CAKE

My partner always asks for his favourite things in baked form. He loves peppermint chocolates, so I made him this cake for his birthday.

For the sponge
260g plain flour, sifted
400g caster sugar
85g cocoa powder, sifted
2 tsp baking powder
1 tsp salt
2 eggs, lightly beaten
240ml whole milk
240ml vegetable oil
1½ tsp vanilla extract
240ml just-boiled water

For the frosting
200g unsalted butter, softened
150g icing sugar, sifted
340g full-fat cream cheese
1 tsp vanilla extract
½–1 tsp mint extract, to taste
green food-colouring paste

For the glaze
6 platinum-grade gelatine leaves
340g caster sugar
265ml double cream
150g white chocolate, chopped
green food-colouring paste

Continues overleaf

1. Make the sponge. Heat the oven to 180°C/160°C fan/Gas 4. Mix together the flour, sugar and cocoa powder in a large mixing bowl. Stir in the baking powder and salt.

2. In a separate mixing bowl, whisk together the eggs, milk and oil with a balloon whisk. Whisk the egg mixture into the dry ingredients.

3. Mix the vanilla with the just-boiled water and gradually beat this into the sponge mixture until smooth and the consistency of pancake batter. Divide the mixture equally between the lined cake tins and bake the sponges on the middle shelves for 20–25 minutes, until just firm to the touch. Leave to cool completely in the tins.

4. Make the frosting. Using an electric hand whisk, whisk the butter and 75g of the icing sugar in a large bowl until smooth, pale and fluffy. Add half the cream cheese and whisk on low speed until combined. Then, use a wooden spoon to beat in the remaining cream cheese and icing sugar with the vanilla, mint and a little green food colouring to make a thick, smooth, pale green frosting. Don't over-whisk or the icing can become runny. Chill until needed.

5. To assemble, trim the top of the cakes to level, if needed. Spread 4 tablespoons of the frosting over one sponge, then top with the second sponge and repeat the frosting. Top with the third sponge, placing it bottom upwards to give the top of the cake a flat surface.

6. Using a palette knife, cover the cake in a smooth, very thin layer of frosting to create a crumb coat, then chill the cake for 15 minutes. Spread the remaining frosting over the top and side of the cake, making it as smooth and even as possible. Return the cake to the fridge for about 1 hour, until firm (this helps to set the glaze).

Continues overleaf

For the decoration
100g 54% dark mint
chocolate, chopped

You will need
18cm sandwich tins
x 3, greased, then
base-lined with
baking paper
8–12cm-square pieces
of baking paper x 8

7. Make the glaze. Place the gelatine in a bowl with 6 tablespoons of cold water and leave the leaves to soften.

8. Place the sugar in a small pan with 120ml of water over a high heat and bring the liquid to the boil. Reduce the heat and simmer for 2 minutes, then stir in the cream and return to the boil. Immediately remove from the heat.

9. Lift the gelatine out of the water and shake off any excess. Stir the gelatine and white chocolate into the sugar and cream mixture until smooth, then, a little at a time, add green food colouring until you have a pale green glaze. Leave to cool until barely warm, stirring occasionally to prevent a skin forming. When ready, the glaze will be at room temperature, and will have thickened but it won't be set.

10. Place a wire rack on your work surface with a sheet of baking paper underneath. Remove the cake from the fridge and place it on the rack. Pour over half the glaze so that it coats the top and side evenly, spreading the side with a palette knife if needed. Chill the cake for 10 minutes, until the glaze is just set, then repeat with a second coat of the glaze. Place the cake on a serving plate and return it to the fridge.

11. Make the decoration. Scrunch each square of baking paper into a ball. Open out the paper a little into a cup shape and place it on a baking tray.

12. Melt the mint chocolate in a small heatproof bowl set over a pan of barely simmering water. Spoon a little of the melted chocolate onto one of the opened-out pieces of paper and swirl, making sure the paper retains its cup shape, so that the chocolate coats the paper. Repeat for all the paper squares and chocolate. Chill for 10 minutes, until set.

13. Peel off the paper from the chocolate cups (don't worry if some of them break). Remove the cake from the fridge and pile on the chocolate pieces to decorate.

WILD GARLIC FLATBREADS

When you begin to smell the pungent scent of wild garlic on woodland walks, you know that spring has finally arrived. Wild garlic, also called ramsons, makes for a great introduction to foraging. It has all the heady aroma of garlic, but a milder flavour when cooked. These simple flatbreads are delicious served with soups, dips and curries, and sprinkled with some pretty white ramsons flowers.

300g strong white bread flour
7g fast-action dried yeast
¼ tsp salt
1 tsp caster sugar
100ml coconut milk
50ml coconut yogurt
3 tbsp extra-virgin olive oil, plus extra for greasing
2 handfuls of wild garlic leaves (about 100g), finely shredded
sea-salt flakes

1. Tip the flour, yeast, salt and sugar into a large mixing bowl, stir to combine and make a well in the centre.

2. Warm the coconut milk until lukewarm, pour it into the dry ingredients, add the yogurt and 2 tablespoons of olive oil and mix until combined.

3. Lightly flour the work surface, tip the dough out of the bowl and knead for 5–10 minutes, until smooth and elastic. Sprinkle over three quarters of the wild garlic and gently knead it into the dough. Do not over-knead or the dough will turn green!

4. Shape the dough into a ball and place it in a lightly oiled bowl. Cover it with a clean tea towel and leave it for about 1 hour, until doubled in size.

5. Meanwhile, mix together the remaining olive oil and wild garlic in a small bowl.

6. Turn out the dough onto a lightly floured work surface and knock out any air pockets. Divide the dough into four equal balls and roll each into a round flatbread, about 20cm in diameter.

7. Heat a griddle or heavy-based frying pan over a medium heat until hot. Add one flatbread and cook it for 2–3 minutes on each side until lightly charred in places, puffed up and beginning to bubble on top. Remove the flat bread from the griddle, cover it with a clean tea towel, and cook the remaining three balls of dough in the same way.

8. Brush the warm flatbreads with the wild garlic oil and sprinkle them with sea-salt flakes before serving.

HAMANTASCHEN

Hamantaschen (meaning 'Haman's pockets') are served at the Jewish holiday of Purim, which usually occurs in early March, and celebrates the Persian Jews' escape from fifth-century-CE King Haman. Traditionally filled with poppy seeds or dates, but now more often with jam, the shape is said to evoke Haman's three-pointed hat.

200g unsalted butter, softened
100g icing sugar, sifted
1 egg
1 tsp vanilla paste
finely grated zest of ¼ unwaxed lemon
300g plain flour
½ tsp baking powder
pinch of salt
10 tbsp of your favourite homemade jam (see page 149)

You will need
9cm round, fluted cutter
2 baking sheets, lined with baking paper

1. Beat the butter and icing sugar in a stand mixer fitted with the beater, on medium speed for 3–5 minutes, until pale and creamy, scraping down the inside of the bowl from time to time. Add the egg, vanilla and lemon zest and mix again to thoroughly combine.

2. Sift the flour, baking powder and salt into the bowl and mix well. Shape the dough into a ball, flatten the ball into a disc, then cover and chill for at least 2 hours, until firm.

3. Roll out the dough on a lightly floured work surface to about 2–3mm thick. Using the cutter, stamp out as many discs as you can from the dough. Gather the scraps together, press them into a ball and re-roll, then stamp out more discs to make about 30 in total.

4. Spoon 1 teaspoon of jam into the middle of each disc, leaving a 1cm border around the edge.

5. Brush the borders with a little water and, one disc at a time, fold one side towards the middle to only partly cover the jam. Fold another third of the border over so that it forms a neat corner with the first fold. Fold the final third over, tucking one end over the previous corner and tucking the other underneath the first corner. Gently pinch the corners to neaten. Repeat for all the discs, arranging the filled biscuits on the lined baking sheets as you go.

6. Chill the biscuits for 20 minutes while you heat the oven to 170°C/150°C fan/Gas 3.

7. Bake the hamantaschen for about 15 minutes, until crisp and golden. Leave them to cool on a wire rack before serving.

SUMMER

RECIPES

PEACH BELLINI CAKE

PAUL'S JAMMY BISCUITS

CHERRY & ALMOND FRIANDS

GOOSEBERRY ROULADE

CHOCOLATE & RASPBERRY RIPPLE CHEESECAKE BROWNIES

FREYA'S PIÑA COLADA CUSTARD SLICE

FREE-FORM TOMATO TART

CHOUXNUTS

ASPARAGUS, PEA & MINT QUICHE

DAIRY-FREE MANGO ICE-CREAM SANDWICHES

APRICOT FRANGIPANE TRAYBAKE

STRAWBERRY & CLOTTED CREAM CAKE

CHOCOLATE & RASPBERRY RUFFLE WEDDING CAKE

CHEESE, HAM & PICCALILLI PASTIES

ROCHICA'S STRAWBERRY-TOPPED COOKIES & CREAM CAKE

TROPICAL PAVLOVA

PRUE'S SABLÉ BRETON

FETA, OREGANO & SUNDRIED TOMATO KNOTS

BLACKCURRANT & ALMOND CAKE

CRUFFINS

AMANDA'S LEMON & ELDERFLOWER PALETTE CAKE

PEACH BELLINI CAKE

Inspired by cocktails for a summer sunset, these fluffy almond sponges are drenched in a sweet prosecco syrup and layered with peach and prosecco compôte and a honey vanilla Chantilly cream. A single slice makes everything seem peachy!

For the sponge
100g ground almonds
160g gluten-free
    self-raising flour, sifted
225g unsalted butter,
    softened
225g golden caster sugar
4 eggs
100ml buttermilk
1 tsp vanilla paste
pinch of salt

**For the peach &
prosecco compôte**
3 large peaches, peeled,
    stoned and chopped
juice of ½ lemon
220g caster sugar
50ml prosecco

For the prosecco syrup
250ml prosecco
200g caster sugar

**For the honey vanilla
Chantilly cream**
500ml double cream
2–3 tbsp runny honey
1 tsp vanilla paste

To decorate
3 peaches, stoned
    and sliced
mint sprigs
icing sugar, for dusting

You will need
15cm sandwich tins x 3
wooden skewer
    or cocktail stick

1. Heat the oven to 180°C/160°C fan/Gas 4.

2. Make the sponge. Mix together the ground almonds and flour. Beat the butter and sugar in a stand mixer fitted with the beater, on medium speed for 10 minutes, until pale and creamy. Add the eggs, one at a time, beating well between each addition. If the mixture starts to curdle, add a spoonful of the flour mixture. Stir in the buttermilk. Fold in the flour mixture, vanilla and salt.

3. Divide the mixture equally between the prepared tins and spread it level. Bake the sponges on the middle shelves for 30–35 minutes, until risen and a skewer inserted into the centres comes out clean. Leave to cool slightly in the tins.

4. While the sponges are baking, make the peach and prosecco compôte. Mix the peaches, lemon juice, sugar and prosecco in a pan and bring the mixture to the boil. Reduce the heat to low and simmer for 30 minutes, stirring occasionally, until the compôte thickens and the peaches are soft. Remove from the heat and leave for 10 minutes, then purée with a hand blender. Leave to cool until needed.

5. Make the prosecco syrup. Warm the prosecco and sugar in a small pan over a low heat until the sugar dissolves.

6. Using a wooden skewer or cocktail stick, make holes over the top of the warm sponges and carefully brush over the syrup. Leave the sponges in the tins for 15 minutes to cool.

7. Make the Chantilly cream. Whip the cream, honey and vanilla together in a bowl to reach soft peaks. Cover and chill until needed.

8. To assemble, place one sponge on a cake board and spread a layer of cream on top. Spoon a ring of cream around the edge of the sponge and fill the centre with the compôte. Place the second sponge on top and repeat with the cream and compôte. Add the third sponge and top with a generous dollop of cream, spreading it to the edge. Decorate with peach slices, drizzle over any remaining prosecco syrup, then finish with mint sprigs and dust with icing sugar.

JUDGE'S RECIPE

PAUL'S JAMMY BISCUITS

We all know that ripe, summer raspberries produce the most delicious jam – here it's sandwiched with a buttercream filling between crisp biscuits. The swirl is optional (if you have a patterned stamp), but it does make for an extra-professional finish.

For the jam
100g raspberries
125g jam sugar

For the biscuits
120g very soft
 unsalted butter
120g caster sugar
1 large egg
½ tsp vanilla extract
215g plain flour
25g cornflour

For the filling
50g unsalted butter,
 softened
100g icing sugar,
 plus extra for dusting
½ tsp vanilla extract

You will need
7cm fluted round cutter
7cm patterned biscuit
 stamp (optional)
2 baking sheets, lined
 with baking paper
2cm heart-shaped cutter

1. Make the jam. Place the raspberries in a small, deep-sided pan and crush them with a potato masher. Add the sugar and bring the liquid to the boil over a low heat until the sugar dissolves. Then, increase the heat and boil for 4 minutes. Remove the pan from the heat and pass the jam through a sieve into a heatproof bowl. Discard the seeds in the sieve. Leave the jam to cool, then chill it to set.

2. Heat the oven to 170°C/150°C fan/Gas 3.

3. Make the biscuits. Place the butter and caster sugar in a mixing bowl and beat well for 3–5 minutes, until pale and fluffy. Add the egg and vanilla and beat again until thoroughly combined.

4. Sift in the flour and cornflour and mix by hand to a crumbly dough. Bring the dough together with your hands and knead it gently on a lightly floured work surface until smooth. Do not overwork.

5. Halve the dough and shape each half into a flat disc. Wrap the discs and chill them for 20 minutes.

6. Unwrap one of the dough discs on a lightly floured work surface and roll it out to about 3mm thick. Using the fluted round cutter, cut out 12 rounds, re-rolling the trimmings as necessary.

7. Lightly flour a biscuit stamp, if you have one, then stamp each round to create a pattern. Re-cut the rounds with the fluted round cutter, then place the 12 discs on one of the lined baking sheets. Chill them while you roll out the remaining dough.

8. Repeat steps 6 and 7 with the remaining dough disc, then, using the heart-shaped cutter, stamp out the centre of 12 of the rounds. Place these on the other baking sheet and chill them for 20 minutes.

Continues overleaf

9. Bake the biscuits for 10–12 minutes, until the edges start to turn a pale golden colour. Leave them to cool on the baking sheets for 5 minutes, then transfer the biscuits to a wire rack to cool completely.

10. Make the filling. Put the butter into a bowl and sift the icing sugar on top. Add the vanilla and, using a wooden spoon or an electric hand whisk, beat until very light and smooth.

11. Dollop a spoonful of the filling onto the smooth side of each of the 12 plain biscuits, spreading it to the edges with a palette knife. Spoon a little jam over the buttercream, then sandwich, smooth side downwards, with the 12 cut-out heart biscuits. Dust with icing sugar to serve.

CHERRY & ALMOND FRIANDS

If you're lucky enough to have a cherry tree in your garden, you'll know that the season for cherries, in the height of summer, is really very short – especially when the birds spy them! These friands are a quick and simple way to make the most of the crop as it ripens.

150g unsalted butter, melted
100g plain flour
225g icing sugar, plus extra for dusting
100g ground almonds
pinch of salt
6 egg whites
1 tsp vanilla extract or paste
finely grated zest of ¼ unwaxed lemon
200g cherries, halved and pitted
50g flaked almonds

You will need
12-hole friand or muffin tin

1. Heat the oven to 180°C/160°C fan/Gas 4.

2. Melt the butter and brush a light coating over the inside of each hole in the friand or muffin tin. Dust the greased tin with a little of the flour and tap out any excess. Leave the remaining butter to cool slightly while you prepare the other ingredients.

3. Sift the remaining flour, and the icing sugar, ground almonds and salt into a large mixing bowl.

4. In another mixing bowl, whisk the egg whites until they just hold soft, floppy peaks.

5. Using a large metal spoon or rubber spatula, fold the dry ingredients, and the vanilla, remaining melted butter and the lemon zest into the egg whites until combined.

6. Divide the mixture equally between the holes in the prepared tin, filling each one three quarters full. Divide the cherry halves between the friands and scatter each friand with flaked almonds.

7. Bake the friands on the middle shelf for 20–25 minutes, until they are well risen, golden brown and a skewer inserted into the centre of each comes out clean.

8. Leave the friands to rest in the tin for 2 minutes, then carefully turn them out onto a wire rack and leave to cool. Dust with icing sugar to finish.

GOOSEBERRY ROULADE

Gooseberries come into season in late June, and give us mostly just the summer months to make the best of them. They pair beautifully with elderflower, another seasonal joy. If you're picking fresh elderflowers to decorate this roulade, give the blossoms a good shake and wash them in cold water to remove any little bugs first.

For the meringue roulade
6 egg whites
pinch of salt
300g caster sugar
2 tsp vanilla paste
1 tsp white wine vinegar
1 tsp cornflour
25g flaked almonds

For the filling
400g gooseberries, topped and tailed
2 tbsp caster sugar
3 tbsp elderflower cordial
600ml double cream
150g full-fat Greek yogurt

To decorate
150ml double cream
1 tbsp icing sugar, sifted, plus extra for dusting
1/2 tsp vanilla paste
handful of elderflower blossoms, to serve (optional)

You will need
40 x 30cm Swiss roll or baking tin (4cm deep), greased, then lined (base and sides) with baking paper
large piping bag fitted with a medium closed star nozzle

1. Heat the oven to 180°C/160°C fan/Gas 4.

2. Whisk the egg whites and salt in a stand mixer fitted with the whisk on medium speed until the egg whites hold soft peaks.

3. Gradually add the sugar, whisking continuously until the meringue is glossy, smooth and holds firm peaks. Add the vanilla, vinegar and cornflour and mix for 30 seconds, until smooth. Spoon the meringue into the lined tin and spread it evenly, but not smoothly. Scatter with the flaked almonds and bake on the middle shelf for 15 minutes.

4. Reduce the oven temperature to 170°C/150°C fan/Gas 3. Turn the tin around in the oven to ensure the meringue cooks evenly, and bake for a further 12–15 minutes, until the top is golden brown and crisp. Leave to cool for 1 hour.

5. Meanwhile, make the filling. Tip the gooseberries into a pan, add the sugar and elderflower cordial and cook, stirring frequently, over a low heat until the gooseberries break down to a soft purée (about 10–15 minutes). Remove the pan from the heat and leave the gooseberry mixture to cool to room temperature.

6. Whisk the cream with the yogurt to very soft peaks. Using a large spoon, lightly fold the gooseberry purée into the cream until barely combined – there should still be pockets of gooseberry purée visible.

7. Turn the meringue out of the tin onto a large, clean, dry tea towel. Peel off the baking paper. Spread the gooseberry filling over the meringue. Then, starting at one short end, roll the meringue into a roulade. Carefully lift it onto a serving plate.

8. To decorate, whisk the cream, icing sugar and vanilla to soft peaks. Spoon it into the large piping bag fitted with a medium closed star nozzle and pipe the cream along the top of the roulade. Chill the roulade until ready to serve. Just before serving, scatter elderflower blossoms (if using) over the top and dust with icing sugar to finish.

CHOCOLATE & RASPBERRY RIPPLE CHEESECAKE BROWNIES

The deep indulgence of chocolate brownie with the tanginess of raspberries on top, these squares of deliciousness take a decadent dessert and give it a summery twist, especially when served with an extra tumble of fresh raspberries on the side.

For the brownie layer
250g 70% dark
   chocolate, chopped
150g unsalted butter,
   cubed
3 eggs
250g golden caster sugar
1 tsp vanilla paste
150g plain flour
1 tbsp cocoa powder
pinch of salt

For the cheesecake layer
350g full-fat cream
   cheese
100g caster sugar
1 tsp vanilla paste
2 eggs
100g soured cream
175g raspberries, plus
   optional extra to serve

You will need
30 x 20cm (4cm deep)
   brownie tin, greased
   and lined (base and
   sides) with baking
   paper
wooden skewer

1. Heat the oven to 170°C/150°C fan/Gas 3.

2. Melt the chocolate and butter in a heatproof bowl set over a pan of barely simmering water. Stir until smooth, then remove the pan from the heat and leave the mixture to cool for 3–4 minutes.

3. Whisk the eggs and sugar in the bowl of a stand mixer fitted with the whisk, on medium speed for about 2 minutes, until well aerated and paler in colour. Add the melted chocolate mixture and vanilla and mix again until just combined.

4. Sift the flour, cocoa powder and salt into the bowl and fold them in using a rubber spatula until the mixture is smooth. Spoon the mixture into the prepared tin and spread it level. Bake the brownie on the middle shelf for 20 minutes, until slightly risen and set.

5. Meanwhile, make the cheesecake layer. In a mixing bowl, beat together the cream cheese and sugar until smooth. Add the vanilla and eggs and beat again to thoroughly combine. Add the soured cream and mix again until smooth.

6. In another bowl, mash the raspberries into a purée with a fork. Pass half of the mashed raspberries through a fine-mesh sieve to remove the seeds, then return the seedless purée to the bowl of remaining mashed raspberries and mix to combine.

7. Remove the brownie from the oven and tap the bottom of the tin sharply on the work surface to deflate slightly. Leave the brownie to cool for 3 minutes, then pour the cheesecake mixture over the top. Spoon the raspberry purée randomly over, then, using a wooden skewer, ripple the mixture through the cheesecake. Return the tin to the oven for a further 22–25 minutes, until the cheesecake sets.

8. Leave the brownie to cool to room temperature in the tin, then chill it for at least 1 hour before cutting it into squares or rectangles to serve (with extra raspberries, if you wish).

BAKER'S RECIPE

FREYA'S PIÑA COLADA CUSTARD SLICE

This was one of the first vegan recipes I created from scratch – for my friend who inspired me to eat a plant-based diet. We couldn't find vegan custard slices anywhere, so I decided to make my own. As for the piña colada, well, nothing says summer more than one of those!

For the rough puff pastry
300g plain flour
pinch of salt
50g vegan block,
    cubed and chilled
8–9 tbsp ice-cold water
120g vegan block, frozen

For the pineapple jam
1 x 227g tin of pineapple
    in light syrup
225g jam sugar
juice of 1 lemon

For the custard
300ml soya milk
4 tbsp cornflour
6 tbsp thick coconut
    milk (from the top
    of the tin)
100g caster sugar
1 tbsp vanilla extract

For the icing
175g icing sugar
yellow food-colouring gel

Continues overleaf

1. Make the vegan rough puff. Mix together the flour and salt in a bowl. Rub in the cubes of vegan block using your fingertips until the mixture resembles breadcrumbs. Gradually add enough ice-cold water to form a dough. Lightly flour the work surface and roll out the dough into a rectangle, about 45 x 15cm, with one of the short ends nearest you.

2. Coarsely grate half the frozen vegan block over the bottom two thirds of the dough. Fold down the top third and fold up the bottom third as if folding a letter.

3. Turn the folded dough through 90 degrees and roll it out into a rectangle, again measuring about 45 x 15cm. Repeat Step 2, using the remaining frozen block. Fold as before. Wrap the dough and leave it to rest in the fridge for 30 minutes.

4. Repeat the rolling and folding process (this time without more vegan block) twice more, chilling the pastry for 30 minutes between each roll and fold.

5. Meanwhile, make the jam. Place a saucer in the freezer (for testing the jam). Drain the pineapple through a sieve over a pan to catch the syrup. Finely chop the pineapple and add it to the pan. Add the sugar and lemon juice and, using a wooden spoon, stir this over a low heat until the sugar dissolves. Increase the heat to medium and bring the liquid to the boil. Cook, stirring for 5–6 minutes, until it reaches 105°C on a sugar thermometer. Remove the pan from the heat.

Continues overleaf

You will need
sugar thermometer
2 baking sheets, lined
    with baking paper
20cm square cake tin,
    lined (base and sides
    with an overhang)
    with foil
small piping bag
cocktail stick

6. To test if the jam is ready, remove the saucer from the freezer and spoon on a little jam. Leave it for 1 minute, then push the jam with your finger – if the jam wrinkles, it has reached setting point. If not, return it to the heat and boil it for a further 1–2 minutes and test again. Leave the jam to cool. (This will make more jam than you need – store any leftover in sterilised jars in the fridge for up to 1 month and use it for spreading on toast, buns, cruffins or scones.) Heat the oven to 200°C/180°C fan/Gas 6.

7. Cut the pastry in half and roll each piece to a 20cm square. Trim the squares neatly, discarding the trimmings, and place them on the lined baking sheets. Bake the pastry sheets for 10–15 minutes, until golden brown and crisp. Remove the sheets from the oven and if they have puffed up and risen a bit, press them gently to flatten, then set aside to cool on the baking sheets while you make the custard.

8. Pour the soya milk into a pan and add the cornflour. Using a wooden spoon, beat them together until smooth. Add the thick coconut milk, the caster sugar and the vanilla. Place the pan over a medium heat and stir continuously for 3–4 minutes, until the mixture is thick. Remove the custard from the heat, pour it into a bowl and cover the surface with cling film to prevent a skin forming. Leave to cool for 15 minutes, then chill for 15 minutes, until starting to set.

9. Assemble the slices. Place one pastry sheet in the bottom of the foil-lined cake tin, reserving the best piece for the top. Spread 3 tablespoons of pineapple jam over the pastry in an even layer. Then, spread a thick layer of cooled custard evenly over that. Top with the second piece of pastry and chill for at least 30 minutes, until set.

10. Make the icing. Sift the icing sugar into a bowl and stir in 2–3 teaspoons of water to give a thick, smooth pouring consistency. Place 2 tablespoons of the icing into a small bowl and add about 2 drops of yellow colouring, or enough to give your desired shade. Spoon the icing into the small piping bag and snip the end.

11. Spread the white icing over the top of the chilled custard slice. Pipe lines of yellow icing, spacing them 2cm apart, over the top. Drag the cocktail stick through the yellow lines in alternate directions to create a feather pattern. Set at room temperature for 30 minutes.

12. Using the foil overhang to help you, carefully remove the custard slice from the tin and then peel away the foil. Cut the custard slice into 8 equal pieces (each measuring 5 x 10cm). Chill before serving.

FREE-FORM TOMATO TART

This tart is a showcase for the best of the summer's tomatoes. Use as many different varieties as you can find. Basil is a natural partner, but any soft herb will work.

For the flaky pastry
125g strong white
   bread flour
125g plain flour
good pinch of salt
250g unsalted butter,
   cut into 2cm cubes
   and chilled
125ml ice-cold water,
   plus extra if needed
1 tsp white wine vinegar
   or lemon juice

For the topping
100g feta
1 egg
1 garlic clove, crushed
1 tbsp whole milk,
   for glazing
1 tsp dried oregano
500g mixed tomatoes,
   tops trimmed and thinly
   sliced horizontally
2 tbsp extra-virgin olive
   oil, plus extra to serve
100g pitted olives,
   roughly chopped
small handful of
   basil leaves
freshly ground
   black pepper

You will need
2 baking sheets, 1 lined
   with baking paper

1. Make the pastry (you can do this a day in advance, if you wish). Combine both flours and the salt in a bowl. Add the butter and cut it into the flour using a knife until the pieces are half their original size.

2. Sprinkle the water and vinegar over the mixture and use the knife to combine, adding more water to bring the dough together, if needed. You should have large pieces of butter still visible. Gather the pastry into a ball, flatten it into a disc, then roll it lengthways, using a tapping motion, into a neat rectangle of about 45 x 15cm.

3. Lightly flour the top of the dough and fold the bottom third up onto the middle third, then the top third down to cover to make a neat three-layered pastry square. Cover and chill for at least 1 hour.

4. Lightly dust the work surface with flour and roll out the dough again to a neat 45 x 15cm rectangle. Fold the bottom third up and the top third down, as before. Turn the square 90 degrees and repeat this rolling and folding one more time. Cover the pastry and chill again for at least a further 1 hour before using.

5. Roll out the pastry on a lightly floured surface to a rectangle measuring about 35 x 25cm, and trim to neaten. Carefully lift the pastry onto the lined baking sheet and, using a knife, 'knock up' the sides of the pastry to create a 1–2cm raised lip all around. Chill the pastry for 30 minutes while you prepare the topping.

6. Heat the oven to 200°C/180°C fan/Gas 6 and place the other baking sheet on the middle shelf.

7. Make the topping. Crumble the feta into a food processor, add the egg and garlic and blitz until smooth. Season with pepper. Spread the feta mixture onto the pastry, leaving a border. Brush the border with milk to glaze. Sprinkle the oregano over the feta and arrange the sliced tomatoes on top. Drizzle with olive oil, season, and transfer to the hot baking sheet to bake for 35–40 minutes, until the pastry is crisp and golden and the tomatoes start to caramelise at the edges. Remove from the oven and cool to room temperature, then drizzle with more olive oil and scatter with olives and basil leaves to finish.

CHOUXNUTS

Think crisp, light choux pastry in a doughnut-like ring. Filled with raspberry ripple Chantilly cream, these chouxnuts are a decadent treat for a garden party. You will have more jam than you need for the recipe, but you can spoon the extra into a small bowl and keep it in the fridge for up to three weeks for toast, cruffins or cakes.

_____

For the raspberry jam
150g raspberries
150g jam sugar
juice of ½ lemon

For the choux pastry
140ml whole milk
135g unsalted butter
1 tsp vanilla sugar
   (or caster sugar)
½ tsp salt
180g plain flour
3 eggs, lightly beaten
1 egg white
1 litre vegetable oil,
   for deep frying

For the Chantilly cream
300ml double cream
3 tbsp icing sugar, sifted
½ tsp vanilla paste

For the icing
200g icing sugar, sifted
juice of ½–1 lemon
freeze-dried raspberries,
   for sprinkling

You will need
2 large piping bags
large closed star nozzle
7cm round cutter
10cm squares of baking
   paper x 12–14
cooking thermometer
small piping bag

1. Make the jam. Put a small saucer in the freezer. Tip the raspberries, jam sugar and lemon juice into a small, heavy-based pan. Place the pan over a medium heat, mash the berries slightly, then simmer for 2–3 minutes, until the sugar dissolves. Bring to the boil and boil for 5–7 minutes, until thickened. Test the jam: remove the saucer from the freezer and spoon a thin layer of jam onto it. Push the jam with your finger – if it wrinkles, it's ready. If not, put the pan back on the heat and boil the jam for another 1–2 minutes, then test again. Once it's ready, transfer the jam to a bowl to cool.

2. Make the choux pastry. Pour 120ml of water into a medium pan and add the milk, butter, sugar and salt and heat gently until the butter melts – don't let the water boil at this stage. Once the butter melts, increase the heat and quickly bring the mixture to the boil.

3. Tip in the flour in one go. Remove the pan from the heat and, using a wooden spoon, beat vigorously until there are no patches of dry flour left.

4. Return the pan to a low heat and beat the dough for 4–5 minutes to slightly cook and dry out, and until the dough comes away from the side of the pan in a smooth, glossy ball.

5. Tip the dough into the bowl of a stand mixer fitted with the beater and mix on low speed until the dough cools to a warm temperature.

6. A little at a time, add the beaten eggs to the dough, beating on medium speed between each addition until shiny and smooth. Beat in the egg white until smooth. Fit one of the large piping bags with the large closed star nozzle and spoon in the dough. Set aside.

7. Using a pencil, draw around the round cutter on each square of baking paper, then turn the pieces of paper over so that they are pencil-side downwards. Set aside.

Continues overleaf

8. Pour the vegetable oil into a large, deep saucepan (it should be no more than one third full) and place it over a high heat. Heat the oil to 180°C on the cooking thermometer, or until a cube of day-old bread sizzles and rises to the surface immediately when dropped into the pan. (Alternatively, heat a deep-fat fryer to 180°C.)

9. While the oil is heating up, pipe a ring of choux dough onto each square of baking paper, using the pencil-drawn circles as a guide. Then pipe another ring of choux on top of each first ring.

10. When the oil has reached the correct temperature, very carefully drop one or two choux rings, and their pieces of paper, into the hot oil. After a few seconds, use tongs to remove the paper. Fry the choux rings for 3–3½ minutes on each side, until golden brown, risen and puffy all over. Remove the choux rings with a slotted spoon and set aside to drain and cool on kitchen paper while you fry the remaining choux rings. (Don't be tempted to cook more than one or two rings at a time, and be sure to let the oil come back to temperature before frying the next batch.)

11. Make the Chantilly cream. Using an electric hand whisk, whisk the cream, icing sugar and vanilla in a mixing bowl to soft peaks. Stir half the cooled jam through the cream, then spoon the mixture into the remaining large piping bag. Snip off the end to make a hole about 1cm in diameter.

12. Using the point of a knife, make three slits evenly spaced apart in the base of each chouxnut. Push the snipped end of the piping bag through each slit into the bun. Pipe in the cream, angling the bag to the side to evenly fill the chouxnut.

13. Spoon 3–4 tablespoons of the remaining jam into the small piping bag. Snip a small hole in the end and pipe a little jam into the chouxnuts through the same slits. Set aside.

14. Make the icing. In a small bowl, mix together the icing sugar and enough of the lemon juice to give a thick, pourable glaze. Using a palette knife, spread a thin layer of glaze over the top of each chouxnut. Sprinkle over the freeze-dried raspberries to decorate, then leave the icing to set before serving. (You can keep the chouxnuts in the fridge to serve the following day, if you wish.)

ASPARAGUS, PEA & MINT QUICHE

A perfect tart to serve al fresco, this quiche is packed with tender new-season vegetables. Vary the herbs depending on your preference and what you might have growing . You can swap the taleggio for feta or crumbly goat's cheese, if you prefer.

For the pastry
300g plain flour
pinch of salt
pinch of freshly ground
  black pepper
175g unsalted butter,
  cubed and chilled
4–5 tbsp ice-cold water
1 tsp white wine vinegar

For the filling
1 tbsp olive oil
1 courgette, trimmed
  and cut diagonally
  into 2mm slices
6–8 spring onions,
  trimmed
400g asparagus,
  trimmed
3 eggs
3 egg yolks
300ml double cream
75g shelled peas
100g taleggio cheese,
  cut into chunks
small handful of mint
  or basil, leaves picked
  and chopped
1 tbsp pine nuts
salt and freshly ground
  black pepper

You will need
23cm fluted tart tin
baking beans or rice

1. Make the pastry. Tip the flour, salt and pepper into a large mixing bowl. Add the butter and cut it into the flour using a table knife. Using your fingertips, rub the butter into the flour until the mixture resembles breadcrumbs.

2. Make a well in the centre, add 4 tablespoons of the water and the vinegar. Using the knife, cut the wet ingredients into the dry, then gather the mixture into a ball, adding more water if needed. Flatten the pastry into a disc, cover it and chill it for at least 1 hour.

3. Lightly flour the work surface and roll out the pastry to a neat disc, about 2–3mm thick and large enough to line the base and sides of the tart tin. Line the tin, trim any excess from the top, prick the base with a fork, then chill the pastry for 20–30 minutes. Meanwhile, heat the oven to 180°C/160°C fan/Gas 4.

4. Line the pastry case with baking paper and baking beans or rice. Place on a solid baking sheet and bake for about 20 minutes, until the edges are golden. Remove the paper and beans or rice and bake it for a further 4–5 minutes to dry out the base. Set the case aside while you prepare the filling.

5. Increase the oven temperature to 190°C/170°C fan/Gas 5.

6. Make the filling. Heat the olive oil in a large frying pan over a medium–high heat. When it's hot, add some courgette slices in an even layer, frying in batches for about 1 minute on each side until golden. Set aside each batch to cool on a baking sheet lined with kitchen paper.

7. Add the spring onions to the hot pan and cook, turning them occasionally, for about 1 minute, until softened and lightly browned. Remove from the pan and leave to cool with the courgettes.

Continues overleaf

8. Meanwhile, cook the asparagus in boiling salted water for about 2 minutes, until just tender (the cooking time will vary depending on the thickness of the stems). Drain the asparagus, then cool them under running cold water. Leave them to dry on kitchen paper.

9. Whisk together the whole eggs and egg yolks, then add the cream. Season well with salt and pepper and whisk to combine.

10. Cut the asparagus spears in half lengthways and arrange them in the pastry case with the courgettes, spring onions and peas.

11. Scatter the taleggio and mint or basil over the vegetables and carefully pour over the egg mixture. Top with the pine nuts and carefully slide the tart, still on the baking sheet, into the oven. Bake for about 30 minutes, until the filling is set and golden brown. Leave the quiche to cool for at least 10 minutes, then serve it warm or at room temperature.

DAIRY-FREE MANGO ICE-CREAM SANDWICHES

What a treat on a hot day! You can make and freeze the coconut, lime and mango ice cream in advance, along with the lightly spiced biscuits, which (uncoated) will keep in an airtight container for up to two days. When you're ready to serve, melt the white chocolate, finish the biscuits, then sandwich with the ice cream to serve. The recipe calls for tinned mango pulp as it makes a creamier ice cream than puréed fresh mango. The results are almost certainly irresistible!

For the ice cream
2 x 160ml tins of
　coconut cream
1 tsp vanilla paste
1 x 450g tin of
　mango pulp
finely grated zest of
　2 large unwaxed limes
125ml maple syrup
2 tsp ground cardamom

For the biscuits
120g Iranian pistachios
280g plain flour, plus
　extra for dusting
40g ground almonds
230g unsalted plant
　butter
130g icing sugar, sifted
2 tbsp caster sugar
1 large egg yolk
½ tsp vanilla paste
¾ tsp ground cardamom
½ tsp salt
200g dairy-free white
　chocolate, chopped

To decorate
1 tbsp pistachios,
　chopped

Continues overleaf

1. Make the ice cream. Place the coconut cream, vanilla paste, mango pulp, lime zest, maple syrup and cardamom in the bowl of a food processor and blitz to a smooth purée.

2. Pour the mixture into a jug and leave it (uncovered) in the freezer for 10 minutes, then transfer it to an ice-cream machine and churn it for 30 minutes, until semi-frozen.

3. Place the silicone mould on a baking sheet. Spoon equal amounts of the mango ice cream into eight of the holes and level it, making sure there are no air pockets. Place the mould on the unlined baking sheet and freeze it for 1–2 hours, while you make the biscuits.

4. Make the biscuits. Tip the pistachios, flour and ground almonds into a food processor and blitz to a fine crumb.

5. Place the plant butter, icing sugar and caster sugar into the bowl of a stand mixer fitted with the beater, and beat on medium speed for 3–5 minutes, until pale and fluffy. Add the egg yolk, vanilla paste and cardamom and beat until combined. Add the flour and pistachio mixture and the salt and mix on low speed until combined.

6. Bring the biscuit dough together with your hands and place it on a lined baking sheet. Cover it with baking paper and roll it out to a rough rectangle about 5mm thick. Place the dough, still on the baking sheet, in the fridge to chill for 20 minutes, until firm. Meanwhile, heat the oven to 180°C/160°C fan/Gas 4.

Continues overleaf

You will need
ice-cream machine
8cm silicone oval
    mould tray
3 baking sheets, 2 lined
    with baking paper
8cm oval biscuit cutter
bristle pastry brush
small piping bag
    fitted with a small
    writing nozzle

7. Remove the dough from the fridge and slide it onto the work surface, using the baking paper. Re-line the baking sheet with baking paper. Using the 8cm oval biscuit cutter, cut out 24 biscuits, re-rolling the trimmings as necessary. Place each biscuit on the lined baking sheets, spacing them 2cm apart.

8. Prick the biscuits all over with a fork and bake them for 15–20 minutes, until they are slightly golden around the edges. Remove them from the oven and while the biscuits are still warm, brush them with the pastry brush to expose the green. Then, transfer the biscuits to a wire rack to cool completely (about 15 minutes).

9. Melt the white chocolate in a heatproof bowl set over a pan of simmering water until smooth. Turn each biscuit upside down and, using the pastry brush, brush the chocolate over the biscuits to coat. Leave for 10 minutes, or until set.

10. To assemble, one at a time, turn out the ice cream blocks from the moulds and sandwich each block between two biscuits, with the white-chocolate side touching the ice-cream. Repeat until you have 12 ice-cream sandwiches.

11. Spoon the remaining white chocolate into the small piping bag fitted with a small writing nozzle and pipe lines of white chocolate back and forth across the centre of the biscuits. Sprinkle with the chopped pistachios to decorate. Serve immediately.

APRICOT FRANGIPANE TRAYBAKE

Wedges of fresh apricots scattered with crumble top these buttery, nutty, fruity shortbread squares, which would be perfect for a bake sale or a cake stall at a village fête. The honey sweetness from ripe apricots is a classic pairing with almonds, as the two come from the same stone-fruit family.

For the shortbread base
250g plain flour
200g unsalted butter,
    cubed and chilled
75g icing sugar, sifted,
    plus extra for dusting
pinch of salt

For the streusel topping
25g unsalted butter
40g flaked almonds
50g light brown
    soft sugar
40g plain flour

For the frangipane
175g unsalted butter,
    softened
175g caster sugar
3 eggs, lightly beaten
finely grated zest of
    ¼ unwaxed lemon
1 tsp vanilla paste
175g ground almonds
25g plain flour
½ tsp baking powder
pinch of salt
2 tbsp soured cream
4 tbsp apricot jam
7–8 apricots, stoned and
    each cut into 6 wedges

You will need
30 x 20cm traybake
    tin (5cm deep),
    greased, then lined
    (base and sides)
large piping bag
    fitted with a large
    plain nozzle

1. Make the shortbread base. Tip the flour, butter, icing sugar and salt into the bowl of a food processor and blitz until the butter is mixed into the flour and the mixture starts to clump together. Tip the mixture into the prepared tin and press it into an even layer to cover the base. Chill the shortbread dough for 20 minutes while you heat the oven to 180°C/160°C fan/Gas 4.

2. Bake the shortbread on the middle shelf for about 20 minutes, until pale golden. Remove it from the oven and leave it to cool while you prepare the rest of the bake.

3. Make the streusel topping. Melt the butter in a small pan or microwave, then leave it to cool for 3 minutes. Add the remaining ingredients and mix them in with your fingertips until the mixture starts to clump together. Set aside.

4. Make the frangipane. Beat the butter and caster sugar in a stand mixer fitted with the beater, on medium speed for 3–5 minutes, until pale and creamy. Add the eggs, a little at a time, mixing well between each addition and scraping down the inside of the bowl from time to time. Add the lemon zest and vanilla and mix again.

5. Sift the ground almonds, flour, baking powder and salt into the bowl and beat until smooth. Add the soured cream and mix again. Spoon the mixture into the large piping bag fitted with a large plain nozzle.

6. Spread the apricot jam evenly over the shortbread base, pipe the frangipane over the top, then spread it level.

7. Arrange the apricots neatly, cut side upwards, on top of the frangipane. Scatter with the streusel topping and bake for about 55 minutes, until the frangipane sets and the top is golden brown.

8. Leave the traybake to cool in the tin, then dust it with icing sugar and cut it into squares or bars to serve.

STRAWBERRY & CLOTTED CREAM CAKE

Nothing says British summer more than strawberries and cream. This cake is made with clotted cream, which gives it an extra richness and a delicate crumb. If you can, find some tiny, pick-your-own strawberries, which would look pretty on the top, too.

For the sponge
125g unsalted butter, softened
75g clotted cream
275g caster sugar
3 large eggs, lightly beaten
1 tsp vanilla paste
300g self-raising flour
½ tsp baking powder
pinch of salt
125ml whole milk

For the filling
350g clotted cream
1 tsp vanilla paste
50g icing sugar, sifted, plus extra for dusting
400g strawberries, hulled
4 tbsp strawberry jam

You will need
17cm round cake tins x 3, greased, then base-lined with baking paper

1. Heat the oven to 170°C/150°C fan/Gas 3.

2. Make the sponge. Beat the butter, clotted cream and sugar in a stand mixer fitted with the beater, on medium speed for 3–5 minutes, until pale and creamy, scraping down the inside of the bowl from time to time.

3. Add the eggs, a little at a time, beating well between each addition. Add the vanilla and mix again. Sift the flour, baking powder and salt into the bowl, add the milk and mix again to thoroughly combine.

4. Divide the mixture equally between the prepared cake tins and spread it level. Bake the sponges on the middle shelves for 25 minutes, until well risen, golden brown and a skewer inserted into the centre of each comes out clean. Leave the sponges to cool in the tins for 5 minutes, then carefully turn them out onto wire racks to cool completely.

5. Meanwhile, make the filling. Using a balloon whisk, whisk the clotted cream, vanilla and icing sugar in a mixing bowl until the cream holds soft, floppy peaks.

6. Weigh out 250g of the strawberries and slice them.

7. To assemble, place one cooled sponge on a serving plate and spread the top of it with 2 tablespoons of the jam. Spoon over one third of the whipped cream and top with half the sliced strawberries.

8. Top with a second sponge and repeat the layering using the remaining jam, another third of the whipped cream and the rest of the sliced strawberries. Top with the third sponge and spread the top with the remaining whipped cream.

9. Arrange the remaining strawberries, whole and cut in half, on the top of the cake, and dust with icing sugar to finish.

CHOCOLATE & RASPBERRY RUFFLE WEDDING CAKE

The romance of a summer wedding comes to life in this pretty-in-pink tiered cake – and no one would ever guess it's vegan. There are three layers of dark chocolate brownie filled with an indulgent raspberry and coconut cream filling. Scattered with plump fruit, this sumptuous cake, served with dollops of whipped coconut cream, can happily double as the dessert for your special celebration, too.

For the brownie layers
700g plain flour
180g cocoa powder
4 tsp bicarbonate of soda
900g light brown soft sugar
270g virgin coconut oil
3 tsp vanilla paste
1 litre coconut milk
4 tsp apple cider vinegar
230g vegan dark chocolate, melted

For the raspberry ruffle filling
250g vegan spread
800g icing sugar, sifted, plus extra for dusting
2 tsp vanilla paste
100g coconut cream
100g desiccated coconut
8 tbsp freeze-dried raspberry powder
6 drops of raspberry pink food-colouring gel

For the coconut vanilla frosting
125g vegan spread
400g icing sugar, sifted
1 tsp vanilla paste
2 tbsp coconut cream
1–2 drops raspberry pink food-colouring gel

Continues overleaf

1. Heat the oven to 180°C/160°C fan/Gas 4.

2. Make the brownie layers. Mix together the flour, cocoa powder and bicarbonate of soda in a large mixing bowl.

3. Put the sugar, coconut oil, vanilla and coconut milk in a very large pan. Place the pan over a low heat and warm the mixture, stirring continuously, until the sugar and oil melt. Remove the pan from the heat and quickly stir in the vinegar.

4. Sift the flour and cocoa mixture over the liquid, then gently mix everything together until combined.

5. Place a sieve over a very large mixing bowl and strain the chocolate batter to remove any lumps, pressing through any cocoa residue with the back of a spoon. You should now have a creamy, thick batter. Whisk the melted chocolate into the batter.

6. Divide the mixture equally between the six lined cake tins (three 20cm and three 15cm) and spread it level. Bake the brownie layers on the middle and lower shelves for 30 minutes, until a skewer inserted into the centre of each comes out clean (there may be a slight sticky residue). Cool in the tins.

7. Make the raspberry ruffle filling. Beat the vegan spread in the bowl of a stand mixer fitted with the beater, adding the icing sugar a cupful at a time, and the vanilla, until you have a thick, smooth paste. Beat in the coconut cream, desiccated coconut, raspberry powder and food colouring until fully combined and you have an even colour.

8. Spoon the filling into a large piping bag fitted with a large plain nozzle (refill the piping bag with the extra filling as needed, when you come to assemble).

Continues overleaf

To decorate
raspberries
mint leaves
edible fresh flowers

You will need
20cm sandwich tins x 3,
    greased, then base-lined
    with baking paper
15cm sandwich tins x 3,
    greased, then base-lined
    with baking paper
2 large piping bags,
    each fitted with a
    large plain nozzle
15cm cake board
20cm cake drum
2 large 40cm cake
    dowel rods
cake scraper
cake-decorating
    turntable (optional)

9. Make the coconut vanilla frosting. With an electric hand whisk or a stand mixer fitted with the beater, beat the vegan spread until pale and soft. Gradually add the icing sugar and add the vanilla, and beat the mixture until light and creamy. Beat in the coconut cream and a drop of food colouring, until smooth. Add more colouring, if desired. Spoon the frosting into the second large piping bag fitted with a large plain nozzle.

10. Carefully turn out the cooled brownie layers onto your work surface. Pipe dots of frosting onto the 15cm cake board and place one 15cm brownie layer on top. Pipe thick circles of the raspberry ruffle filling on top and spread them out evenly with a palette knife. Place another 15cm layer on top. Repeat with the raspberry ruffle filling. Place the third 15cm layer on top.

11. Pipe dots of frosting onto the 20cm cake drum and place one 20cm brownie layer on top. Pipe thick circles of the raspberry ruffle filling on top and spread them out evenly. Place another 20cm layer on top. Repeat with the raspberry ruffle filling. Place the third 20cm layer on top.

12. To assemble, measure and cut the cake dowels to the same height as the assembled 20cm cake tier and push 4 rods in a square shape in the middle of the cake to fit within a 15cm circle.

13. Using an offset spatula, spread the coconut vanilla frosting over the top and side of the 20cm tier. Using a cake scraper, scrape away the excess into a clean bowl to give a semi-naked finish. (You can use a cake-decorating turntable to do this, if you have one.)

14. Spread the remaining coconut vanilla frosting over the top and side of the 15cm tier and scrape away the excess into a clean bowl to give a semi-naked finish. Carefully place the 15cm cake tier (on its board) on top of the 20cm cake tier.

15. Decorate the cake with raspberries, mint leaves and fresh flowers and dust with icing sugar, then serve to impress your guests.

CHEESE, HAM & PICCALILLI PASTIES

These little pasties – a perfect size to hold – are just the thing to tuck into a picnic when you're out walking with the family. Alternatively, serve them warm, with drinks, at a casual, grown-up gathering on a summer's evening – prepare them in advance and bake them just before your guests arrive.

For the pastry
225g plain flour
pinch of salt
pinch of freshly ground
  black pepper
125g unsalted butter,
  cubed and chilled
¼ tsp ground turmeric
¼ tsp cayenne pepper
3 tbsp ice-cold water
1 tsp white wine vinegar
1 tbsp whole milk, to glaze

For the filling
7 tbsp piccalilli (see p.128)
100g mature cheddar,
  grated
100g smoked ham,
  shredded

You will need
10cm plain, round cutter
large baking sheet, lined
  with baking paper

1. Make the pastry. Tip the flour, salt and pepper into a large mixing bowl. Add the butter and cut it into the flour using a table knife. Using your fingertips, rub the butter into the flour until the mixture resembles breadcrumbs. Add the turmeric and cayenne pepper and mix again to combine.

2. Make a well in the centre and add the ice-cold water and vinegar. Using the knife, cut the wet ingredients into the dry, then gather the mixture into a ball. Flatten the ball into a disc, cover and chill the pastry for at least 1 hour, until firm.

3. Roll out the pastry on a lightly floured work surface to about 2mm thick. Using the cutter, stamp out discs, re-rolling the trimmings as necessary, until you have about 20 discs in total.

4. Place 1 teaspoon of piccalilli in the middle of each disc. Divide the cheese and ham between the pastry discs on top of the piccalilli, leaving a 1cm border around the edge. Brush a little water on each pastry border and fold each disc over to encase the filling and make a little parcel. Press the edges together to seal, then crimp the edges between your fingers.

5. Arrange the pasties on the lined baking sheet and chill for 20 minutes. Meanwhile, heat the oven to 190°C/170°C fan/Gas 5.

6. Brush the top of each pasty with a little milk to glaze, and cut a little steam hole in the top. Bake the pasties for about 25 minutes, until the pastry is crisp and golden and the filling is piping hot. Leave the pasties to cool for 2–3 minutes before serving.

MAKES 3 JARS / **HANDS ON** 30 MINS, PLUS BRINING & INFUSING / **COOK** 15 MINS

PICCALILLI

Piccalilli is a pickle full of crisp, summer vegetables in a mustardy turmeric sauce. Perfect both inside and as an accompaniment for our pasties, it's also delicious alongside charcuterie or with a cheese board.

1 small cauliflower, cut into very small florets
2 carrots, diced
125g French beans, cut into 1cm lengths
125g runner beans, cut into 1cm lengths
½ cucumber, halved, deseeded and diced
10 silverskin onions, peeled
75g sea-salt flakes
500ml white malt vinegar
1 bay leaf
2 tsp yellow mustard seeds
8 black peppercorns
½ tsp coriander seeds
3 allspice berries
2 garlic cloves, peeled
25g plain flour
1 tbsp English mustard powder
2 tsp ground turmeric
1 tsp ground ginger
75g caster sugar

1. Mix together all the vegetables in a large mixing bowl. Dissolve the sea-salt flakes in 1 litre of cold water and pour this over the vegetables to cover. Mix, cover and leave to brine for 4 hours.

2. Meanwhile, combine the vinegar, bay leaf, mustard seeds, peppercorns, coriander seeds, allspice berries and garlic in a pan and bring the liquid to the boil over a low heat. Remove the pan from the heat and leave to cool and infuse for 2 hours.

3. In a bowl, mix together the plain flour, mustard powder, turmeric and ginger.

4. Strain the infused vinegar into a bowl and discard the aromatic spices. Add 2 tablespoons of the strained vinegar to the flour mixture and mix to a paste.

5. Pour the remaining vinegar back into the pan. Add the sugar and bring to the boil, stirring continuously, until the mixture is glossy, thickened and coats the back of a spoon.

6. Drain the vegetables and pat them dry on kitchen paper. Add them to the hot vinegar mixture and cook over a low heat for 3–4 minutes, until just tender.

7. Spoon the piccalilli into sterilised jars and immediately cover with a lid. Store unopened in a cool cupboard for 2 weeks before using, and keep them in the fridge for up to 1 month after opening.

ROCHICA'S STRAWBERRY-TOPPED COOKIES & CREAM CAKE

My birthday treat, this is an indulgent cake full of all my favourite flavours. I thoroughly recommend it for a party with friends – there's certainly plenty for everyone – when strawberries are at their best. The quantity of Irish cream liqueur buttercream is generous, so you'll need a large stand mixer to make it in one go.

For the vanilla sponge
250g unsalted butter
250g caster sugar
4 eggs, lightly beaten
1 tsp vanilla extract
250g self-raising flour
20ml Irish cream liqueur
20g icing sugar, sifted

For the biscuit sponge
125g unsalted butter
125g caster sugar
2 eggs, lightly beaten
½ tsp vanilla extract
125g self-raising flour
7 chocolate & vanilla
   sandwich biscuits,
   finely crushed

For the chocolate sponge
250g caster sugar
200ml sunflower oil
4 eggs, lightly beaten
40ml whole milk
1 tsp vanilla extract
180g self-raising flour
90g cocoa powder
2 tsp apple cider vinegar
50ml just-boiled water

Continues overleaf

1. Heat the oven to 170°C/150°C fan/Gas 3.

2. Make the vanilla sponge. Melt the butter either in a small pan over a low heat or in a suitable bowl in the microwave, then add the sugar and stir to combine. Leave to cool.

3. Pour the cooled butter and sugar mixture into a large bowl. Add the eggs and vanilla and, using a wooden spoon, beat to combine. Sift in the flour and fold it in with a large metal spoon or a rubber spatula.

4. Divide the mixture between the lined cake tins and spread it level. Bake the sponges on the middle shelf for about 25 minutes, until well risen, golden and a skewer inserted into the centre of each comes out clean. Turn out the sponges onto a wire rack and leave to cool, then trim the top of each sponge to level, if needed.

5. In a small bowl, combine the liqueur and icing sugar and mix until the sugar dissolves. Brush the mixture over the top of each cold cake.

6. Make the biscuit sponge. Grease and line one of the cake tins again and follow steps 2 and 3 as for the vanilla sponge, above. Fold the crushed biscuits into the sponge mixture, then spoon the mixture into the lined tin and spread it level.

7. Bake the sponge (at the same temperature as before) on the middle shelf for 25–30 minutes, until well risen, golden and a skewer inserted into the centre comes out clean. Turn out the sponge onto a wire rack and leave to cool, then trim the top to level, if needed.

Continues overleaf

For the buttercream
8 egg whites
450g caster sugar
600g unsalted butter,
    softened
5 tbsp Irish cream liqueur
1 tsp vanilla extract
5 chocolate & vanilla
    sandwich biscuits,
    finely crushed

For the chocolate drip
100g double cream
75g 70% dark chocolate,
    chopped

To decorate
8–12 chocolate & vanilla
    sandwich biscuits, some
    whole, some halved
8–10 strawberries, some
    whole, some halved

You will need
20cm round cake tins x 2,
    greased, then base-lined
    with baking paper
small piping bag

8. Make the chocolate sponge. Grease and line both cake tins again. In a mixing bowl, whisk together the sugar and sunflower oil until combined. Add the eggs, milk and vanilla and beat to combine. Sift the flour and cocoa into the bowl and fold them in with a metal spoon. Add the vinegar and just-boiled water and beat until smooth.

9. Bake the sponges (at the same temperature again) on the middle shelf for 20–22 minutes, until well risen and a skewer inserted into the centre of each comes out with a moist crumb. Turn out the sponges onto a wire rack to cool, then trim the tops to level, if needed.

10. Make the buttercream. Whisk the egg whites and sugar together in a heatproof bowl until combined. Set the bowl over a pan of barely simmering water and whisk until the sugar dissolves and the meringue just holds a ribbon trail when you lift the whisk.

11. Transfer the egg mixture to a stand mixer and whisk on medium speed until the meringue cools completely. Add the butter, a little at a time, whisking well between each addition until thick, smooth and spreadable. Add the liqueur and vanilla and whisk again to combine. Spoon 150g of the buttercream into a separate bowl and stir in the crushed biscuits until combined.

12. Assemble the cake. Place one of the vanilla sponges on a serving plate and, using a palette knife, spread 3 tablespoons of the Irish liqueur buttercream evenly over the top. Top with a chocolate sponge and spread with half the biscuit buttercream. Put the biscuit sponge on top and spread with the remaining biscuit buttercream. Top with the second chocolate sponge and spread over 3 tablespoons of the Irish liqueur buttercream. Finally, top with the second vanilla sponge.

13. Using a palette knife, cover the top and side of the cake in a smooth, very thin layer of liqueur buttercream to crumb coat, then chill for 30 minutes, until firm. Then, spread the remaining liqueur buttercream evenly over the top and side of the cake and smooth it out using a palette knife. Chill for a further 30–40 minutes, until firm.

14. Make the chocolate drip. Warm the cream in a pan until hot, but not boiling. Meanwhile, tip the chocolate into a heatproof bowl and, when it's ready, pour the cream over. Leave for 2 minutes, then stir to melt the chocolate. Cool to room temperature, then spoon the drip into the piping bag and snip the end to give a 5mm hole. Pipe the drip around the top edge of the cake, allowing it to run down the side, then use the remainder to fill in and coat the top of the cake. To finish, top with the biscuits and strawberries for decoration.

TROPICAL PAVLOVA

This indulgent pavlova is shaped in a ring and decorated using upward sweeps of a palette knife, to make it look like a crown. The blueberries – ripe and ready to pick during summer – are the perfect complement for intensely sweet mango.

For the meringue
6 large egg whites
330g caster sugar
2½ tsp cider vinegar
1 tbsp cornflour
1 tsp vanilla paste

For the pistachio praline
50g caster sugar
35g pistachios

For the topping
3 mangoes, peeled,
    stoned, and flesh
    finely chopped
1 tbsp icing sugar, sifted
3 passionfruits, halved
90g 54% dark chocolate,
    finely chopped
150g blueberries
few mint sprigs,
    to decorate

For the Chantilly cream
600ml double cream
20g icing sugar, sifted
finely grated zest of
    2 unwaxed limes
    and the juice of 1
1½ tsp vanilla paste

You will need
large baking tray
small baking tray, lined
    with baking paper
cooking thermometer
sheet of acetate, cut into
    three 8 x 10cm strips
3 mugs or tall glasses

1. Heat the oven to 140°C/120°C fan/Gas 1. Using a pencil, draw a 26cm-diameter circle on a sheet of baking paper the same size as the large baking tray, then draw a 15cm diameter inner circle in the centre of the large circle to make the outline of a wreath. Turn the sheet over and place it on the large baking tray.

2. Make the meringue. Whisk the egg whites in the bowl of a stand mixer fitted with the whisk, on low speed for 1 minute, until foamy. Increase the speed to high and whisk until the egg whites hold soft peaks. Add the caster sugar, 1 tablespoon at a time, whisking well between each addition, until the mixture is firm and glossy, and you cannot feel any grains of sugar between your fingertips. Mix the vinegar with the cornflour in a cup until smooth, then whisk this into the egg whites with the vanilla, until just combined.

3. Spoon the meringue between the two circles drawn on the baking paper to make a wreath shape. Using a palette knife, smooth the edges and make sure the top of the wreath is wide enough to give plenty of room for the topping. Make a slight dip in the meringue around the top so that the fruit and cream topping can sit in the dip.

4. Using the palette knife, make light upward strokes all the way around the outside of the wreath. Bake the meringue for 1¼ hours, until pale golden and crisp. Turn off the oven and leave the meringue inside to cool for 1 hour, then wedge the door open with a wooden spoon and leave it for a further 20 minutes. (This helps prevent cracking.) Remove it from the oven and leave it to cool completely.

5. Meanwhile, make the pistachio praline. Heat the sugar and 2 tablespoons of water in a small pan over a medium–high heat, swirling the pan from time to time (do not stir), until the sugar turns golden amber (about 3–4 minutes). Add the pistachios, turn until coated, then tip out the mixture onto the lined small baking tray.

Continues overleaf

6. Leave the praline to set for 15 minutes. Once set and cool, break it into shards, then tip it into a food processor and pulse to break it up – don't over-blitz as you want a few large pieces of praline.

7. Make the topping. Purée one of the chopped mangoes in a blender with the icing sugar. Set aside. Using a teaspoon, scoop out the seeds from the passionfruits into a sieve set over a bowl, then press the pulp through and discard the seeds. Set aside.

8. Make the chocolate curls. Melt 60g of the chocolate in a heatproof bowl set over a pan of barely simmering water until it reaches 44°C on the cooking thermometer. Remove the bowl from the heat and add the remaining 30g of chocolate, stirring until it melts and cools to 32°C.

9. Place the strips of acetate on the work surface so that the long sides are nearest you. Using a palette knife, spread two thick lines (each about 1cm wide) of chocolate along the length of each acetate strip. Curl each strip inside a mug or a tall, straight glass laid on its side, then chill for 10–15 minutes, until set. When set, remove the acetates from the mugs or glasses and carefully lift off the curls of chocolate.

10. Make the Chantilly cream. Pour the double cream into a mixing bowl. Add the icing sugar, half the lime zest, the lime juice and the vanilla paste and whisk to soft peaks.

11. To assemble, lightly crack the top of the meringue with a spoon. Carefully, spoon the Chantilly cream evenly on top to cover, then drizzle with a little of the mango purée and all the passionfruit pulp. Top with the remaining chopped mango and the blueberries and then pour over any remaining mango purée. Scatter the ring with the pistachio praline and the remaining lime zest and, finally, decorate with mint leaves and chocolate curls.

PRUE'S
SABLÉ BRETON

This is a classic pâtissérie-style fruit tart made with a sablé Breton base – the salt (fleur de sel) comes from Brittany. The base is thick, buttery and crisp, and is easy to make in a sandwich tin, and the berry topping is the very essence of summer.

For the sablé dough
170g plain flour
1 tsp baking powder
¼ tsp fleur de sel
125g unsalted butter,
    at room temperature,
    cubed
4 egg yolks
100g caster sugar

For the meringue kisses
1 egg white
60g caster sugar
pinch of salt

For the raspberry jam
350g raspberries
120g jam sugar
2g pectin

For the chocolate decorations
90g 54% dark chocolate,
    chopped into pieces

For the pistachio paste
75g pistachios
2 tsp pistachio oil
10 drops pistachio
    extract

Continues overleaf

1. Make the sablé dough. Sift the flour, baking powder and salt together into a bowl.

2. Beat the butter in the bowl of a stand mixer fitted with the beater, on medium speed for 2–3 minutes, until soft and creamy.

3. In a separate bowl, whisk together the egg yolks and caster sugar until thick and mousse-like, and the mixture leaves a ribbon trail when you lift the whisk. Using a wooden spoon, beat in the softened butter until fluffy. Fold in the flour mixture to make a dough, then wrap the dough and chill it for 1 hour.

4. Make the meringue kisses. Heat the oven to 120°C/100°C fan/ Gas ½. Tip the egg white into a large, clean bowl and, using an electric hand whisk, whisk it slowly until small bubbles form. Increase the speed to medium and beat until white and foamy.

5. Increase the speed to high and add the caster sugar, 1 teaspoon at a time, whisking well between each addition. Add the salt and continue whisking until you have added all the sugar and the meringue is smooth, glossy and very stiff.

6. Spoon the meringue into the small piping bag fitted with a small open star nozzle. Pipe small 'kisses' onto the lined baking sheet in neat rows, leaving a little space between each meringue: squeeze lightly on the piping bag without touching the baking paper, then pull up quickly to create the tip of the kiss. (You'll have more kisses than you need. They will keep in a sealed container for up to 5 days – eat them as treats just as they are, or use them to decorate other bakes.)

7. Bake the meringue kisses on the middle shelf for 45 minutes, until dry and they peel easily off the baking paper. Remove them from the oven and leave them to cool on the baking sheet. Leave the oven on.

Continues overleaf

For the crème mousseline
250ml whole milk
½ vanilla pod, split
    lengthways and
    seeds scraped out
4 egg yolks
50g caster sugar
35g plain flour, sifted
100g unsalted butter,
    at room temperature,
    cubed

To decorate
30 strawberries,
    hulled and halved
10 raspberries
2 sheets of gold leaf

You will need
small piping bag
    fitted with a small
    open star nozzle
large baking sheet,
    lined with baking paper
sugar thermometer
20cm sandwich tin,
    greased, then base-lined
    with baking paper
15 x 8cm piece of acetate
chocolate comb
inside tube from a kitchen
    roll or tall, narrow glass
medium piping bag, fitted
    with a small plain nozzle
small cake-decorating
    paint brush

8. Make the raspberry jam. Tip the raspberries and 75g of the sugar into a pan and mash with a potato masher, then place the pan over a low heat and slowly bring the liquid to the boil.

9. Mix the remaining 45g of sugar with the pectin in a small bowl, then whisk this into the contents of the pan. Continue to boil until the raspberry mixture reaches 105°C on the sugar thermometer. Remove the pan from the heat and carefully pass the jam through a sieve into a heatproof bowl. Leave to cool and set.

10. Increase the oven temperature to 180°C/160°C fan/Gas 4.

11. Roll out the chilled sablé dough to a 20cm-diameter disc. Place the pastry disc in the prepared tin and bake it for 20–25 minutes, until risen and golden brown.

12. Meanwhile, make the chocolate decorations. Melt 60g of the chocolate in a heatproof bowl set over a pan of barely simmering water until it reaches 44°C on the sugar thermometer. Remove the bowl from the heat and add the remaining 30g of chocolate, stirring until it melts and cools to 32°C.

13. Using a palette knife, spread a spoonful of the chocolate onto the rectangular piece of acetate. Drag the chocolate comb across the chocolate from the top left-hand corner to the bottom right-hand corner to form diagonal lines of chocolate. Carefully roll the acetate rectangle until the shorter edges are just about touching and place it in the cardboard tube or tall, narrow glass. Leave to set.

14. Make the pistachio paste. Tip the pistachios into a food processor with the pistachio oil and blitz to a smooth paste, scraping down the inside of the processor bowl as necessary. Add the pistachio extract and blitz for a further 30 seconds, then set aside.

15. Make the crème mousseline. Pour the milk into a pan, add the vanilla seeds and bring the milk to the boil.

16. Meanwhile, in a mixing bowl, whisk the egg yolks and caster sugar together, then add the flour and whisk until smooth.

17. Pour the hot milk over the egg mixture, whisking continuously, then pour the mixture back into the pan and heat it until it comes to the boil again. Reduce the heat and simmer for 3–5 minutes, until smooth and the mixture no longer tastes floury.

18. Pour the mixture into a clean bowl and cover the surface with cling film to prevent a skin forming. Leave to cool, then transfer to the fridge and chill for 1 hour, until set.

19. Remove the chilled mixture from the fridge and place it in the bowl of a stand mixer fitted with the whisk. With the whisk on low speed, add the butter, a little at a time, until combined, then fold in the pistachio paste. Spoon the mixture into the medium piping bag fitted with a small plain nozzle and chill until needed.

20. Make the glaze for the sablé. Place 2 tablespoons of the set jam into a small pan with 3 tablespoons of water. Over a low heat, bring the mixture slowly to simmering point, stirring until smooth, then remove the pan from the heat and set aside.

21. To assemble, spread the remaining jam over the baked sablé round, leaving a 1.5cm border around the edge. Pipe the crème mousseline in a spiral over the jam, working from the outside into the middle, and chill for 15 minutes.

22. Arrange the strawberries and raspberries on top of the chilled mousseline layer. Using a pastry brush, dab the top of the fruit with the raspberry glaze.

23. Finally, using a small cake-decorating paint brush, top 12 of the meringue kisses with gold leaf, then peel the chocolate spirals off the acetate. Decorate the sablé Breton with the meringue kisses and chocolate spirals.

FETA, OREGANO & SUNDRIED TOMATO KNOTS

Sundried tomatoes preserve the flavours of summer far beyond the height of the tomato season. Left on the vine in the heat of the sun, then picked and further dried out on screens, the tomatoes develop an intense tartness. These buns are a savoury version of Swedish cinnamon buns and are perfect for a picnic.

500g strong white
   bread flour
7g fast-action dried yeast
2 tsp caster sugar
1 tsp salt
1 tsp dried oregano
½ tsp garlic granules
250ml whole milk,
   plus extra for glazing
75g unsalted butter,
   cubed
1 egg, lightly beaten
freshly ground
   black pepper
4 tsp sesame seeds,
   to garnish

For the filling
200g feta, crumbled
100g drained sundried
   tomatoes in oil,
   finely chopped
small handful of oregano
   or basil, leaves picked
   and chopped

You will need
large, sharp knife
   or pizza wheel
2 large baking trays,
   lined with baking paper

1. Combine the flour, yeast, sugar, salt, oregano and garlic granules in the bowl of a stand mixer fitted with the dough hook and season well with pepper. Make a well in the centre.

2. Warm the milk until lukewarm, add the butter and pour the mixture into the bowl with the dry ingredients. Add the egg and mix on low speed until combined, then continue mixing for about 4 minutes, until the dough is smooth, elastic and cleanly leaves the side of the bowl.

3. Shape the dough into a ball and place it in a large, oiled bowl, cover and leave it to rise at room temperature for about 1 hour, until doubled in size.

4. Meanwhile, make the filling. Tip the feta into a mixing bowl. Add the sundried tomatoes and oregano or basil, mashing everything together into a rough paste. Cover the filling and chill it until needed.

5. Turn out the risen dough onto a lightly floured work surface and knead it for 10 seconds to knock out any large air bubbles. Roll the dough into a neat rectangle, about 60 x 30cm. This may take a few minutes as the dough stretches and relaxes, so roll it a little, rest a little, then roll some more.

6. With one of the long sides of the dough nearest you, scatter the feta mixture over the bottom half of the dough. Fold the top half of the dough over the filling so that the long edges meet. Lightly roll to press the filling into the dough and to get rid of any air pockets.

7. Trim the short ends to neaten, then, using a large, sharp knife or a pizza wheel, cut the dough vertically into 12 equal strips of 5 x 15cm. Take the first strip and, starting at the bottom, end cut upwards into three long strands stopping 1cm from the top.

Continues overleaf

8. Gently separate the strands, and plait them together. Carefully turn the plait over and roll it into a neat ball with the ends tucked underneath. Place the knot on a lined baking tray and repeat with the remaining dough, arranging six buns on each tray.

9. Loosely cover the buns and leave them at room temperature for 45 minutes to 1 hour, until almost doubled in size.

10. Heat the oven to 180°C/160°C fan/Gas 4.

11. Brush the buns with milk to glaze, scatter them with sesame seeds and bake them for 20–25 minutes, until well risen and golden brown and the undersides sound hollow when tapped. Transfer the buns to a wire rack, then serve warm or at room temperature.

BLACKCURRANT & ALMOND CAKE

This showstopper of a cake brims with blackcurrants, which are in full swing in midsummer. Light, with a touch of almonds, lemon and vanilla, the cake is turned into a giant Swiss roll, filled and coated in swathes of buttercream. You could frost some fresh blackcurrants (see page 270) to add to the top for decoration, if you like.

For the sponge
50g unsalted butter,
   melted, plus extra
   for greasing
100g plain flour,
   plus extra for dusting
6 eggs
150g caster sugar, plus
   1 tbsp for scattering
finely grated zest of
   ¼ unwaxed lemon
1 tsp vanilla paste
1 tsp baking powder
50g ground almonds
pinch of salt

For the blackcurrant purée
400g blackcurrants
3 tbsp caster sugar
juice of ½ lemon

For the buttercream
250g caster sugar
4 egg whites
pinch of salt
325g unsalted
   butter, softened
1 tsp vanilla paste
pink, white or purple
   edible sprinkles

Continues overleaf

1. Heat the oven to 180°C/160°C fan/Gas 4. Brush the inside of the lined Swiss roll tin with melted butter, then dust it with plain flour and tip out the excess.

2. Whisk the eggs and caster sugar in a stand mixer fitted with the whisk, until tripled in volume, pale in colour and the mixture holds a firm ribbon trail when you lift the whisk. Add the lemon zest and vanilla and whisk to combine.

3. Sift the flour, baking powder, ground almonds and salt into the bowl and gently fold them together with a metal spoon. Pour the melted butter around the inside edge of the bowl and fold it in. Pour the mixture into the prepared tin and gently spread it level, trying not to knock out too much air or volume.

4. Bake the sponge on the middle shelf for 15 minutes, until golden and risen, and the top is firm but springy when you gently press it with a fingertip. Leave the sponge to cool in the tin for 5 minutes, then scatter 1 tablespoon of caster sugar over the top.

5. Lay a clean tea towel on top of the sponge and a large baking sheet on top of the towel. Carefully flip the baking sheet and tin over, releasing the sponge onto the tea towel. Peel off the baking paper. Using the tea towel, roll the sponge into a spiral starting at one of the short ends and with the tea towel inside the roll. This helps to 'train' the sponge into shape for rolling later. Leave to cool.

6. Meanwhile, prepare the blackcurrant purée and the buttercream. Tip the blackcurrants into a small pan, add the sugar and lemon juice and stir to combine. Cook over a low heat, stirring often, for 5 minutes, until the fruit softens and becomes a jammy slump. Press the mixture through a sieve into a clean bowl, discard the seeds in the sieve and leave the purée in the bowl to cool.

Continues overleaf

You will need
40 x 30cm Swiss roll tin,
  greased, then lined
  (base and sides)
  with baking paper
2 small piping bags,
  one fitted with
  a medium closed
  star nozzle

7. Make the buttercream. Whisk the sugar, egg whites and 2 tablespoons of water together in a large, heatproof mixing bowl until combined. Set the bowl over a pan of barely simmering water and whisk continuously for about 6 minutes to a thick, glossy meringue that leaves a ribbon trail when you lift the whisk.

8. Scoop the meringue into the bowl of a stand mixer. Add the salt and whisk on medium speed for 4–5 minutes, until cold and very thick and holding firm peaks. Add the butter, a little at a time, whisking well between each addition. Add the vanilla and mix again to make a thick, smooth buttercream. Spoon 200g of the buttercream into a bowl, then cover it and set it aside.

9. Carefully unroll the sponge, remove the tea towel and cut the sponge into three long, equal strips, each about 40 x 9cm. Trim the ends and brush the top of each strip with some blackcurrant purée.

10. Add all but 1 tablespoon of the remaining blackcurrant purée to the buttercream in the mixer and mix to combine. Using a palette knife, spread 4 tablespoons of blackcurrant buttercream onto each sponge strip on top of the purée.

11. To assemble, one strip at a time and working from one of the short ends, roll up the strip into a tight spiral and place it flat-side down in the middle of a serving plate. Take the next strip of sponge and wrap this around the rolled-up sponge strip, buttercream innermost so that the cake starts to become a wide, upright Swiss roll. Continue with the third sponge strip. Gently but firmly press the sponge strips together, then chill the roll for 15 minutes to firm up.

12. Reserve 3–4 tablespoons of blackcurrant buttercream to decorate. Using a palette knife, spread a smooth, even layer of the remaining blackcurrant buttercream over the top and side of the cake.

13. Spoon the reserved vanilla buttercream into the small piping bag fitted with a medium closed star nozzle and pipe rosettes in different sizes across the top and down one side of the cake. Spoon the reserved blackcurrant buttercream into the same piping bag and pipe blackcurrant rosettes around the vanilla ones.

14. Spoon the reserved 1 tablespoon of blackcurrant purée into the remaining small piping bag and snip the end. Pipe the purée between the buttercream rosettes, then scatter with sprinkles to finish.

CRUFFINS

A cruffin is essentially a croissant baked in a muffin tray and coated in sugar while still warm. Delicate and sophisticated, filled with delicious homemade summer berry jam and topped with cream, these cruffins would not look out of place at a VIP breakfast before a Wimbledon final.

For the cruffin dough
500g strong white
    bread flour
50g caster sugar
7g fast-action dried yeast
2 tsp salt
160ml whole milk
2 x 125g blocks of
    unsalted butter,
    chilled, plus 20g

To finish
250g caster sugar
1 tbsp ground cinnamon
6 tbsp homemade
    raspberry, strawberry
    or blackberry jam
    (see p.149)

You will need
large baking tray or large
    plastic food box, oiled
large, sharp knife
    or a pizza wheel
12-hole muffin tray,
    brushed with melted
    butter and dusted
    with caster sugar

1. Make the cruffin dough. Combine the flour, sugar, yeast and salt in the bowl of a stand mixer fitted with the dough hook.

2. Pour the milk into a small pan with 160ml of water over a low heat. Add the 20g of butter and leave it to soften and melt for 30 seconds. Pour the warm milk mixture into the bowl of the stand mixer and mix on low–medium speed to combine. Scrape down the inside of the bowl and mix again for 4 minutes, to a smooth and elastic dough.

3. Turn out the dough onto a lightly floured work surface and shape it into a square. Transfer it to the large, oiled baking tray or oiled plastic box, cover it and chill it for at least 4 hours, but ideally overnight.

4. About 45 minutes before you're ready to use the dough, cut one block of butter into 1cm-thick slices. Lay these slices side-by-side on a sheet of baking paper and cover with more paper. Using a rolling pin, press and roll the butter into a neat 18 x 12cm rectangle, then transfer the butter rectangle, sandwiched in the paper, to the fridge to chill. Repeat with the other block, chilling both for 30 minutes.

5. Weigh the dough and cut it equally in half. Cover and return one half to the fridge. Roll out the first piece of dough on a lightly floured work surface to a neat rectangle, about 30 x 20cm and with one of the long sides nearest you.

6. Place one chilled butter rectangle vertically in the centre of the dough (to give about 6cm of dough either side). Fold the two sides of dough inward, so that the edges meet in the middle. Press the edges together to join and the ends together, sealing in the butter.

7. Lightly flour the work surface. Start at the middle of the dough and using a short, sharp tapping motion with the rolling pin, flatten and gently roll the dough into a rectangle, about 45 x 15cm. Trim the ends if they are slightly rounded – you want the rectangle to be neat.

Continues overleaf

8. Fold the top quarter of the dough back down on itself and fold the bottom quarter up to meet it. Gently press the edges together, brush off any excess flour, then fold the dough in half again so that you have a dough package four-layers thick. (This is called a book fold.) Cover and chill the dough for 30–45 minutes to relax and firm up.

9. Meanwhile, repeat this rolling, folding and chilling with the second piece of dough and second slab of butter.

10. Lightly flour the work surface. Place the first dough portion with the book opening on the right-hand side and roll it into a neat rectangle three times as long as it is wide, about 45 x 15cm. Fold the top of the dough down to cover two thirds and the bottom up to cover this. Cover and chill for 1 hour. Repeat for the second portion.

11. Roll out one piece of dough on a lightly floured work surface to a 32 x 29cm rectangle with one of the short ends nearest you. Using the sharp knife or pizza wheel, trim the edges to a neat rectangle, about 30 x 27cm. Cut the dough down its length into 9 strips, each 3cm wide. Cut these strips in half to make 18 strips of 15 x 3cm.

12. Take one strip and lay it vertically in front of you. Place a second strip neatly on top, about 3cm up from the bottom edge of the first strip. Place a third strip on top of this, 3cm from the bottom edge of the second strip. Starting at the bottom, roll the pastry strips into a neat coil. Tuck the loose ends underneath the coil and place it in the prepared muffin tin, gently pressing the cruffin into the bottom. Repeat to make 6 cruffins from each batch of dough (12 altogether).

13. Loosely cover the cruffins. Leave them at a cool room temperature for about 2 hours, until puffy and almost doubled in height.

14. Heat the oven to 200°C/180°C fan/Gas 6. Bake the cruffins for 15 minutes, then reduce the oven to 190°C/170°C fan/Gas 5 and bake for 10–12 minutes, until well risen, crisp and deep golden brown.

15. Meanwhile, combine the caster sugar and cinnamon in a roasting tin. Leave the cruffins to cool in the muffin tray for 2–3 minutes, then toss them in the cinnamon sugar to coat. Transfer them to a wire rack and, once cool, fill each cruffin with ½ tablespoon of jam, then serve.

QUICK & EASY BERRY JAM

This tangy, fruit-packed jam is perfect for filling your cruffins. It will make more than you need (you'll have about 425g of jam altogether), but enjoy the excess on toast, or for sandwiching biscuits and sponges, and topping scones.

250g raspberries, strawberries or blackberries
250g jam sugar

You will need
sugar thermometer (optional)
2 sterilised, warmed small jam jars with wax discs (optional) and lids

1. Tip the berries into a large, heavy-based pan. Add the sugar and gently squash the fruit with a potato masher, or the back of a wooden spoon, making sure you keep a bit of texture in the mash.

2. Set the pan over a low heat and, using a wooden spoon, stir gently as the juice starts to run. Keep the heat low, and keep stirring until the sugar has dissolved (it won't take long).

3. Turn up the heat and boil the liquid rapidly, stirring to prevent the jam 'catching' around the base of the pan, until the jam reaches 105°C on a sugar thermometer (this is setting point). (See also the tip, below.)

4. Carefully pour the jam into the sterilised, warm jars. Put a wax disc on the surface (waxed-side down), if using, then leave until cold. Cover tightly with a lid. Store the jam in a cool spot and use within a month. Once opened, store in the fridge and use within a month.

TIP If you don't have a sugar thermometer, test the jam using a saucer that has been left in the freezer for at least 30 minutes. After the jam has been boiling for 4 minutes (see Step 3), take the pan off the heat, put ½ teaspoon of jam onto the chilled saucer, leave it for a few seconds, then draw your finger through it. If the jam forms a skin that wrinkles, it has reached setting point. If not, boil it for another 1 minute and test again, using another freezer-chilled saucer.

BAKER'S RECIPE

AMANDA'S LEMON & ELDERFLOWER PALETTE CAKE

*Cake and flowers all in one, with the bonus of a bit of booze
(optional, of course!), this is the cake I make for all of my girlies' birthdays.*

For the sponge
350g unsalted butter,
    softened
350g caster sugar
6 eggs, lightly beaten
300g plain flour
1 tsp vanilla paste
finely grated zest of
    1 unwaxed lemon
50g cornflour
3 tsp baking powder
pinch of salt
3–4 tbsp whole milk

For the lemon curd
3 eggs
3 egg yolks
175g caster sugar
juice and finely
    grated zest of
    3 unwaxed lemons
100g unsalted butter,
    cubed

For the buttercream
6 egg whites
375g caster sugar
pinch of salt
450g unsalted butter,
    softened
2 tbsp elderflower syrup,
    plus 4 tbsp to assemble
various food-colouring
    pastes, including green,
    red and orange

Continues overleaf

1. Heat the oven to 180°C/160°C fan/Gas 4.

2. Make the sponge. Beat the butter and sugar in a stand mixer fitted with the beater, on medium speed for 3–5 minutes, until pale and creamy, scraping down the inside of the bowl from time to time. Add the eggs, a little at a time, beating well between each addition and adding a little of the flour if the mixture curdles. Add the vanilla and lemon zest and mix to combine.

3. Sift the flour, cornflour, baking powder and salt into the bowl, add the milk and mix again until smooth.

4. Divide the sponge mixture equally between the prepared tins and spread it level. Bake the sponges on the middle shelves for about 20 minutes, until risen, pale golden and a skewer inserted into the centre of each comes out clean. Leave the sponges to cool in the tins for 5 minutes, then turn them out onto a wire rack to cool completely.

5. Meanwhile, make the lemon curd. Whisk the whole eggs, egg yolks and sugar in a small pan over a low heat. Add the lemon juice and zest and whisk to combine. Add the butter and cook the curd over a low heat, whisking continuously, for about 4 minutes, until the butter melts and the curd thickens enough to coat the back of a spoon. Pass the lemon curd through a sieve into a clean bowl.

6. Spoon the lemon curd into a large piping bag fitted with a medium plain nozzle, twist the top and leave to cool, then chill it for at least 1 hour or until ready to use.

7. Make the buttercream. Whisk the egg whites with the caster sugar and 2 tablespoons of water in a medium, heatproof bowl until combined.

Continues overleaf

You will need
20cm sandwich tins x 4,
    greased, then base-lined
    with baking paper
2 large piping bags,
    each fitted with a
    medium plain nozzle
cake scraper or
    palette knife
1 small piping bag

8. Set the bowl over a pan of barely simmering water and whisk continuously for about 6 minutes, until the sugar dissolves and the mixture thickens to become smooth and glossy, and leaves a thick ribbon trail when you lift the whisk.

9. Scoop the meringue into the bowl of a stand mixer fitted with the whisk, add the salt and whisk on medium speed for 6–7 minutes, until the meringue cools completely, is very thick and holds firm peaks. Add the butter, a little at a time, whisking well between each addition until the buttercream is thick and silky smooth. Add the 2 tablespoons of elderflower syrup and mix again to combine. Spoon one third of the buttercream into the second large piping bag fitted with a medium plain nozzle (set the rest aside).

10. To assemble, lay three of the sponges on the work surface and brush the top of each sponge with a third of the elderflower syrup. Pipe a ring of buttercream around the top outer edge of each sponge. Pipe two more buttercream circles on top of each sponge, leaving equal gaps between each circle for the lemon curd, and dividing the buttercream equally between the sponges. Pipe the lemon curd in between the buttercream circles.

11. Place one of the sponges on a cake board or plate, then top with the two buttercream- and curd-topped sponges followed by the fourth sponge, gently pressing the layers together.

12. Using a cake scraper or palette knife, cover the top and side of the cake with a smooth, very thin layer of some of the set-aside buttercream to crumb coat, then chill for 20 minutes to firm up.

13. Spoon 10 tablespoons of the buttercream into a bowl and set it aside. Cover the top and side of the cake with the rest of the buttercream, spreading it with a cake scraper or palette knife to give a smooth finish.

14. Spoon 2 tablespoons of the reserved buttercream into a small bowl and tint it using the green food-colouring paste. Spoon this into the small piping bag, snip the end to a fine point and pipe flower stalks and leaves around the side and over the top of the cake.

15. Divide the remaining 8 tablespoons of buttercream between 4 small bowls (2 tablespoons of buttercream for each) and tint each one a different, bright colour. Using a small palette knife, 'paint' flowers in the different-coloured buttercreams on top of the green stalks to decorate the top and side of the cake.

AUTUMN

RECIPES

BANANA, TAHINI & CARAMEL LOAF

PEAR & WALNUT CAKE

GIUSEPPE'S CELEBRATION CAKE

PUMPKIN ROLLS

DOUBLE CHOCOLATE BEETROOT DEVIL'S FOOD CAKE

PRUE'S VEGAN SAUSAGE ROLLS

FIG, HONEY & ALMOND CAKE

TOFFEE APPLE CAKE

VEGETABLE SAMOSAS

FETA, GRAPE & FENNEL FOCACCIA

JÜRGEN'S PEAR & CHOCOLATE CHARLOTTE

PECAN PIE

CHOCOLATE HAZELNUT TORTE

PLUM & GINGER CAKE

PAUL'S CIABATTA BREADSTICKS

BLACKBERRY & PEAR CRUMBLE CAKE

APPLE & QUINCE CHAUSSONS

TOM'S BLACKBERRY & APPLE CAKE WITH CHAI BUTTERCREAM

APPLE, PECAN & MISO CARAMEL TART

BANANA, TAHINI & CARAMEL LOAF

In early autumn, the pods of the sesame plant begin to ripen, and eventually split, releasing their precious seeds. In this recipe, those seeds become sesame caramel, broken into pieces to take the humble banana loaf to new heights. If you can wait, the loaf tastes even better a day after making it.

For the sesame caramel
100g caster sugar
3 tsp sesame seeds

For the loaf
125g unsalted butter,
    plus extra for greasing
75g light brown soft or
    light muscovado sugar,
    plus extra for dusting
50g dark brown
    soft sugar
2 eggs
75g full-fat plain yogurt
3 tbsp tahini
3 very ripe bananas
    (about 200–225g
    peeled weight),
    well mashed
250g self-raising flour
1 tsp baking powder
½ tsp ground cinnamon
pinch of salt

To decorate
1 banana, peeled and
    halved lengthways

You will need
1 small baking tray,
    lined with baking paper
900g loaf tin,
    greased and lined
    (base and ends)
    with baking paper

1. Make the sesame caramel. Tip the sugar into a small pan or non-stick frying pan. Add 1 tablespoon of water, place the pan over a low heat to dissolve the sugar (do not stir), then increase the heat and bring the syrup to the boil. Cook until the syrup starts to turn golden, swirling the pan from time to time. When the caramel is a deeper amber colour (about 5–6 minutes), remove it from the heat and pour it into the lined baking tray. Scatter with the sesame seeds and leave it for about 30 minutes, until crisp.

2. Heat the oven to 170°C/150°C fan/Gas 3.

3. Meanwhile, brush the lined loaf tin with butter and dust the base and sides with 1 tablespoon of light brown soft or muscovado sugar.

4. Make the loaf. Melt the butter in a small pan over a low heat and cook, swirling the pan, until it smells nutty and the milk solids start to brown. Remove from the heat and strain the butter through a metal sieve into a bowl. Leave it to cool slightly.

5. In a large mixing bowl, whisk together both types of brown sugar and the eggs until smooth and creamy and there are no lumps of sugar. Add the yogurt, tahini and melted butter and mix well, then add the mashed bananas and mix again.

6. Sift the flour, baking powder, cinnamon and salt into the bowl and stir until thoroughly combined.

7. Break the sesame caramel into 1–2cm pieces and fold half of them into the loaf mixture. Scoop the mixture into the prepared tin and spread it level. Lay the banana halves for decoration cut side up on top of the cake. Scatter with the remaining sesame caramel and bake the loaf on the middle shelf for 55–60 minutes, until well risen and a skewer inserted into the centre comes out clean.

8. Leave the cake in the tin for 3 minutes, then transfer it to a wire rack, peel off the baking paper and leave to cool.

PEAR & WALNUT CAKE

This beautiful, showstopper of a cake captures everything that is bountiful in our trees and hedgerows in autumn. Walnuts, although originating from southern Europe, were introduced to the UK by the Romans. The trees now appear all over our countryside – thanks to a little help from the squirrels.

For the poached pears
4 small pears, peeled
    with stalks left on
200g caster sugar
1 cinnamon stick
2 star anise
juice of ½ lemon
2 bay leaves

For the sponge
125g walnut halves
    or pieces
200g unsalted
    butter, softened
175g caster sugar
100g light muscovado
    or light brown soft sugar
3 large eggs
1 tsp vanilla paste
325g plain flour
2 tsp baking powder
1 tsp bicarbonate of soda
1 tsp ground cinnamon
¼ tsp ground cloves
¼ tsp grated nutmeg
pinch of salt
120ml whole milk

For the buttercream
150g blackberries
275g caster sugar,
    plus 1 tbsp
4 large egg whites
pinch of salt
350g unsalted
    butter, softened
1 tsp vanilla paste

Continues overleaf

1. Poach the pears the day before serving. Place the pears in a medium pan, add the sugar, cinnamon stick, star anise, lemon juice, bay leaves and enough water to just cover the pears (about 750ml). Place the pan over a low–medium heat, and bring the liquid to a gentle simmer, stirring occasionally to dissolve the sugar. Cover the surface of the syrup with a disc of baking paper to keep the pears submerged and cook gently for about 20 minutes, until the pears are tender to the point of a sharp knife. Remove the pan from the heat and leave the pears to cool in the syrup. Chill overnight.

2. Make the sponge. Heat the oven to 180°C/160°C fan/Gas 4.

3. Tip the walnut halves onto a large baking tray and toast them in the oven for 5 minutes, until crisp. Leave to cool completely, then finely chop them in a food processor. Set aside.

4. Beat the butter and both sugars in a stand mixer fitted with the beater, on medium speed for 3–5 minutes, until pale and creamy, scraping down the inside of the bowl from time to time. One at a time, add the eggs, beating well between each addition. Stir in the vanilla and the finely chopped toasted walnuts.

5. Sift the flour, baking powder, bicarbonate of soda, cinnamon, cloves, nutmeg and salt into the bowl. Add the milk and mix with a spatula to just combine, then beat with an electric hand mixer on low speed for 20 seconds, until the mixture is smooth.

6. Divide the mixture equally between the lined cake tins and spread it level. Bake the sponges on the middle shelves for about 25 minutes, until well risen, golden brown and a skewer inserted into the centre of each comes out clean. Leave the sponges to cool in the tins for 2–3 minutes, then turn them out onto wire racks to cool completely.

Continues overleaf

For the caramel sauce

200g caster sugar
125g soured cream
30g unsalted butter
1 tsp vanilla paste
pinch of salt

To decorate

150g blackberries
bay leaves or blackberry
    leaves (optional)
50g walnut halves

You will need

18cm round cake tins x 3,
    greased, then base-lined
    with baking paper
medium piping bag
    fitted with a medium
    plain nozzle
cake scraper (optional)

7. Meanwhile, cook the blackberries for the buttercream. Tip the blackberries into a small pan, add the 1 tablespoon of caster sugar and 2 tablespoons of the pear poaching syrup and cook over a low heat, stirring frequently, for about 4 minutes, until the berries burst and release their juice. Cook for a further 4–5 minutes, until the berries are a soft jammy mixture and most of the excess juice has evaporated. Remove the pan from the heat and leave to cool.

8. Finish the buttercream. Whisk the egg whites with the 275g of caster sugar and 2 tablespoons of water in a medium, heatproof bowl until combined. Set the bowl over a pan of barely simmering water and whisk continuously for about 6 minutes, until the sugar dissolves and the mixture thickens to a smooth, glossy meringue that leaves a thick ribbon trail when you lift the whisk.

9. Scoop the meringue into the bowl of a stand mixer fitted with the whisk. Add the salt and whisk on medium speed for 5–6 minutes, until the meringue cools completely, is very thick and holds firm peaks. Add the butter, a little at a time, whisking well between each addition until the buttercream is thick and silky smooth. Add the vanilla and mix again to combine.

10. Spoon 6 rounded tablespoons of the buttercream into a small bowl and mix in the cooled blackberry mixture until combined. Spoon another 6 tablespoons of the buttercream into the medium piping bag fitted with a medium plain nozzle.

11. Assemble the cake. Place one of the sponges on a cake board or serving plate and pipe a ring of vanilla buttercream around the top edge. Fill the middle of the buttercream ring with half of the blackberry buttercream and spread it level. Place a second sponge on top and repeat with the vanilla and blackberry buttercreams. Top with the third sponge, gently pressing the layers together.

12. Using a cake scraper or palette knife, cover the top and side of the cake with a very thin layer of vanilla buttercream, to create a crumb coat. Chill for 30 minutes, until firm.

13. Meanwhile make the caramel sauce. Tip the sugar into a medium, heavy-based pan, add 2 tablespoons of water and place the pan over a low heat, swirling the pan from time to time to dissolve the sugar (do not stir). Brush the inside of the pan with water to melt any sugar crystals that may have stuck there.

14. Once the sugar has dissolved, increase the heat to medium, bring the syrup to the boil and cook to a deeper amber colour (about 5–6 minutes), swirling the pan from time to time to ensure that the caramel cooks evenly.

15. Slide the pan off the heat and carefully stir in the soured cream and butter until combined. Return the pan to a low heat to remelt any hardened caramel, then mix in the vanilla and salt. Pour the caramel into a bowl, leave it to cool to room temperature, then chill it for 20 minutes, until it thickens slightly.

16. Cover the side of the cake in a second layer of vanilla buttercream. To create a semi-naked look, run a cake scraper or palette knife around the outside of the cake with a firm pressure, so that parts of the cake show through the buttercream. Spread the top of the cake with any remaining buttercream and chill it for a further 15 minutes.

17. Meanwhile, take the pears out of the syrup with a slotted spoon and leave them to dry on kitchen paper for 10 minutes (discard the syrup). Cut one pear in half through the stalk and leave the remaining pears whole.

18. Spoon the caramel sauce over the top of the cake, letting it drip down the side. Arrange the halved and whole pears, and the blackberries, bay or blackberry leaves (if using) and walnut halves on top of the cake to finish.

GIUSEPPE'S CELEBRATION CAKE

As a child, I remember vividly waiting for the next celebration just so that I could dive into a substantial slice of light sponge generously smothered in cream! My chocolate and hazelnut cake is a perfect treat for an autumn birthday. I recommend the grown-ups enjoy it with a glass of chilled prosecco valdobbiene alongside, to cut through the sweetness.

———————

For the sponge
6 eggs
190g caster sugar
1½ tsp vanilla paste
finely grated zest of
    1 unwaxed lemon
95g plain flour
95g potato starch
    (or additional plain flour)

For the hazelnut paste
200g ready-roasted
    hazelnuts, chopped

For the crème pâtissière
500ml whole milk
1 tsp vanilla paste
6 egg yolks
120g caster sugar
50g cornflour
pinch of salt
50g unsalted butter
50g 54% dark chocolate,
    finely chopped
100g ready-roasted
    hazelnuts, chopped

Continues overleaf

1. Make the sponge. Heat the oven to 180°C/160°C fan/Gas 4. Put the eggs, sugar, vanilla and lemon zest in a large mixing bowl set over a pan of barely simmering water. Whisk with an electric hand whisk, on high speed for about 10 minutes, until thick and mousse-like, and the mixture leaves a ribbon trail when you lift the whisk (or whisk in a stand mixer on high speed for 6–7 minutes).

2. Sift the flour and potato starch (or additional plain flour) together into a bowl. Carefully fold half the flour mixture into the egg mixture with a metal spoon. Repeat with the remaining flour mixture. Pour the sponge mixture into the lined tin and spread it level.

3. Bake the sponge on the middle shelf for 20–25 minutes, until well risen and the top of the cake springs back when lightly pressed with your fingertip. Leave the sponge to cool in the tin for a few minutes, then carefully turn it out onto a wire rack to cool completely.

4. Meanwhile, make the hazelnut paste. Blitz the hazelnuts to a paste in a food processor. Set aside until needed. (This will make more paste than you need – the remainder will keep in the fridge in an airtight container for up to 1 month. It's delicious on toast!)

5. Make the crème pâtissière. Pour the milk into a pan and add the vanilla. Slowly bring the milk to the boil, then remove the pan from the heat and set aside.

6. Whisk the egg yolks and caster sugar in a heatproof mixing bowl until pale, then whisk in the cornflour. Whisking continuously, pour in the hot milk in a thin, steady stream.

Continues overleaf

For the vanilla syrup
50g caster sugar
1cm length of unwaxed
   lemon peel
1 tsp vanilla paste

For the Chantilly cream
250ml double cream
40g icing sugar, sifted
½ tsp vanilla paste

To decorate
small handful of whole
   ready-roasted
   hazelnuts

You will need
23cm springform tin
   (6cm deep), greased,
   then base-lined with
   baking paper
large piping bag fitted
   with a large closed
   star nozzle

7. Return the mixture to the pan and place it over a medium heat. Bring the mixture to the boil, whisking continuously, and cook for 1 minute, until smooth and thick. Add the salt, butter and chocolate and stir until smooth.

8. Pour the crème pâtissière into a bowl and cover the surface with cling film to prevent a skin forming. Leave it to cool, then stir in 3 tablespoons of the hazelnut paste and chill it until needed.

9. Make the vanilla syrup. Place the sugar in a small pan with the lemon peel, vanilla and 100ml of water. Bring the mixture to the boil, then reduce the heat and simmer it for 2 minutes, until syrupy. Remove the pan from the heat and leave the syrup to cool. Discard the lemon peel.

10. To assemble, using a large serrated knife, cut the sponge horizontally into three layers. Place the first layer onto a cake plate and drizzle with half the syrup. Spread with a third of the hazelnut crème pâtissière and sprinkle over half the chopped hazelnuts. Cover with the second layer of sponge and repeat. Top with the third layer.

11. Make the Chantilly cream. Whisk the double cream, icing sugar and vanilla together in a mixing bowl to firm peaks, then whisk in the final third of the hazelnut crème pâtissière. Spread half the Chantilly cream evenly over the top and side of the cake with a palette knife.

12. Spoon the remaining Chantilly cream into the large piping bag fitted with a large closed star nozzle and pipe it around the bottom edge and top edge of the cake. Finish with a ring of whole hazelnuts, placed neatly just inside the piped top edge to decorate.

PUMPKIN ROLLS

These little rolls not only look like pumpkins, but they have pumpkin purée in the dough, which makes them perfect for using up the flesh of a scooped-out pumpkin lantern. Just peel and deseed the pumpkin (or squash) flesh, cut it into chunks and steam it until tender. Leave it to cool and then blend until smooth.

500g strong white
   bread flour
7g fast-action dried yeast
2 tsp caster sugar
1 tsp salt
¼ tsp ground turmeric
225–250ml whole milk,
   plus 1 tbsp to glaze
150g pumpkin purée
2 tbsp olive oil
1 egg, to glaze
6–7 walnut halves,
   cut in half

You will need
12–14 pieces of fine
   kitchen string, each
   about 60–70cm long
   (1 per dough ball)
2 baking trays, lined
   with baking paper

1. Tip the flour into the bowl of a stand mixer fitted with the dough hook. Add the yeast, sugar, salt and turmeric and mix to combine.

2. Warm the milk until lukewarm and add it to the bowl with the pumpkin purée and olive oil. Mix on low speed until combined, then increase the speed slightly and knead for a further 5 minutes, until the dough is smooth and cleanly leaves the side of the bowl.

3. Shape the dough into a neat ball. Lightly oil a mixing bowl and place the dough ball inside. Cover and leave the dough in a draught-free place at room temperature for about 1 hour, until doubled in size.

4. Turn out the dough onto a lightly floured work surface and knead it lightly for 20 seconds. Divide the dough into 12–14 portions – it doesn't matter if they're not exactly the same size. Shape each dough portion into a tight, smooth and neat ball.

5. Lay a length of kitchen string on the work surface. Place one dough ball in the middle of the string, then bring each end up and cross them over the dough ball as if wrapping a parcel. Without tightening the string around the dough (you don't want the string to cut into it), carefully turn the dough ball over. Repeat this wrapping with the string so that it marks out 8 sections of the dough ball. Tie the string in a knot to secure it and place the ball on a lined baking tray with the knot underneath. Repeat with the remaining dough balls. Cover the balls loosely and leave them to prove at room temperature for about 45 minutes, until nearly doubled in size.

6. Meanwhile, beat the egg with the 1 tablespoon of milk and heat the oven to 180°C/160°C fan/Gas 4.

7. Carefully brush the rolls with egg wash and bake them for 25 minutes, until they are risen and deep golden brown. Leave to cool for 2–3 minutes, then carefully snip off the string. Press a piece of walnut into the top of each pumpkin for a stalk. Leave to cool.

DOUBLE CHOCOLATE BEETROOT DEVIL'S FOOD CAKE

The addition of beetroot purée to this cake brings both natural sweetness and more than just a hint of seasonal earthiness. Topped with berries, nuts and apple and beetroot crisps, it's a gorgeous centrepiece for an autumnal get-together.

For the sponge
2 raw beetroot, trimmed
225g plain flour, sifted
1¼ tsp baking powder
¾ tsp bicarbonate of soda
120g cocoa powder, sifted
pinch of salt
225g dark brown soft sugar
380ml almond milk
120ml light olive oil
1 tsp vanilla paste
150g vegan dark
   chocolate chips

For the crisps
1 eating apple
1 small raw beetroot

For the ganache
200g vegan dark
   chocolate, chopped
100ml almond cream

To decorate
thyme sprigs
lemon balm or mint sprigs
edible flower petals
   and lavender
5 pistachios,
   finely chopped
handful of blackberries
   and blueberries

You will need
2 baking trays, lined
   with baking paper
25cm deep, round cake
   tin, greased, then lined
   with baking paper

1. Cook the beetroot in a pan of boiling water, covered, for 1 hour, until tender. Drain, then rub off the skins and chop the flesh into chunks. Blitz to a purée in a food processor and set aside to cool.

2. Meanwhile, heat the oven to 160°C/140°C fan/Gas 2½.

3. Make the crisps. Slice the apple and beetroot into 1–2mm rounds, removing the apple seeds. Place a layer of apple slices on one lined baking tray and a layer of beetroot slices on the other. Bake for 45–60 minutes, turning halfway through, until coloured and crinkled. Leave to cool and crisp up on the tray.

4. Make the sponge. Increase the oven temperature to 180°C/160°C fan/Gas 4. Mix the flour, baking powder, bicarbonate of soda, cocoa powder and salt together in a large mixing bowl.

5. Whisk the sugar, almond milk, olive oil and vanilla in a stand mixer fitted with the whisk, for about 2 minutes, until thick and creamy, then fold in the beetroot purée. Gently fold in the flour mixture and chocolate chips.

6. Pour the mixture into the prepared tin and spread it level. Bake the sponge on the middle shelf for about 35 minutes, until risen, dark brown and a skewer inserted into the centre comes out with a sticky residue. The top will be slightly cracked. If the sponge is still runny in the middle, bake it for another 5–10 minutes and test again. Leave the sponge to cool completely in the tin, then turn out onto a wire rack.

7. Make the chocolate ganache. Melt the chocolate with the almond cream in a large bowl set over a pan of barely simmering water. Stir until smooth and shiny. Leave to cool for 5 minutes before using.

8. Pour the ganache over the top of the cake and, using the back of a spoon, make a large swirl over the top. Decorate with the beetroot and apple crisps (you can eat any you don't use), and the herbs, flowers, pistachios, blackberries and blueberries.

PRUE'S VEGAN SAUSAGE ROLLS

Packed with a rich autumnal mixture of mushrooms, lentils, nuts and seeds, these vegan 'sausage' rolls are warming and filling and the perfect finger food for an evening around the bonfire. Vegan or not – everyone will love them.

For the rough puff pastry
300g plain flour
pinch of salt
50g vegan block,
    cubed and chilled
8–9 tbsp ice-cold water
120g vegan block, frozen
2 tbsp almond milk
1 tsp agave syrup

For the filling
7g dried porcini
    mushrooms
100ml just-boiled water
200g chestnut
    mushrooms
70g walnuts
1 tbsp olive oil
1 small onion,
    finely chopped
2 garlic cloves, crushed
1 x 400g tin of
    lentils, drained
2 tbsp brown miso paste
1 tbsp ground flaxseeds
juice of ½ lemon
large handful of flat-leaf
    parsley, leaves picked
    and finely chopped
3 sage sprigs, leaves
    picked and chopped
3 thyme sprigs, leaves
    picked and chopped

Continues overleaf

1. Make the rough puff pastry. Mix together the flour and salt in a bowl. Rub in the cubes of vegan block using your fingertips until the mixture resembles breadcrumbs. Gradually add enough ice-cold water to form a dough. Tip out the dough onto a lightly floured work surface and roll it out into a rectangle, about 15 x 30cm, with one of the short ends nearest you.

2. Coarsely grate half the frozen vegan block over the bottom two thirds of the dough. Fold down the top third and fold up the bottom third as if folding a letter.

3. Turn the folded dough through 90 degrees and roll it out into a 15 x 30cm rectangle again. Repeat Step 2, using the remaining frozen vegan block and fold as before. Wrap the dough and leave it to rest in the fridge for 20 minutes.

4. Repeat the rolling and folding process twice more, chilling for 20 minutes between each roll and fold.

5. Make the filling. Place the dried porcini in a heatproof bowl, pour over the just-boiled water, then set aside for 10 minutes, until rehydrated and softened. Drain, reserving the soaking liquid, and finely chop the porcini.

6. Tip the chestnut mushrooms and walnuts into a food processor and pulse until finely chopped, but do not over process.

7. Heat the olive oil in a large frying pan over a medium–high heat. Add the onion and cook for 5 minutes, until it is beginning to soften. Add the walnut and mushroom mixture and cook for 5 minutes, until the mushrooms begin to release their liquid.

Continues overleaf

2 tbsp Dijon mustard
salt and freshly ground
    black pepper

*For the caramelised
red onion chutney*
2 tbsp olive oil
2 red onions,
    finely chopped
1 red chilli,
    finely chopped
1 garlic clove, crushed
3 tbsp dark
    muscovado sugar
3 tbsp balsamic vinegar

You will need
baking sheet, lined
    with baking paper

8. Add the garlic, the chopped porcini and the soaking liquid. Season with salt and pepper and reduce the heat to low. Cook the filling for 5–10 minutes, until the liquid has boiled and bubbled away. Add the lentils, miso paste, flaxseeds, lemon juice, parsley, sage and thyme and simmer for 2–3 minutes, until dry. Set aside to cool.

9. Once the mixture has cooled, return it to the food processor and pulse it to a sausagemeat texture. Divide the filling into 8 equal portions and shape each one into a 10cm-long cylinder. Place the cylinders on the lined baking sheet and chill until needed.

10. Heat the oven to 220°C/200°C fan/Gas 7.

11. Roll out the pastry on a lightly floured work surface to a rectangle, about 40 x 30cm. Cut this into 8 smaller rectangles of 10 x 15cm.

12. Cut 5 or 6 diagonal slits, about 1cm apart, down one side of each pastry rectangle (this will be the side that overlaps the filling).

13. Spread each rectangle with Dijon mustard, then place a filling cylinder just off centre on the uncut side.

14. Fold the cut side of the pastry over the filling and seal the edges together. Crimp the edges with a fork so you have a visible seam running down the side of each roll and the diagonal slits are on the top of the filling.

15. Place the sausage rolls back on the lined baking sheet. Mix the almond milk and agave syrup together and brush this over the sausage rolls to glaze.

16. Place the baking sheet of sausage rolls into the oven and bake the rolls for 25–30 minutes, until the pastry is golden brown and the filling is cooked through.

17. Meanwhile, make the caramelised red onion chutney. Heat the olive oil in a small pan. Add the onions and chilli and cook for 10–15 minutes, until the onions are soft and just beginning to colour. Add the garlic and sugar, then cook for a further 5 minutes. Add the vinegar and bring the liquid to the boil. Boil, stirring, until the vinegar has evaporated. Remove the pan from the heat and leave the chutney to cool. Serve the chutney with the sausage rolls.

FIG, HONEY & ALMOND CAKE

Local honey really makes a difference to the aromatic flavours of this rich and succulent fig cake. Perfectly ripe, plump figs have a delicate, sweet flavour and will 'give' slightly (but hold their shape) when lightly squeezed. Inside, they have ruby-coloured flesh – the only decoration you need for this bake.

For the vanilla honey drizzle
120g runny honey, plus extra to serve
juice of ½ lemon
1 tsp vanilla paste
50g light brown soft sugar

For the sponge
240g ground almonds
140g gluten-free self-raising flour
330g unsalted butter, softened
150g light brown soft sugar
100g golden caster sugar
80ml runny honey
6 eggs, lightly beaten
200ml full-fat Greek yogurt, plus optional extra to serve
1½ tsp vanilla paste
large pinch of salt
4–6 figs, cut into thin slices
flaked almonds, for sprinkling

You will need
23cm round cake tin (7cm deep), greased, then base-lined with baking paper
cocktail stick

1. Heat the oven to 180°C/160°C fan/Gas 4.

2. Make the vanilla honey drizzle. Place all the ingredients in a small pan with 100ml of water and simmer over a low heat for 10 minutes, stirring occasionally, until syrupy. Leave to cool.

3. Make the sponge. In a bowl, mix together the ground almonds and flour.

4. Beat the butter, both sugars and the honey in a stand mixer fitted with the beater, on medium speed for 7–10 minutes, until pale and creamy, scraping down the inside of the bowl from time to time.

5. Add the eggs, a little at a time, beating well between each addition. Beat in the Greek yogurt, then fold in the ground almond mixture, and the vanilla and salt.

6. Pour the mixture into the prepared tin and spread it level. Arrange the fig slices over the surface and gently press them into the mixture. Brush the figs with a little of the vanilla honey drizzle. Sprinkle a few flaked almonds between the gaps, around the figs.

7. Bake the cake on the middle shelf for 45 minutes, then check if the surface of the cake is turning too brown. If it is, place a disc of baking paper on top. Return the cake to the oven for a further 10–15 minutes, until risen and a skewer inserted into the centre comes out coated in just a few sticky crumbs.

8. Remove the cake from the oven and prick holes all over the top with a cocktail stick. Trickle over the remaining vanilla honey drizzle and leave the cake in the tin to cool completely. Remove the cake from the tin and serve it drizzled with extra honey and with Greek yogurt for spooning over, if you wish.

TOFFEE APPLE CAKE

An ode to apples! You'll need two types of apple here – sharp Bramleys and crisp Braeburns – among the best of autumn fruit. Whiz any leftover apple pieces into juice, or grate and fold them into overnight oats – or eat them as baker's perks.

For the apple butter
4 Braeburn apples,
    peeled, cored
    and diced
100g golden caster sugar
juice and finely grated zest
    of ½ unwaxed lemon

For the apple purée
2 Bramley apples,
    peeled, quartered,
    cored and diced
50g light brown
    soft sugar
juice of ½ lemon

For the sponge
250g unsalted
    butter, softened
150g golden caster sugar
125g dark brown
    soft sugar
4 large eggs
350g plain flour
2 tsp baking powder
1 tsp bicarbonate of soda
1 tsp ground cinnamon
¼ tsp ground allspice
¼ tsp grated nutmeg
pinch of salt
125ml whole milk

Continues overleaf

1. Make the apple butter. Tip the Braeburn pieces into a heavy-based pan with the sugar, lemon juice and zest and 100ml of water. Cover and cook over a low–medium heat, stirring from time to time, for about 5 minutes, or until the apples are soft. Remove the lid, reduce the heat and cook, stirring often, for about 45 minutes, until you have a thick paste that cleanly leaves the side of the pan. Spoon the paste into a bowl, leave it to cool, then cover it and chill it until needed.

2. Make the apple purée. Tip the Bramley pieces into a pan, add the sugar and lemon juice, cover and cook over a low heat until the apples have softened (about 5–10 minutes). Remove the lid and cook, stirring often, for about 20 minutes, to a thick purée. Leave to cool.

3. Meanwhile, heat the oven to 170°C/150°C fan/Gas 3.

4. Make the sponge. Beat the butter and both sugars in a stand mixer fitted with the beater, on medium speed for about 5 minutes, until pale and creamy, scraping down the inside of the bowl from time to time. Add the eggs, one at a time, beating well between each addition.

5. Sift the flour, baking powder, bicarbonate of soda, cinnamon, allspice, nutmeg and salt into the bowl. Measure 200g of the cold apple purée and add this to the bowl with the milk. Fold in the purée with a spoon until almost combined, then beat for 20 seconds until silky smooth. (Reserve any leftover apple purée for later.)

6. Divide the mixture equally between the cake tins, spread it level and bake the sponges on the middle shelves for 25 minutes, until well risen, golden brown and a skewer inserted into the centre of each comes out clean. Leave the sponges to cool in the tins for 2–3 minutes, then turn them out onto wire racks to cool completely.

Continues overleaf

*For the salted
toffee frosting*
150g caster sugar
125g soured cream
280g unsalted butter
2 tsp vanilla paste
½ tsp sea-salt flakes
400g icing sugar, sifted
3–4 tbsp whole milk

*For the mini
toffee apples*
3 Braeburn apples,
    peeled
200g caster sugar

You will need
20cm round cake tins x 3,
    greased, then base-
    lined with greased
    baking paper
melon baller
9 long wooden skewers
large piping bag
    fitted with a large
    plain nozzle

7. Make the salted toffee frosting. Tip the sugar into a small, heavy-based pan with 2 tablespoons of water. Set the pan over a low heat, swirling it from time to time to dissolve the sugar (do not stir). Increase the heat to medium, bring the syrup to the boil, then cook, swirling occasionally, to a deeper amber colour (about 5–6 minutes).

8. Carefully slide the pan off the heat and gently stir the soured cream and 30g of the butter into the caramel. Return the pan to a low heat to remelt any hardened caramel. Stir in the vanilla and salt, then pour the sauce into a bowl and cool to room temperature.

9. To finish the frosting, beat the remaining 250g of butter in a stand mixer for 2–3 minutes, until pale and creamy. Add the cooled toffee sauce and mix again. Gradually beat in the icing sugar and enough of the milk to give a smooth, combined consistency. Scrape down the inside of the bowl and beat for a further 2 minutes, until the frosting is light and fluffy. Spoon the frosting into the large piping bag fitted with a large plain nozzle.

10. To assemble, place one sponge on a serving plate and spread half the apple butter over the top. Then, using one third of the frosting in the piping bag, pipe frosting 'kisses' in concentric circles, over the apple butter (start at the outside edge and work inwards). Spoon any leftover apple purée over the frosting. Top with a second sponge and repeat with the apple butter and frosting, then top with the third sponge. Use the remaining frosting to pipe kisses in neat concentric circles on the top of the cake. Set aside in the fridge.

11. Make the mini toffee apples. Lay a sheet of newspaper on the floor underneath the edge of your work surface. Place a heavy chopping board or marble slab on your work surface. Using a melon baller, scoop 3 balls from each apple and pat them dry on kitchen paper. Push a long wooden skewer into the middle of each ball. Tip the sugar into a small, heavy-based pan and add 1 tablespoon of water. Make a caramel following the method in Step 7.

12. Working quickly, dip each apple ball into the caramel until evenly coated, then wedge the wooden skewer under the chopping board or slab, leaving the caramel to drip onto the newspaper below, forming strands as it does so. Let the caramel cool and harden, then use scissors to cut the caramel strands to your desired length. The strands are very sticky, so trim them first, then remove each skewer from under the chopping board. Gently pull the toffee apples from the skewers, arranging them on top of the cake to finish.

VEGETABLE SAMOSAS

Crispy pastry filled with spiced autumn vegetables and served with pickles and relishes, these veggie samosas are what cosy Friday nights with friends were made for. It is easier to make, fill and fry the samosas with one person filling and another frying. Serve with an assortment of Indian pickles and chutneys and a mint raita.

For the filling

350g mixture of peeled
   and diced squash
   (or pumpkin) and
   sweet potato
1 potato, peeled and
   diced (about 125g
   prepared weight)
1 parsnip, peeled and
   diced (about 125g
   prepared weight)
75g spring greens
   or about 5 Brussels
   sprouts, shredded
1 small onion, chopped
2 garlic cloves, crushed
1 green chilli, deseeded
5cm piece of fresh ginger,
   peeled and grated
2 tbsp olive oil
1 tsp black mustard
   seeds
1 tsp cumin seeds
½ tsp ground coriander
½ tsp ground turmeric
½ tsp garam masala
¼ tsp cayenne pepper
1 litre sunflower oil,
   for deep frying
salt and freshly ground
   black pepper
lime wedges, to serve

For the pastry

300g plain flour
½ tsp salt
4 tbsp sunflower oil

Continues overleaf

1. Make the filling. Steam the squash (or pumpkin) and sweet potato for about 20 minutes, until tender. Remove from the heat and leave the vegetables in the pan to steam dry for 5 minutes, then tip them into a large mixing bowl.

2. Meanwhile, cook the potato and parsnip in boiling salted water for about 20 minutes, until tender. Drain and leave to dry before adding them to the squash or sweet-potato mixture. Using a fork, mash the vegetables until nearly smooth but still with some texture.

3. Steam the spring greens or Brussels sprouts for 2 minutes, until tender and add them to the other vegetables.

4. Put the onion, garlic, chilli and ginger in a food processor and blitz them together until finely chopped.

5. Heat the olive oil in a frying pan over a low–medium heat, add the onion mixture and cook for 8 minutes, stirring frequently, until the onion has softened.

6. Add the mustard and cumin seeds and the coriander, turmeric, garam masala and cayenne pepper to the pan and cook for a further 1 minute before adding them to the vegetable mixture. Season with salt and pepper and mix to combine. Cover the filling and set it aside while you make the pastry.

7. Tip the flour and salt into a large mixing bowl. Add the oil and rub it in using your fingertips until the mixture is crumbly and the oil is thoroughly combined. Add 7–8 tablespoons of water and, using your hands, mix until everything comes together, but do not overwork the dough. Cover the dough and set it aside for 30 minutes.

8. Tip out the dough onto a lightly floured work surface and roll it into a sausage shape. Cut it into ten equal pieces.

Continues overleaf

You will need
baking tray, lined with
a double-thickness
of baking paper
cooking thermometer

9. Roll each piece into a ball and return all but one ball to the bowl. Cover the balls to prevent them drying out. Take the first dough ball and roll it out into a neat 15cm-diameter disc, about 2mm thick.

10. Cut the disc in half to make two semi-circles. Lightly brush the edge of the straight side of one semi-circle with water, then form it into a cone shape by sticking the straight edges together, slightly overlapping them, then press them together to seal.

11. Spoon a dessertspoon of the filling into the cone, lightly brush the inside edge of one side of the open cone with water and press the cone edges together to seal the filling inside. Place the parcel on the double-lined baking tray, cover and repeat with the remaining dough semi-circle. Repeat this rolling and filling process with the remaining dough balls to make 20 samosas in total.

12. Meanwhile, heat the sunflower oil in a large, deep pan (the oil shouldn't come more than a third of the way up the side of the pan) to 170°C on the cooking thermometer, or until a cube of day-old bread sizzles and rises to the surface quickly when dropped into the pan. (Alternatively, heat a deep-fat fryer to 170°C.) Fry the samosas in batches of four or five at a time for about 5 minutes per batch, turning occasionally, until crisp and golden brown all over.

13. Using a slotted spoon, remove the cooked samosas from the oil and set aside each batch to drain on kitchen paper. Allow the oil to come back up to temperature before frying the next batch. Serve warm or hot with pickles, chutneys and mint raita, and lime wedges for squeezing over.

FETA, GRAPE & FENNEL FOCACCIA

One of the simplest breads to make, focaccia is a brilliant base for adding your favourite seasonal flavours – in this case, wafer-thin sliced fennel and sweet black grapes. For a complete meal, serve it with a platter of cold meats and a salad.

For the dough
250g strong white
   bread flour
1 tsp salt
7g fast-action dried yeast
20ml extra-virgin olive oil,
   plus extra for greasing
200ml lukewarm water

For the infused oil
50ml extra-virgin olive oil
6–8 thyme sprigs, leaves
   picked and chopped
1 garlic clove, peeled
   but left whole

For the topping
1 fennel bulb, finely
   sliced lengthways,
   any fronds reserved
juice of ½ lemon
10 walnut halves
200g feta, cut into
   small cubes
200g seedless
   black grapes
1½ tbsp runny honey
few thyme sprigs

You will need
30 x 20cm (3cm deep)
   baking tin, oiled

1. Make the dough. Tip the flour into the bowl of a stand mixer fitted with the dough hook. Add the salt to one side of the bowl and the yeast to the other, then pour the olive oil into the middle. Add the water and mix on low speed for 5 minutes to a sticky, slightly shaggy dough.

2. Place the dough in the oiled tin and press it out so that it covers the base and goes neatly into the four corners. Cover the dough with oiled cling film and leave it for 40–60 minutes, until doubled in size.

3. Meanwhile, make the infused oil. Warm the olive oil with the thyme and garlic in a small pan over a low heat for 2–3 minutes, until the oil is sizzling and fragrant. Turn off the heat and leave the oil to infuse.

4. Prepare the topping. Put the fennel in a bowl with the lemon juice. Season the fennel with salt, mix it all together and set aside.

5. Toast the walnuts in a dry frying pan over a medium heat for about 7 minutes, tossing the pan occasionally until they start to colour. Remove the pan from the heat and when the nuts are cool enough to handle, break them into small pieces. Set aside.

6. When the dough is ready, firmly press the feta, walnuts and grapes evenly over the top. Cover the dough with oiled cling film again and leave it to prove for 30–60 minutes, until it rises to the top of the tin.

7. Heat the oven to 220°C/200°C fan/Gas 7.

8. Drizzle 2 tablespoons of the infused oil over the risen dough and bake it for 10 minutes. Increase the oven temperature to 240°C/220°C fan/Gas 9 and bake the focaccia for a further 5 minutes, until risen and golden.

9. To finish, drizzle any remaining infused oil and the honey over the focaccia, then scatter it with the fennel and thyme sprigs, and fennel fronds if available. Serve warm or cold in slices.

JÜRGEN'S PEAR & CHOCOLATE CHARLOTTE

A popular dessert in Germany, 'Birne Helene' combines chocolate and poached pears and provides the inspiration for this charlotte. Fruit charlottes are my most popular birthday cakes – this is one I created for my father-in-law.

For the génoise sponge
2 eggs
60g caster sugar
60g plain flour
10g unsalted butter, melted

For the sponge fingers
3 eggs, separated
pinch of salt
100g caster sugar
100g plain flour
1 tsp orange blossom water (optional)
1 tbsp icing sugar

For the chocolate bavarois
3 platinum-grade gelatine leaves
300ml whole milk
1 tsp vanilla paste
4 egg yolks
150g caster sugar
100g 70% dark chocolate, finely chopped
75g milk chocolate, finely chopped
300ml double cream

Continues overleaf

1. Heat the oven to 180°C/160°C fan/Gas 4.

2. Make the génoise sponge. Whisk the eggs and sugar in a stand mixer fitted with the whisk, on medium speed for 3–4 minutes, until pale, doubled in volume and the mixture holds a firm ribbon trail. Sift in the flour and fold it in with a metal spoon. Pour the melted butter down the inside of the bowl and fold to combine.

3. Spoon the mixture into the lined cake tin and gently spread it level. Bake the sponge on the middle shelf for about 8 minutes, until golden and the sponge springs back when pressed gently with a fingertip. Leave the sponge to cool in the tin on a wire rack.

4. Make the sponge fingers (biscuits à la cuillère). Whisk the egg whites and salt in the clean bowl of a stand mixer fitted with the whisk until they form firm peaks. Add 50g of the sugar and continue to whisk until the meringue is glossy and smooth. Using a rubber spatula, scoop the meringue into a clean bowl.

5. In the same mixer bowl (no need to wash), whisk the egg yolks and the remaining sugar until pale and doubled in volume, and the mixture holds a firm ribbon trail when you lift the whisk.

6. Using a spoon, fold one third of the meringue into the egg-yolk mixture. Sift in the flour, add the orange blossom water, if using, and fold until nearly combined. Fold in the remaining meringue.

7. Scoop the mixture into the piping bag fitted with a large plain nozzle and pipe neat 7cm-long biscuits onto the lined baking sheets. Dust them with icing sugar and bake them for 8 minutes, until golden. Leave them to cool on the baking sheets.

Continues overleaf

For the pear bavarois
5 platinum-grade
    gelatine leaves
200ml whole milk
1 tsp vanilla paste
4 egg yolks
125g caster sugar
1 tbsp pear brandy
375ml double cream
2 ripe pears, peeled,
    cored and diced

For the glaze
2 platinum-grade
    gelatine leaves
75g caster sugar
1 tbsp pear brandy
    (optional)
2 pears, cored
    and thinly sliced

You will need
23cm springform tin,
    greased, then base-lined
    with baking paper
large piping bag
    fitted with a large
    plain nozzle
2 baking sheets, lined
    with baking paper

8. Make the chocolate bavarois. Soak the gelatine in a bowl of cold water for 5 minutes, until soft. Meanwhile, heat the milk with the vanilla over a medium heat until just boiling. Whisk the egg yolks with the sugar in a mixing bowl until combined.

9. Pour half the hot milk into the egg-yolk mixture, whisking until smooth. Return this to the pan and cook it over a low heat, stirring until the custard thickens to coat the back of a spoon. Strain the custard into a clean bowl, add the drained gelatine leaves and both types of chocolate and whisk until smooth. Leave the chocolate custard to cool to room temperature and it just starts to thicken.

10. While the custard is cooling, prepare the charlotte tin. Remove the cooled sponge from the springform tin and set aside. Lightly oil the side of the tin and line it with a strip of baking paper or acetate. Cut the génoise into a 21cm disc and lay this in the bottom of the tin. Cut the sponge fingers to the same height as the depth of the tin and arrange them, cut side down and rounded side facing outwards, neatly around the inside wall of the tin, packing them tightly side-by-side so when the filling goes in, it can't escape.

11. Whip the cream to soft peaks and, half at a time, fold it into the cooled chocolate custard. Pour the custard into the prepared tin in an even layer and chill it for about 1 hour, until nearly set.

12. Meanwhile, make the pear bavarois. Soak the gelatine in a bowl of cold water for 5 minutes, until soft. Meanwhile, heat the milk with the vanilla over a medium heat until just boiling. Whisk the egg yolks with the sugar in a mixing bowl until combined. Pour all the hot milk into the egg-yolk mixture, whisking until smooth. Return the mixture to the pan and cook it over a low heat, stirring continuously, until the custard thickens enough to coat the back of a spoon. Strain the custard into a clean bowl, add the pear brandy and the drained gelatine and whisk until smooth. Leave until cold and thickened.

13. Whip the cream to soft peaks and, half at a time, fold it into the cold vanilla custard. Pour half the custard into the tin, scatter over the diced pears and pour over the remaining custard. Chill for 1 hour.

14. Make the glaze. Soak the gelatine in a bowl of water for 5 minutes, until soft. Pour 125ml of water into a small pan, add the sugar and heat until the sugar dissolves. Add the pear brandy, if using, and stir in the drained gelatine leaves until they melt. Cool to room temperature. Arrange the pears on top of the chilled charlotte, then carefully spoon over the glaze to cover. Chill until set, then serve in slices.

PECAN PIE

This classic American dessert is a popular feature at Thanksgiving celebrations, when it is perfectly timed for the pecan harvest. You can make the pie the day before you intend to serve it – just leave it to cool, then wrap it tightly and store it at room temperature until you're ready.

For the pastry

175g plain flour
good pinch of salt
100g unsalted butter, cubed and chilled
2 tbsp golden caster sugar
1 egg yolk
1½ tbsp ice-cold water
1 tsp lemon juice

For the filling

300g pecans
4 eggs
125g dark brown soft sugar
125g maple syrup
1 tsp vanilla paste
50g unsalted butter
1 tsp lemon juice
good pinch of sea-salt flakes
50g 54% dark chocolate chips

You will need

20cm fluted tart tin (about 4cm deep)
baking beans or rice

1. Make the pastry. Tip the flour and salt into a large mixing bowl. Add the butter and cut it into the flour using a table knife. Using your fingertips, rub the butter into the flour until the mixture resembles breadcrumbs. Mix in the sugar.

2. Make a well in the centre of the mixture, and add the egg yolk, ice-cold water and lemon juice. Using the knife, cut the wet ingredients into the dry, then gather the mixture into a ball. Flatten the ball into a disc, cover it and chill it for at least 1 hour, until firm.

3. Roll out the pastry on a lightly floured work surface to a neat disc, about 2–3mm thick and large enough to line the base and side of the tin. Line the tin, trim any excess, prick the base with a fork, then chill the case for 20–30 minutes. Heat the oven to 180°C/160°C fan/Gas 4.

4. Line the pastry case with baking paper and baking beans or rice, place it on a solid baking sheet and bake it for about 20 minutes, until the edges are golden. Remove the paper and beans or rice and bake the case for a further 4–5 minutes to dry it out. Remove the pastry case from the oven and set it aside while you prepare the filling.

5. Tip the pecans into a baking tray and toast them in the oven for about 4 minutes, until starting to colour. Remove them from the oven and, when they're cool enough to handle, reserve about 30 pecans for decoration. Roughly chop the remainder and set aside. Reduce the oven temperature to 170°C/150°C fan/Gas 3.

6. Whisk together the eggs, brown sugar, maple syrup and vanilla until smooth. Melt the butter and add it to the bowl, along with the lemon juice and salt. Stir through the pecans and chocolate chips.

7. Pour the filling into the tart case and spread it out evenly. Arrange the reserved pecans around the edge of the filling. Bake the pie on the middle shelf for 30–35 minutes, until the filling is set but has a very slight wobble in the middle. Leave the pie to cool to room temperature – the filling will continue to cook and set as it cools.

CHOCOLATE HAZELNUT TORTE

If you're foraging for hazelnuts, bear in mind they need to be fully ripe to be edible. During September and October, look for nuts that have started to shed their outer, green-brown, leafy skin and are drying out a little, so that they 'pop' free. Serve this indulgent cake as a dessert, in small, elegant slices.

For the sponge
275g blanched hazelnuts
225g 54% dark chocolate, chopped
225g unsalted butter, softened
250g caster sugar
6 eggs, separated
pinch of salt
1 tbsp cocoa powder, sifted

For the praline
100g caster sugar

For the chocolate glaze
125g 70% dark chocolate, chopped
75g milk chocolate, chopped
100ml whipping cream
20g unsalted butter, cubed
1 tbsp liquid glucose

You will need
23cm springform tin, greased, then base-lined with greased baking paper
baking tray, lined with baking paper
medium piping bag fitted with a medium open star nozzle

1. Heat the oven to 170°C/150°C fan/Gas 3.

2. Tip the hazelnuts onto a baking tray and toast them in the oven for 4–5 minutes, until golden. Leave them to cool, then weigh out 175g and blitz these in a food processor until ground. Set aside the remaining nuts for now.

3. Make the sponge. Melt the chocolate in a heatproof bowl set over a pan of barely simmering water. Stir until smooth, remove the chocolate from the heat and leave it to cool slightly.

4. Beat the butter and 125g of the caster sugar in a stand mixer fitted with the beater, on medium speed for 3–5 minutes, until pale and creamy, scraping down the inside of the bowl from time to time. Add the egg yolks, one at a time, beating well between each addition.

5. In a separate large bowl, whisk the egg whites with the salt to soft peaks. One third at a time, add the remaining 125g of caster sugar, whisking well between each addition, until the egg whites hold firm but not dry, glossy peaks.

6. Fold the melted chocolate, ground hazelnuts and cocoa into the butter mixture. Using a large metal spoon, fold one third of the egg whites into the mixture until almost combined. Fold in the remaining egg whites in two batches, until smooth and no streaks remain.

7. Spoon 250g of the sponge mixture into the lined tin and spread it level. Place the tin on a baking tray and bake the sponge on the middle shelf for 12 minutes, until the top is firm. Remove the sponge from the oven, tap the tray sharply on the work surface and leave the sponge to cool for 3 minutes.

Continues overleaf

8. Spoon the remaining sponge mixture into the tin over the first layer, spread it level and bake it for 45 minutes, until risen and the top is firm but with a slight wobble. Leave it to cool in the tin.

9. Make the praline. Tip the caster sugar into a small, heavy-based pan and add 1 tablespoon of water. Set the pan over a low heat, swirling the pan from time to time to dissolve the sugar (do not stir). Increase the heat to medium, bring the syrup to the boil and cook until it turns a deep amber colour (about 5–6 minutes).

10. Add the remaining 100g of whole toasted hazelnuts to the pan and stir them to coat them in the caramel. Turn out the mixture onto the lined baking tray and, using a fork, separate out 24 whole caramel-coated hazelnuts and set them aside – the remaining praline mixture can remain as one piece. Leave the praline piece to cool, then break it up and blitz it in the food processor until it's finely chopped.

11. Make the glaze. Tip all the glaze ingredients into a pan and place the pan over a low heat. Stir gently until the butter and chocolate melt. Pour the glaze into a bowl and leave it to cool for 5 minutes.

12. Carefully remove the torte from the tin, turning it upside down onto a wire rack. Pour three-quarters of the chocolate glaze over the top and side of the cake, spreading it with a palette knife, and allowing any excess to drip off the edge. Leave the glaze to set for 2 minutes, then neatly press the crushed praline around the side of the torte. Carefully transfer the torte to a serving plate.

13. Using a balloon whisk, beat the remaining glaze until thickened. Spoon it into the piping bag fitted with a medium open star nozzle and pipe rosettes around the top outer edge of the torte. Press the caramel-coated hazelnuts evenly spaced into the ring of rosettes, then leave the torte for 30 minutes for the glaze to completely set before serving.

PLUM & GINGER CAKE

Large, red-skinned plums are usually the most widely available variety in our stores at this time of year, but if you're lucky enough to find or grow some of the more unusual varieties, use these instead – just bear in mind that Mirabelles and greengages are small, so you'll need more to top your cake.

50g blanched hazelnuts
175g unsalted butter,
    softened
150g caster sugar
3 eggs, lightly beaten
3 nuggets of stem ginger
    in syrup, drained
    and finely chopped
125g self-raising flour
½ tsp baking powder
1 tsp ground ginger
pinch of salt
4 tbsp crème fraîche,
    plus optional extra
    to serve
5–6 large plums, halved,
    stoned and each half
    cut into 4–6 wedges
2 tbsp stem ginger syrup
whipped cream or ginger
    or vanilla ice cream,
    to serve (optional)

You will need
23cm springform tin,
    greased, then base-lined
    with baking paper

1. Heat the oven to 170°C/150°C fan/Gas 3.

2. Tip the hazelnuts onto a small baking tray and toast them in the oven for 3–4 minutes, until light golden brown. Leave them to cool completely, then blitz them in a food processor until very finely chopped.

3. Beat the butter and sugar together in a stand mixer fitted with the beater, on medium speed for 7 minutes, until pale and creamy, scraping down the inside of the bowl from time to time. Add the eggs, a little at a time, beating well between each addition, then add the stem ginger and mix again.

4. Sift the flour, baking powder, ground ginger and salt into the bowl, then add the finely chopped hazelnuts and crème fraîche and beat again until smooth and thoroughly combined.

5. Spoon the sponge mixture into the lined tin and spread it level. Arrange the plums neatly and tightly in two concentric circles on top of the sponge mixture. Bake the cake on the middle shelf for 45–50 minutes, until well risen and golden, and a skewer inserted into the centre comes out clean (don't worry if some of the plums sink during baking).

6. Brush the top of the cake with the stem ginger syrup and leave it in the tin to cool for 10 minutes, then remove it from the tin and transfer it to a wire rack to cool. Serve the cake warm or at room temperature with crème fraîche, softly whipped cream or a scoop of ginger or vanilla ice cream.

JUDGE'S RECIPE

PAUL'S CIABATTA BREADSTICKS

*The olive harvest is one of those events that truly marks a specific time of year –
in this case, when the intense heat of the summer sun gives way to a warm
autumnal glow. Enjoy Paul's breadsticks with some cooling tzatziki for dipping.*

For the breadsticks
750g strong white
   bread flour
1 tbsp salt
14g fast-action
   dried yeast
600ml lukewarm water
3 tbsp olive oil, plus
   extra for greasing
350g pitted green
   queen olives, halved
200g manchego cheese,
   cut into 2cm cubes
1 red onion,
   finely chopped
large handful of
   coriander, leaves
   picked and roughly
   chopped
semolina, for dusting

For the tzatziki
¼ cucumber
¼ tsp salt
150g full-fat Greek yogurt
1 small garlic clove,
   crushed or finely grated
1 tbsp extra-virgin olive oil
1 tsp white wine vinegar
1 tsp tzatziki seasoning

You will need
5-litre plastic food
   tub with a lid, oiled
3 baking trays,
   dusted with flour

1. Tip the flour into the bowl of a stand mixer fitted with the dough hook. Add the salt to one side of the bowl and the yeast to the other. Add three quarters of the water and mix on low speed. As the dough starts to come together, gradually add the remaining water. Mix for a further 5–8 minutes on medium speed. The dough should be wet and stretch easily when pulled. Add the olive oil and mix for 3 minutes.

2. Add the olives, manchego, onion and coriander and mix to evenly distribute. Tip the dough into the oiled container, cover and leave it for 1–2 hours at room temperature, until at least doubled in size.

3. Meanwhile, make the tzatziki. Grate the cucumber into a sieve set over a bowl and sprinkle over the salt. Mix the salt into the cucumber, then leave the cucumber to drain for 10 minutes. Squeeze any remaining liquid out of the cucumber, then spoon the yogurt into a bowl, add the cucumber, garlic, olive oil, vinegar and tzatziki seasoning and fold everything together. Transfer the tzatziki to a serving bowl and chill until needed.

4. Dust the work surface heavily with semolina. Carefully tip the dough onto the surface. It will be very loose and flowing, but don't worry. Handle it gently to keep as much air in it as possible.

5. Dust the top of the dough with semolina, then stretch it out gently to a rough rectangle. Starting at one long edge, cut the dough into about 18 strips. Stretch each piece out until 30cm long. Place six strips, equally spaced, onto each of the prepared baking trays. Cover and leave the dough strips to rise for 15 minutes. Meanwhile, heat your oven to 240°C/220°C fan/Gas 9, or to its hottest setting.

6. Bake the breadsticks for 15–20 minutes, until brown, then remove them from the oven and transfer them to wire racks to cool. Serve the breadsticks with the tzatziki for dipping.

BLACKBERRY & PEAR CRUMBLE CAKE

Juicy pears and blackberries are a wonderful match for each other and both are abundant during autumn. Comprising layers of cake, nutty crumble and juicy fruit, this bake would make a delicious pudding, served with a bowl of crème fraîche or ice cream, or an ideal weekend teatime treat just as it is.

225g unsalted
   butter, softened
150g caster sugar,
   plus 1 tbsp
3 pears, peeled,
   cored and each
   cut into 8 wedges
50g demerara sugar
1 tsp ground cinnamon
275g plain flour
50g blanched hazelnuts,
   toasted and roughly
   chopped
3 large eggs,
   lightly beaten
2 tsp baking powder
pinch of salt
150g soured cream
150g blackberries,
   plus optional extra
   to decorate
crème fraîche, or double
   cream, lightly whipped,
   to serve (optional)

You will need
20cm springform tin,
   greased, then base-
   lined with greased
   baking paper

1. Melt 25g of the butter in a large frying pan over a low–medium heat. Add the 1 tablespoon of caster sugar and the pears. Cook for about 10 minutes, turning frequently, until the pears are tender and lightly caramelised. Remove from the heat and leave to cool. Meanwhile, heat the oven to 180°C/160°C fan/Gas 4 and make the crumble topping.

2. Melt 50g of the butter, pour it into a bowl and leave it to cool slightly. Add the demerara sugar, cinnamon and 75g of the plain flour and mix well. Stir in the toasted hazelnuts and set aside.

3. Beat together the remaining 150g of butter and the 150g of caster sugar in a stand mixer fitter with the beater, on medium speed for 3–5 minutes, until pale and creamy, scraping down the inside of the bowl from time to time. Add the eggs, a little at a time, beating well between each addition. Sift the remaining 200g of plain flour, along with the baking powder and the salt into the bowl. Add the soured cream and mix again until smooth.

4. Spoon about two thirds of the sponge mixture into the prepared tin, spread it level and scatter over one third of the crumble topping. Top with the remaining sponge mixture and spread it level again.

5. Scatter another third of the crumble topping over the sponge mixture and arrange the cooked pear wedges and the blackberries on top. Scatter over the remaining crumble topping.

6. Bake the cake on the middle shelf for about 1½ hours, until risen and a skewer inserted into the centre comes out clean. (Loosely cover the top of the cake with baking paper or foil halfway through baking if the top is browning too quickly.)

7. Leave the cake to cool in the tin for 10 minutes, then remove it and transfer it to a wire rack and cool to room temperature before serving – with a few extra blackberries and with crème fraîche or lightly whipped double cream, if you wish.

APPLE & QUINCE CHAUSSONS

A chausson (literally meaning 'slipper') is the French equivalent of a turnover. These are filled with the best of the season's firm fruit – apples and delicious, often-underrated, quince. Although they're too firm to eat raw, quince have a brilliantly long shelf-life, so if a friend offers you their windfalls, always say yes!

For the puff pastry
250g unsalted
    butter, chilled
150g plain flour
100g strong white
    bread flour
pinch of salt
1 egg yolk
100ml ice-cold water
1 tsp lemon juice

For the filling
4 crisp eating apples
    (such as Braeburn),
    peeled, cored
    and thinly sliced
1 large quince, peeled,
    cored and thinly sliced
2 tbsp golden caster
    sugar
juice of ½ lemon
25g unsalted butter
½ tsp ground cinnamon
½ tsp vanilla paste
1 egg, beaten
2 tbsp demerara sugar
vanilla ice cream, or
    crème fraîche, to serve

You will need
12cm round cutter
    or small plate
baking tray, lined
    with baking paper

1. Make the puff pastry. Cut 50g of the butter into cubes. Combine both flours in a mixing bowl and add the salt and cubed butter. Using your fingertips, rub the butter into the flour until the mixture resembles breadcrumbs.

2. Make a well in the centre and add the egg yolk. Mix the water with the lemon juice and add this to the well, too. Using a table knife, cut the wet ingredients into the dry (you may need to add a drop more water), then gather the mixture into a ball. Flatten and shape the ball into a neat rectangle, then cover it and chill it for 1 hour, until firm.

3. Place the pastry on a lightly floured work surface and roll it out lengthways into a neat rectangle three times as long as it is wide (about 45 x 15cm), with one of the short ends nearest you.

4. Place the remaining 200g of butter between two sheets of baking paper and roll it into a neat square, slightly smaller than a third of the pastry rectangle. Place the butter on the middle section of the pastry and fold the bottom third up over it. Brush off any excess flour, then fold the top third down so that the butter is completely encased in the dough. Brush off any excess flour and turn the square 90 degrees clockwise.

5. Roll out the pastry again into a neat rectangle, about 45 x 15cm. Fold the bottom third of the rectangle up over the middle third and the top third down, as if you were folding a letter, and brush off any excess flour. Lightly press the pastry edges together, turn the square 90 degrees clockwise, cover it and chill it for 1 hour, until firm.

6. Repeat this rolling and folding twice more, turning the pastry 90 degrees clockwise each time, then chill it again for 1 hour. Roll the dough out one further time, so that you have rolled it out five times in total. Fold it, then cover it and chill it for 2 hours before use.

Continues overleaf

7. Make the filling. Tip the apples and quince into a medium pan. Stir in the golden caster sugar, lemon juice, butter, cinnamon and vanilla and cook for 10–15 minutes over a low–medium heat, half-covered, until the fruit is really soft and any excess juice has evaporated. Leave to cool.

8. Lightly flour the work surface and roll out the pastry to a circle, about 2mm thick. Using the 12cm cutter or plate as a guide, stamp out 12–14 discs, or as many as you can, re-rolling any trimmings to make more discs.

9. Lay the pastry discs on the work surface and spoon a tablespoon of the cooked apple and quince mixture on one side of each disc, leaving a 1cm border. Lightly brush each border with beaten egg, fold the pastry over to encase the filling and press the edges together to seal. Arrange the pastry parcels on the lined baking tray and chill them for 15 minutes.

10. Using a paring knife, knock up the rounded edge of each pastry parcel and brush the top with a little beaten egg. Chill the parcels again for 15 minutes. Meanwhile, heat the oven to 190°C/170°C fan/Gas 5.

11. Brush the parcels with beaten egg again and, using the point of a small, sharp knife, score a decorative pattern into the top of each one, cutting into but not through the pastry. Scatter the chaussons with the demerara sugar and bake them on the middle shelf for about 25 minutes, until the pastry is crisp and golden brown.

12. Serve the chaussons hot, warm or at room temperature, with ice cream or crème fraîche.

TOM'S BLACKBERRY & APPLE CAKE WITH CHAI BUTTERCREAM

Inspired by a traditional apple and blackberry crumble with custard, this recipe turns the pudding into something fitting for a celebration. I initially created the cake specifically for my Gran's birthday and it is now a family favourite.

For the sponge

150g unsalted
  butter, softened
300g golden caster sugar
150g mild, odourless
  coconut oil, at room
  temperature
6 eggs, lightly beaten
300g self-raising flour
1½ tsp baking powder
½ tsp ground cinnamon
1 large Bramley apple,
  peeled, cored and
  cut into 1cm dice

For the blackberry coulis

150g blackberries
100g caster sugar

For the chai-custard buttercream

300ml whole milk
2 vanilla chai tea bags
  (or other flavoured tea)
70g golden caster sugar
15g plain flour
15g cornflour
4 egg yolks
175g unsalted butter,
  softened
3 tbsp icing sugar, sifted

Continues overleaf

1. Heat the oven to 180°C/160°C fan/Gas 4.

2. Make the sponge. Beat the butter, sugar and coconut oil in a stand mixer fitted with the beater, on medium speed for 3–5 minutes, until pale and creamy. Add the eggs, a little at a time, and combine.

3. Sift the flour, baking powder and cinnamon into the bowl and fold everything together with a metal spoon. Stir in the apple pieces.

4. Divide the mixture equally between the lined tins and spread it level. Bake the sponges on the middle shelves for about 25 minutes, until well risen, golden brown and a skewer inserted into the centre of each sponge comes out clean. Leave the sponges to cool in the tins for 10 minutes, then turn them out onto wire racks to cool completely.

5. Meanwhile, make the blackberry coulis. Place the blackberries and caster sugar in a pan, add 50ml of water and cook over a low–medium heat for 2–3 minutes, or until the berries are soft.

6. Using a potato masher, squash the berries. Increase the heat to medium and bring the liquid to the boil, then cook, stirring occasionally, for about 5 minutes, until thickened to a coulis consistency. Press the blackberry mixture through a sieve into a bowl to remove the seeds, then leave the coulis in the bowl to cool.

7. Make the custard for the buttercream. Pour the milk into a pan, add the tea bags and warm them over a low heat to scalding temperature, but do not let the milk boil. Remove the pan from the heat and leave the milk to infuse for 20 minutes.

Continues overleaf

To decorate
150g blackberries
blackberry or mint leaves

You will need
20cm round cake tins x 3,
    greased, then base-lined
    with baking paper

8. In a bowl, whisk the sugar, flour, cornflour and egg yolks together until smooth and combined.

9. Remove the tea bags from the milk and squeeze them to extract as much flavour as possible, then reheat the milk to just below boiling point. Pour half the milk into the egg mixture, whisking continuously to prevent the eggs scrambling. When combined, pour the contents of the mixing bowl back into the pan and cook over a low-medium heat, whisking continuously, until the custard thickens to coat the back of the spoon and it no longer tastes floury.

10. Strain the custard into a heatproof bowl, cover the surface with cling film to stop a skin forming, then cool it to room temperature.

11. Whisk the cooled custard in a stand mixer fitted with the whisk until loosened. Add the butter, 1 tablespoon at a time, whisking continuously until combined. Add the icing sugar and continue to mix until the buttercream is thick and spreadable.

12. To assemble, place one of the sponges on a serving plate or cake stand. Spread half the blackberry coulis over the sponge, then spread one third of the buttercream over the coulis. Top with a second sponge and spread that with the remaining coulis and another third of the buttercream.

13. Place the third sponge on top and spread it with the remaining buttercream, creating a swirly pattern with the back of a spoon or offset spatula. Decorate the cake with the blackberries and blackberry or mint leaves.

APPLE, PECAN & MISO CARAMEL TART

This sweetness of this beautiful tart is delicately balanced by the saltiness of the miso in the caramel. Cooking the apples so that they keep a little bite adds texture.

For the pâte sucrée
15g pecans
125g plain flour
45g caster sugar
¼ tsp salt
75g unsalted butter,
    cubed and chilled
1 egg yolk
1 tbsp ice-cold water

For the apple filling
20g unsalted butter
2 Bramley apples,
    peeled, cored and
    cut into 1cm dice
½ tsp ground cinnamon
½ tsp apple cider vinegar

For the miso caramel
115g unsalted butter
125ml double cream
200g caster sugar
1 tsp liquid glucose
1 tbsp brown miso paste

For the pecan crunch
125g pecans
½ tsp vanilla paste
pinch of salt

For the caramelised pecans
50g caster sugar
6 pecans

Continues overleaf

1. Make the pâte sucrée. Blitz the pecans in a food processor until finely ground. Add the flour, sugar, salt and butter and blitz until the mixture resembles breadcrumbs. Add the egg yolk and ice-cold water, and pulse until the mixture begins to clump together. Then, tip the dough onto the work surface and bring it together into a ball. Flatten it slightly, then wrap it and chill it for 10 minutes.

2. Meanwhile, cook the apple filling. Melt the butter in a medium pan, then cook it over a low heat for 5 minutes, until lightly browned and smelling nutty. Remove the pan from the heat.

3. Stir the apples into the butter with the cinnamon and vinegar and place this over a medium heat. Cover with a lid and cook the apples for 4–5 minutes, until the apples are tender, but still have a bite and hold their shape. Tip the apples onto a plate and leave them to cool.

4. Remove the pâte sucrée from the fridge and set aside 30g for the flower decorations. Lightly flour the work surface and roll out the remaining pâte sucrée to a 28cm-diameter circle. Flip the pâte sucrée over the rolling pin, lift it into the tart tin, pressing it into the base and up the side. Trim the edge. Chill the case for 15 minutes. Thinly roll out the reserved pâte sucrée with any trimmings, and cut out six medium and six small flowers. Place them on a baking tray and chill.

5. Make the miso caramel. Fill a large bowl with cold water and ice and set it aside.

6. Warm the butter and cream in a medium pan over a low heat until the butter melts. Leave the mixture on a very low heat.

7. Place the sugar, 50ml of water and the liquid glucose in a separate medium pan. Set the pan over a low heat, swirling it from time to time to dissolve the sugar (do not stir). Increase the heat to medium and bring the syrup to the boil, then cook it, swirling the pan occasionally, until it turns a deeper amber colour (about 5–6 minutes).

Continues overleaf

For the topping
250ml double cream
125g full-fat cream cheese
1 tbsp icing sugar, sifted
1 tbsp vanilla paste

You will need
20cm fluted tart tin
    (4cm deep)
medium and small
    daisy/flower cutters
sugar thermometer
baking beans or rice
large piping bag fitted
    with a large closed
    star nozzle

8. Remove the pan from the heat and gradually whisk in the warm cream and butter mixture, taking care as the mixture will foam up and spit. Return the pan to the heat, stir in the miso paste and cook, stirring continuously over a medium heat, for about 5 minutes, until the mixture reaches 118°C on a sugar thermometer and becomes thick and toffee-like. Place the base of the pan in the bowl of iced water to prevent the sauce cooking any further. Leave it to cool to 35–40°C, and it has a thick, pouring consistency.

9. Heat the oven to 180°C/160°C fan/Gas 4. Line the pastry case with baking paper and fill it with baking beans or rice. Bake the case for 15 minutes, then remove the paper and beans or rice and return it to the oven for a further 15 minutes, until golden brown. Bake the pastry flowers alongside the tart case for 15 minutes, until golden brown. Leave the tart case and flowers to cool on a wire rack.

10. Make the pecan crunch. Scatter the pecans over a baking tray and bake them for 10 minutes, until toasted and a little darker in colour. Leave them to cool, then blitz about two thirds of them in a food processor until well chopped. Add the remaining pecans with the vanilla and salt and blitz for a few seconds to break up the pecans a little, but leave some chunkier pieces.

11. Remove the tart case from the tin and place it on a serving plate. Spread the pecan crunch evenly over the base, then top with the apple mixture (reserve a few pieces for decoration), spreading it out evenly. Pour over the miso caramel in an even layer and chill the tart for at least 30 minutes to set the caramel to a soft toffee.

12. Meanwhile, make the caramelised pecans. Place the sugar in a small, heavy-based pan with 1 tablespoon of water. Set the pan over a low heat, swirling the pan from time to time to dissolve the sugar (do not stir). Then, increase the heat to medium and bring the syrup to the boil, swirling the pan occasionally and cooking until the syrup turns a deeper amber colour (about 5–6 minutes). Add the pecans, then lift them, out one at a time, onto a sheet of baking paper and leave them to set for 10 minutes.

13. Make the topping. Whisk the double cream, cream cheese, icing sugar and vanilla in a mixing bowl with an electric hand whisk until smooth and the mixture holds soft peaks. Spoon it into the large piping bag fitted with a large closed star nozzle and pipe rosettes over the top of the tart, then decorate the tart with the pastry flowers, caramelised pecans and the reserved pieces of apple.

WINTER

RECILES

PARSNIP, MAPLE & PECAN CAKE

PAUL'S CARAMEL BISCUIT BARS

SEVILLE ORANGE LAMINGTONS

DARK MASALA & STOUT CHRISTMAS CAKE

BLOOD ORANGE GALETTE

LIZZIE'S SPROUT & CHESTNUT TARTS

PERSIAN LOVE CAKE

DATE & WALNUT M'HANNCHA

NEW YORK CHEESECAKE WITH CRANBERRIES

PANETTONE

BEEF & POTATO PIES

ST CLEMENT'S SQUARES

PRUE'S MALT LOAF

SPICED APPLE BRANDY SNAP BASKETS

GEORGE'S KOURABIETHES

WINTER NO-KNEAD LOAF

PAUL'S BAKLAVA

PRAWN & PORK POTSTICKERS

MINCEMEAT & MARZIPAN COURONNE

MAGGIE'S ORANGE & LEMON CAKE

PARSNIP, MAPLE & PECAN CAKE

Imagine your favourite lightly spiced carrot cake but with the fragrance of parsnip, the crunch of pecan and the subtle, mellow notes of maple syrup. The cream cheese and maple filling perfectly offsets the sweetness of this cake. A generous slice is pure comfort on dark, cold afternoons in front of a restorative roaring fire.

For the sponge
180g gluten-free
   self-raising flour
80g ground almonds
½ tsp bicarbonate
   of soda
2 tsp ground mixed spice
pinch of salt
235ml vegetable oil
320g light brown
   soft sugar
120g full-fat plain yogurt
4 large eggs
100ml maple syrup
1 tsp vanilla paste
250g parsnips
   (about 3), peeled
   and coarsely grated
100g pecans, toasted
   and roughly chopped

For the cream-cheese filling
50g unsalted
   butter, softened
2 tbsp maple syrup
1 tsp vanilla paste
200g full-fat
   cream cheese
icing sugar, for dusting

You will need
20cm sandwich tins x 2,
   oiled, then base-lined
   with baking paper
maple leaf stencil
   (optional)

1. Heat the oven to 180°C/160°C fan/Gas 4.

2. Mix the flour, ground almonds, bicarbonate of soda, mixed spice and salt in a large mixing bowl.

3. Whisk the vegetable oil, sugar, yogurt, eggs, maple syrup and vanilla in a stand mixer fitted with the whisk, on medium speed for 3 minutes, until the mixture leaves a ribbon trail when you lift the whisk.

4. Add the dry ingredients to the mixer bowl and, using a large spoon, mix until combined. Fold in the parsnips and pecans.

5. Divide the mixture between the prepared tins and spread it level. Bake the sponges on the middle shelf for about 35 minutes, until a skewer inserted into the centre of each comes out clean. Leave the sponges to cool completely in the tins.

6. Make the cream-cheese filling. Beat the butter in a stand mixer fitted with the beater until pale and creamy, scraping down the inside of the bowl from time to time. Mix in the maple syrup and vanilla. Add spoonfuls of the cream cheese, a little at a time, and mix gently until smooth and creamy. Chill until needed.

7. Turn out the cooled sponges from the tins. Place one sponge, top downwards, on a board and spread it with the cream-cheese filling. Sandwich with the second sponge, top upwards. Dust the cake with icing sugar, using a maple leaf as a stencil to create a pattern, if you like.

PAUL'S CARAMEL BISCUIT BARS

If there's one thing we deserve after a freezing-cold walk, it's a sweet hit with a hot mug of tea or, even better, hot chocolate. These biscuit bars are just the thing – crisp shortbread biscuit topped with shiny set caramel and coated in smooth milk chocolate. Add a few sprinkles of sea salt over the caramel for a salted caramel version, if you like.

For the shortbread biscuit base
55g unsalted
   butter, softened
25g caster sugar
55g plain flour
25g cornflour

For the caramel filling
90g caster sugar
15g liquid glucose
45ml double cream
50g unsalted butter

For the chocolate coating
300g milk chocolate,
   chopped

You will need
900g loaf tin, greased,
   then lined (base and
   short sides, leaving
   the ends overhanging)
   with baking paper
medium piping bag
   fitted with a medium
   plain nozzle
baking sheet, lined
   with baking paper
small piping bag fitted
   with a small plain nozzle

1. Make the shortbread biscuit base. Using a wooden spoon, beat the butter and sugar together until light and creamy, but not aerated. Sift in the plain flour and cornflour and mix to a dough.

2. Tip the dough onto a sheet of baking paper and place a second sheet of paper on top. Roll out the dough to a rectangle the same size as the base of the loaf tin, trimming to fit, if necessary. Carefully lift the shortbread dough into the tin, then chill it for 20 minutes.

3. Heat the oven to 170°C/150°C fan/Gas 3.

4. Prick the chilled dough all over with a fork and bake it for 15–20 minutes, until a pale biscuit colour. Remove the shortbread from the oven and leave it to cool and firm up in the tin for 5 minutes.

5. Using the baking paper to help you, remove the shortbread from the tin. While it's slightly warm, cut the shortbread into 10 equal fingers (about 1.5cm wide), then set them aside to cool completely while you make the caramel.

6. Make the caramel. Tip the caster sugar and liquid glucose into a small heavy-based pan and heat the mixture over a low heat until the sugar begins to melt, shaking the pan from time to time (do not stir). Bring the mixture to the boil, then cook the caramel to a light amber caramel colour (about 2–3 minutes). Meanwhile, prepare a bowl of ice-cold water.

7. Carefully remove the pan from the heat and plunge the base into the cold water to stop the cooking process and prevent the caramel from burning.

Continues overleaf

8. Add the cream and butter to the pan and stir until the butter melts. Tip the caramel into a clean bowl and leave it to cool (about 1 hour), then chill it until thick enough to pipe.

9. Spoon the chilled caramel into the medium piping bag fitted with the medium plain nozzle and pipe a line of caramel on the top of each shortbread finger. Set aside.

10. Make the chocolate coating. Melt the chocolate in a heatproof bowl set over a pan of barely simmering water, stirring occasionally until smooth.

11. Remove the bowl from the heat and pour about one quarter of the chocolate into a shallow bowl. Dip the base of each caramel biscuit finger into the chocolate to coat, then place them on the lined baking sheet. Chill the fingers for 5 minutes, until the chocolate sets.

12. Spoon 2 tablespoons of the chocolate into the small piping bag fitted with a small plain nozzle and set aside.

13. Pour the remaining chocolate into a jug. Place the biscuit fingers on a cooling rack set over a sheet of baking paper to catch the drips, then pour the chocolate in the jug over the caramel to evenly coat the biscuits. Leave the chocolate coating to set for 2 minutes, then pipe thin lines across the top of the biscuits in a zig-zag motion. Leave the chocolate to set completely (about 15 minutes) before tucking in.

SEVILLE ORANGE LAMINGTONS

The first Seville oranges ripen in November and the season lasts not much longer than the end of December, so snaffle them up when you see them. Their sour tang is perfect for the curd filling in these lamingtons (and any leftover is yummy on toast).

For the sponge
150g unsalted
  butter, softened
150g caster sugar
3 eggs, lightly beaten
1 tsp vanilla paste
175g self-raising flour
1 tsp ground mixed spice
½ tsp baking powder
good pinch of salt
2 tbsp soured cream
2 tbsp whole milk

For the orange curd
juice and finely grated
  zest of 2 unwaxed
  Seville oranges
100g caster sugar
75g unsalted
  butter, cubed
pinch of salt
2 eggs
2 egg yolks
1 platinum-grade
  gelatine leaf

For the coating
150g 54% dark
  chocolate, chopped
40g unsalted butter
150ml whole milk
225g icing sugar
25g cocoa powder
finely grated zest of
  ½ Seville orange
300g desiccated coconut

Continues overleaf

1. Heat the oven to 180°C/160°C fan/Gas 4.

2. Make the sponge. Beat the butter and sugar in a stand mixer fitted with the beater, on medium speed for about 3–5 minutes, until pale and creamy, scraping down the inside of the bowl from time to time. Gradually add the eggs, beating well between each addition. Add the vanilla and mix again.

3. Sift the flour, mixed spice, baking powder and salt into the bowl. Add the soured cream and milk and mix again until smooth.

4. Scoop the mixture into the prepared tin and spread it level using a palette knife. Bake the sponge on the middle shelf for 25–30 minutes, until golden brown, well risen and a skewer inserted into the centre comes out clean.

5. Leave the sponge to cool in the tin for 5 minutes, then turn it out onto a wire rack to cool completely. Wrap the sponge and leave it until the next day before cutting and coating.

6. Meanwhile, prepare the orange curd (this also needs overnight chilling). Put the orange zest in a heatproof mixing bowl. Measure 175ml of the orange juice (drink any leftover) and add it to the zest with the sugar, butter and salt. Place the bowl over a pan of barely simmering water (don't let the bottom of the bowl touch the water, otherwise the curd will scramble).

7. In another bowl, whisk the whole eggs and egg yolks together, then add these to the orange mixture. Whisk frequently until the butter melts and the sugar dissolves. Continue to cook for about 10 minutes, stirring frequently, until the curd thickens enough to coat the back of a spoon and holds a ribbon trail when you lift the whisk.

Continues overleaf

You will need
20cm square cake tin,
    greased, then lined
    (base and sides)
    with baking paper
medium piping bag
    fitted with a small
    plain nozzle
baking sheet, lined
    with baking paper

8. Meanwhile, soak the gelatine in a bowl of cold water for 5 minutes, until soft. Drain the gelatine, squeezing out any excess, then add it to the curd. Stir to melt and combine.

9. Pour the curd into a clean bowl and cover the surface with cling film to prevent a skin forming. Leave it to cool, then chill it overnight.

10. The following day, make the coating. Melt the chocolate and butter in a heatproof bowl set over a pan of barely simmering water. Stir until smooth, remove from the heat and leave to cool slightly.

11. Warm the milk in a small pan or in a suitable bowl in the microwave. Sift the icing sugar with the cocoa into a large bowl, gradually add the warmed milk and mix until smooth. Add the melted chocolate mixture and orange zest and mix again until smooth.

12. Cut the cake into 16 equal-sized squares. Spoon the orange curd into the medium piping bag fitted with a small plain nozzle. Push the nozzle into the middle of one cake and pipe in about 1 teaspoonful of curd. Repeat for all of the cakes.

13. Tip half the desiccated coconut onto a baking tray. Sit one cake on the tines of a large fork and dip the cake into the chocolate coating to completely cover. Hold the cake above the bowl and sharply tap to allow any excess chocolate coating to drip off. Place the chocolate-coated cake in the desiccated coconut and roll it around until completely covered. Transfer it to the lined baking sheet until set firm (at least 1 hour).

14. Repeat for all the cakes – the coconut will get messy and full of chocolate drips halfway through, so swap it for the remaining coconut, as necessary.

DARK MASALA & STOUT CHRISTMAS CAKE

Both stone and vine fruits are steeped in a blend of aromatic fresh chai masala tea and dark rum, which combine deliciously with dark stout, to create this rich and intense cake that's less sweet than more traditional festive offerings.

For the fruit
100g dried apricots,
    chopped
100g dried pitted dates
    or prunes, chopped
150g raisins
1 small eating apple,
    peeled, cored
    and grated
300ml freshly brewed
    chai masala tea
100ml dark rum,
    plus optional 3 tbsp
    for pouring

For the date purée
100g dried pitted dates
100ml freshly brewed
    hot chai masala tea

For the cake
100ml light olive
    or any neutral oil
200g dark brown
    soft sugar
150ml maple syrup
200ml dark stout
100ml coconut milk
4 tsp apple cider vinegar
1 tsp vanilla paste
1 tsp almond extract
400g plain flour, sifted
50g ground almonds
1½ tsp bicarbonate
    of soda
½ tsp salt

Continues overleaf

1. Prepare the fruit. Place the apricots, dates or prunes, raisins and apple in a bowl, pour in the hot tea and the rum and leave the mixture to cool. Once the liquid is cool, transfer the bowl to the fridge and leave the fruit to soak overnight.

2. Meanwhile, prepare the date purée. Place the dates and hot tea in a small bowl. Leave the mixture to cool, then transfer it to the fridge and leave to soak overnight. The next day, tip the soaked date mixture into a food processor and blitz it to a purée.

3. Make the cake. Heat the oven to 160°C/140°C fan/Gas 2½. Mix the oil, sugar and maple syrup together in a large mixing bowl. Whisk in the date purée, stout and coconut milk, then whisk in the vinegar, vanilla and almond extract.

4. Fold the flour, ground almonds, bicarbonate of soda, salt, cinnamon, ginger and mixed spice into the wet ingredients until combined. Remove the soaked fruit from the fridge and add it to the cake mixture with any liquid left in the bowl. Fold in the chopped nuts, then pour the mixture into the lined tin and spread it level.

5. Bake the cake on the middle shelf for 2 hours, until dark and risen, and a skewer inserted into the centre comes out almost clean. Remove from the oven. Prick holes all over the cake using a wooden skewer or cocktail stick and pour over the extra 3 tablespoons of rum, if you wish. Leave the cake to cool completely in the tin.

6. Make the vegan marzipan. Place the ground almonds and icing sugar in a food processor and blitz them together to a fine powder. Stir in 4½ tablespoons of water and the almond extract to form a thick paste – if the paste is too dry, add a few more drops of water, or (if it's too wet) extra ground almonds. Knead the paste for 1 minute, until combined, then cover it and chill it until needed.

Continues overleaf

2 tsp ground cinnamon
1 tsp ground ginger
1 tsp ground mixed spice
200g chopped mixed
    nuts (such as almonds,
    walnuts and pecans)
1 tbsp smooth apricot jam

For the vegan marzipan
300g ground almonds,
    plus extra if needed
240g icing sugar, sifted,
    plus extra for dusting
1½ tsp almond extract

For the vegan royal icing
6 tbsp aquafaba
    (the liquid from
    a tin of chickpeas)
500g icing sugar, sifted
1 tbsp cornflour (optional)

*For the frosted rosemary
and redcurrants*
200g caster sugar
6–8 long rosemary sprigs
about 5–6 redcurrant
    clusters

You will need
20cm springform or
    loose-bottomed deep
    cake tin, greased,
    then double-lined
    with baking paper
wooden skewer
    or cocktail stick
cake scraper (optional)
offset spatula
cake-decorating turntable
    (optional)

7. Make vegan the royal icing. Whisk the aquafaba in the bowl of a stand mixer fitted with the whisk, until foamy and doubled in volume. Add the icing sugar and continue to whisk until smooth, thick and spreadable. Thicken the icing by adding the cornflour if it is too thin. Set aside.

8. Make the frosted rosemary and redcurrants. Put 100ml of water and half the sugar into a small pan over a low heat and stir until the sugar dissolves. Simmer for 5 minutes, until syrupy. Allow the syrup to cool slightly, then add the rosemary sprigs and turn them to coat them in the syrup. Lift them out, drain them and place them on a sheet of baking paper. Brush the redcurrant clusters with the syrup, then dust the sprigs and clusters with the remaining caster sugar, and leave to set.

9. Lightly dust the work surface with icing sugar. Roll out the marzipan into a disc, about 5mm thick and large enough to cover the top and side of the cake.

10. Remove the cold cake from the tin and peel off the lining paper. Brush the cake with the apricot jam and lay the marzipan on top, pressing slightly to fix it in place and smoothing it over the edges and down the side (you can use a cake scraper for this, if you have one). Pour the royal icing over the cake and spread it across the top and down the side, using an offset spatula to create a smooth, even finish (use a cake-decorating turntable, if you have one).

11. Position the frosted redcurrants around the top edge of the cake in a ring and the frosted rosemary sprigs upright around the side, to decorate.

BLOOD ORANGE GALETTE

The blood-orange season begins in December, but the fruit tends to be most abundant in January and February, when the dark, almost purple moro variety ripens for just a short few months. Blood oranges are generally smaller (and more juicy) than regular oranges, but if yours are larger, reduce the quantity to six.

For the pastry
200g plain flour, sifted
1 tbsp caster sugar
½ tsp ground cinnamon, ground mixed spice or ground cardamom
good pinch of salt
140g unsalted butter, cut into 1cm cubes and chilled
3 tbsp ice-cold water

For the filling
70g unsalted butter, softened
70g caster sugar, plus extra for sprinkling
70g ground almonds
1 egg, separated
finely grated zest of ¼ blood orange
pinch of salt
8–9 blood oranges
2 tbsp flaked almonds
crème fraîche, to serve

You will need
large baking sheet, lined with baking paper

1. Make the pastry. Tip the flour into a large mixing bowl and add the sugar, cinnamon (or other ground spice) and salt. Using your fingertips, rub the butter into the flour until the pieces of butter are the size of peas. Drizzle in the ice-cold water and, using your hands, gather the mixture into a scrappy dough without over-mixing. Add a little more water if needed, but maintain the large butter pieces throughout the dough. Flatten the pastry into a disc, wrap it and chill it for 1 hour, until firm.

2. Roll out the pastry on a lightly floured work surface to a 30cm disc. Trim the edges to neaten. Slide the pastry onto the lined baking sheet and chill it for 30 minutes while you prepare the filling. Meanwhile, heat the oven to 190°C/170°C fan/Gas 5.

3. Using a wooden spoon, beat together the butter and sugar until pale and creamy. Add the ground almonds, egg yolk, orange zest and salt, then mix again until combined.

4. Using a small, serrated knife, cut a thin slice off the top and bottom of each blood orange. Stand the oranges upright and, working around each fruit from top to bottom, cut off the skin and pith in strips, so that you have beautifully neat, peeled fruit. Cut each orange into 5–10mm-thick slices.

5. Spread the almond mixture over the pastry disc, leaving a 4cm border around the edge. Arrange the orange slices on top of the almond paste. Fold and roll the pastry edge over to form a crust.

6. Lightly beat the egg white and brush this over the pastry crust. Sprinkle caster sugar over the pastry and oranges and scatter the galette with the flaked almonds. Bake for 35–40 minutes, until the pastry is crisp and golden and the oranges start to caramelise at the edges. Serve warm or at room temperature with crème fraîche.

BAKER'S RECIPE

LIZZIE'S SPROUT & CHESTNUT TARTS

I created this recipe as an alternative to bubble and squeak for the leftover veggies after a roast. Now they are my Brussels sprouts go-to.

For the pastry
150g plain flour
1 tsp salt
pinch of sugar
75g unsalted butter,
    cubed and chilled
3–4 tbsp ice-cold water

For the filling
125g smoked
    bacon lardons
1 tbsp olive oil
1 garlic clove, crushed
1 rosemary sprig,
    leaves picked and
    finely chopped
200g Brussels sprouts,
    outer layers removed,
    finely shredded
100g peeled, cooked
    chestnuts
1 x 125g ball of mozzarella
    cheese, drained
    (liquid reserved)
    and finely chopped
3 tbsp double cream
1 egg
salt and freshly ground
    black pepper

You will need
12cm loose-bottomed
    tart tins x 4
baking beans or rice

1. Make the pastry. Place the flour, salt and sugar in a food processor. Add the butter and blitz until the mixture resembles breadcrumbs. Add 3 tablespoons of the ice-cold water and blitz again until the pastry begins to clump (add the remaining tablespoon of water a little at a time, if necessary). Turn out the dough onto your work surface and bring it together into a ball. Cut it into four equal pieces.

2. Roll out each piece of dough on a lightly floured work surface into a circle about 16cm in diameter and large enough to line the base and side of the tart tin. Lift one of the pastry circles into the first tin, press it into the base and side and trim off any excess. Repeat to line all four tart tins, then chill the pastry cases for 20 minutes.

3. Heat the oven to 180°C/160°C fan/Gas 4. Line each pastry case with baking paper and fill it with baking beans or rice. Place the pastry cases on a baking sheet and bake them for 10 minutes, until the edges turn pale golden. Remove the paper and beans or rice and bake for a further 5 minutes, until the bases are pale golden, too.

4. Meanwhile, make the filling. Fry the bacon lardons in a dry frying pan over a medium heat for about 5 minutes, until cooked and slightly golden. Add the olive oil, garlic and rosemary to the pan and fry for 1 minute, then add the Brussels sprouts and stir-fry for 2–3 minutes, until slightly softened. Remove the pan from the heat and crumble in the chestnuts. Divide the mixture equally between the pastry cases and scatter the mozzarella over.

5. Mix the reserved mozzarella liquid with the cream and egg, season with salt and pepper, and pour the mixture over the filling in the pastry cases. Bake the tarts for 15–20 minutes, until the custard sets. Leave the tarts to cool in the tins, then gently remove them and serve at room temperature.

PERSIAN LOVE CAKE

This Persian love cake (so called for the story of the Persian woman who baked a cake with the flavours of love to woo her prince) makes the most of winter stores of nuts, seeds and dried produce.

For the sponge
3 tbsp whole milk
pinch of saffron
150g unsalted
    butter, softened
175g caster sugar
3 eggs, lightly beaten
juice and finely
    grated zest of
    ½ unwaxed lemon
2–3 tsp rosewater
100g ground almonds
50g ground pistachios
125g plain flour
1 tsp baking powder
½ tsp ground cardamom
pinch of salt

For the syrup
juice of ½ lemon
juice of ¼ orange
1 tsp rosewater
4 tbsp caster sugar

To decorate
150g icing sugar, sifted
juice of ½ lemon
juice of ¼ orange
few drops of rosewater
1 tbsp edible dried
    rose petals or fresh,
    if available
25g nibbed pistachios

You will need
20cm springform
    cake tin, greased,
    then base-lined with
    greased baking paper
wooden skewer
    or cocktail stick

1. Make the sponge. Lightly warm the milk with the saffron in a small pan over a low heat, then remove the pan from the heat and set the milk aside for 15 minutes to infuse.

2. Meanwhile, heat the oven to 170°C/150°C fan/Gas 3.

3. Beat the butter and sugar in a stand mixer fitted with the beater, on medium speed for about 3–5 minutes, until pale and creamy, scraping down the inside of the bowl from time to time. Gradually add the eggs, beating well between each addition.

4. Add the lemon juice and zest, the rosewater and the ground almonds and pistachios. Sift the flour, baking powder, cardamom and salt into the bowl, add the saffron-infused milk and mix again until smooth.

5. Spoon the mixture into the prepared tin and spread it level. Bake the cake on the middle shelf for about 45 minutes, until golden brown, risen and a skewer inserted into the centre comes out clean. Leave the cake to cool slightly in the tin while you prepare the syrup.

6. In a small bowl, combine the lemon and orange juices, the rosewater and the sugar, then stir to dissolve the sugar. Using a wooden skewer or cocktail stick, make holes over the top of the cake, then carefully spoon over the syrup. Leave the cake in the tin for another 15 minutes, then carefully remove it and leave it to cool completely, right-side up, on a wire rack.

7. Once the cake is cold, prepare the decoration. In a small bowl, beat the icing sugar with the lemon and orange juices and a few drops of rosewater to make a smooth, thick, but pourable icing. Carefully spoon this over the cake, allowing it to run down the side. Leave the icing for 3–5 minutes to set slightly, then scatter the cake with rose petals and nibbed pistachios. Leave the icing to set completely before serving.

DATE & WALNUT M'HANNCHA

A m'hanncha is a coil of crisp filo pastry, filled in this case with a mixture of dates and pears that are caramelised to become almost toffee-like. The date palm produces fruit for several harvests that begin in autumn and run into winter. The tree is prolific – a single bunch of dates can comprise more than a thousand fruit.

For the filling
6 ripe pears, peeled, cored and diced
40g unsalted butter
2 tbsp caster sugar
½ tsp ground cinnamon
juice of ½ lemon
125g soft, pitted dates, finely chopped
100g walnut pieces, toasted and chopped small

For the m'hanncha
170–200g filo pastry (5 sheets each of about 40 x 32cm)
75g unsalted butter, melted
25g flaked almonds
1–2 tbsp runny honey, warmed
icing sugar, for dusting

You will need
1m-long sheet of baking paper
20cm springform tin, greased, then base-lined with baking paper

1. Make the filling. Tip the pears into a sauté pan, add the butter, sugar, cinnamon and lemon juice. Cover with a disc of baking paper and cook, stirring often, for about 20 minutes, until the pears start to soften. Stir in the dates, replace the paper and cook for 10 minutes, until all the fruit is tender. Mix in the walnut pieces and leave to cool.

2. For the m'hanncha, unroll the filo pastry and, with the long side nearest you, cut the sheets in half horizontally.

3. Lay the 1-metre long sheet of baking paper on the work surface. Lay one sheet of filo horizontally at the right-hand end of the baking paper and brush it with melted butter. Lay a second sheet of filo to the left of the first, overlapping them by 5–7cm. Brush with butter. Lay a third sheet to the left of the second, overlapping by 5–7cm and brushing with butter to give a 1-metre long x 16cm-wide strip. Repeat, stacking the sheets each time to create three layers of buttered filo and using 9 of the sheets altogether (set aside the last sheet).

4. Spoon the cold pear mixture in a long sausage along the bottom edge of the pastry, 1cm in from the edge and leaving a 2cm gap at each end. Using the baking paper to support the pastry, roll the pastry up and over the filling into a long snake shape, with the filling completely encased in filo and the join on the underside.

5. Heat the oven to 180°C/160°C fan/Gas 4. Fold one end of the filo underneath to seal in the filling and wind the pastry snake into a coil using your hands to support the pastry and prevent the filo cracking. Using the paper, slide it into the springform tin and tuck the tail end of the pastry underneath to prevent the filling oozing out. Brush the pastry with melted butter and patch up any cracks with buttered filo 'bandages' from the remaining sheet. Scatter with the flaked almonds.

6. Bake the m'hanncha for 45 minutes, until the pastry is crisp and golden, turning the tin halfway through baking. Remove it from the oven, brush it with honey and cool. Dust with icing sugar to serve.

NEW YORK CHEESECAKE WITH CRANBERRIES

The compôte on top of this creamy, smooth NY cheesecake makes use of wonderful winter cranberries and clementines, giving a seasonal twist to this classic American baked dessert.

150g digestive
   biscuits, crushed
50g unsalted butter,
   melted, plus extra
   for greasing
½ tsp ground mixed
   spice
700g full-fat cream
   cheese
200g caster sugar
4 large eggs
juice and finely
   grated zest of
   ½ unwaxed lemon
2 tsp vanilla paste
150g soured cream
1 tbsp plain flour, sifted

For the cranberry topping
300g cranberries
100g caster sugar
juice and finely grated
   zest of 1 unwaxed
   clementine
2 tsp cornflour

You will need
20cm springform tin,
   greased, then base-lined
   with baking paper

1. Heat the oven to 170°C/150°C fan/Gas 3.

2. Tip the crushed digestives into a bowl and mix in the melted butter and mixed spice. Tip the mixture into the lined tin and, using the base of a glass, press into a smooth, even, firm layer. Bake the base on the middle shelf for 5 minutes, until starting to crisp, then leave it to cool while you prepare the cheesecake layer.

3. In a large mixing bowl, whisk the cream cheese until smooth. Add the sugar and mix again. Add the eggs, one at a time, mixing well between each addition. Scrape down the inside of the bowl with a rubber spatula, then add the lemon juice and zest, the vanilla and the soured cream. Mix again. Add the flour and whisk to combine. Tap the bowl on the work surface to expel any large air bubbles.

4. Pour the mixture into the tin. Place the tin on a baking sheet and bake the cheesecake on the middle shelf for about 45 minutes, until just set. The top of the cheesecake should look firm and dry but the middle will have a gentle wobble. Turn off the oven and leave the cheesecake to cool in the oven for 5–10 minutes, to prevent cracking.

5. Remove the cheesecake from the oven and leave it to cool completely. Run a palette knife around the edge to loosen it from the side of the tin, then cover it and chill it overnight before serving.

6. Meanwhile, make the topping. Tip the cranberries into a pan, add the sugar and the clementine juice and zest and cook over a low heat for about 5 minutes, stirring from time to time, until the sugar dissolves and the cranberries soften but retain their shape. In a small bowl, whisk the cornflour with 50ml of water. Add this to the cranberry mixture, stir and continue to cook for 30 seconds, until glossy and thick. Leave to cool, then cover and chill until ready to use.

7. Carefully remove the chilled cheesecake from the tin, place it on a serving plate and finish it off with the cranberry topping.

PANETTONE

This traditional Italian yeasted cake, now synonymous with Christmas, is flavoured with vanilla and citrus zests and packed full of rum-soaked dried fruit. You'll need a high-sided cake tin and a paper collar to accommodate the height of the finished bake, or a traditional panettone paper case (1kg size).

500g strong white
    bread flour
150g caster sugar
7g fast-action dried yeast
1 tsp salt
¼ tsp grated nutmeg
150ml whole milk
3 eggs, lightly beaten
2 tsp vanilla paste
finely grated zest of
    ¼ unwaxed lemon
finely grated zest of
    ¼ small orange
175g unsalted butter,
    softened
3 egg yolks
40g dried cranberries
40g sultanas
40g raisins
2 tbsp dark rum
1 tbsp orange juice
50g candied peel,
    chopped
40g nibbed pistachios

To decorate
1 egg, beaten
10g unsalted butter
1–2 tbsp pearl sugar

You will need
dough scraper
18cm round cake tin
    (12cm deep), greased,
    then double-lined
    (base and sides) with
    baking paper to give
    a total height of 13cm
kitchen string

1. Combine 400g of the flour, 1 teaspoon of the caster sugar, the yeast, salt and nutmeg in the bowl of a stand mixer fitted with the dough hook.

2. Warm the milk until lukewarm and add it to the bowl with the beaten whole eggs, the vanilla and the lemon and orange zests. Mix on low speed until combined. Scrape down the inside of the bowl and continue mixing for 1 minute, until the dough is smooth. Cover the dough and leave it at room temperature for 1 hour.

3. In another bowl, using a wooden spoon, beat together the butter, remaining caster sugar, remaining flour and the egg yolks for 1 minute, until smooth and thoroughly combined.

4. Add the butter mixture to the dough and mix everything on low speed to combine. Increase the mixer speed to medium and continue kneading for about 10 minutes, scraping down the inside of the bowl from time to time, until the dough cleanly leaves the side of the bowl and is silky smooth and very elastic. Cover and leave the dough at cool room temperature for about 5½ hours, until it is very puffy and has doubled in size.

5. Meanwhile, combine the cranberries, sultanas and raisins in a small pan. Add the rum and orange juice and warm over a low heat for 30 seconds. Stir to coat the fruit, then remove the pan from the heat and leave the mixture to infuse, cool and plump up until the dough is risen. Then, when the dough is ready, tip the soaked fruit, candied peel and pistachios into the risen dough and mix well.

6. Tip out the dough onto a lightly floured work surface and, using lightly floured or damp hands and a dough scraper, shape the dough into a tight ball. Place the ball into the lined tin and cover.

Continues overleaf

7. Leave the dough to prove at cool room temperature for another 5½ hours, until puffy, doubled in size and it reaches the top of the tin.

8. Heat the oven to 190°C/170°C fan/Gas 5.

9. Wrap the outside of the tin in a double thickness of baking paper and secure it with string – this will prevent the side of the panettone browning too much during baking. Brush the top of the loaf with beaten egg to glaze, and cut a cross in the middle using a sharp knife or scissors.

10. Divide the 10g of butter into four equal portions and put one piece into each cut of the cross. Scatter the panettone with the pearl sugar and bake it in the bottom third of the oven for 10 minutes.

11. Reduce the heat to 170°C/150°C fan/Gas 3 and continue baking for 40 minutes. Cover the top loosely with foil and bake for a further 30–35 minutes, until the panettone is well risen, deep golden brown and a skewer inserted into the centre comes out clean.

12. Leave the panettone to cool in the tin for 10 minutes, then remove it from the tin and leave it to cool completely on a wire rack.

BEEF & POTATO PIES

These pies are proper winter-weekend baking – the well-deserved meal after a blustery walk. Make the beef filling the day before you want to eat it, as the flavours will improve overnight. Or, completely assemble the pies in advance, so that they are ready to pop in the oven as soon as you arrive home in need of sustenance.

For the filling
2 tbsp plain flour
2–3 tbsp olive oil
1kg beef shin, trimmed
  and cut into 4cm chunks
2 onions, sliced
2 carrots, diced
4 garlic cloves, crushed
150g smoked bacon lardons
  or diced pancetta
1 tbsp tomato purée
300ml amber ale
350ml beef stock
dash of Worcestershire
  sauce
2 bay leaves
1 thyme sprig
2 Maris Piper potatoes,
  peeled and cubed
25g unsalted butter
200g chestnut
  mushrooms, sliced
salt and freshly ground
  black pepper

For the hot water pastry
300g plain flour
300g strong white
  bread flour
150g unsalted
  butter, cubed
100g lard, cubed
1 egg, lightly beaten

You will need
lidded casserole dish
10cm-diameter round pie
  dishes (4cm deep) x 6

1. Heat the oven to 150°C/130°C fan/Gas 2.

2. Tip the flour into a large bowl and season well with salt and pepper.

3. Heat 1 tablespoon of the olive oil in a large frying pan over a high heat. Toss half the beef in the seasoned flour to coat, shake off any excess, then add it to the hot pan, turning it for 1–2 minutes, until browned all over. Transfer the browned meat to the casserole dish and repeat with the remaining beef, adding another 1 tablespoon of the olive oil to the pan if needed.

4. Add the remaining 1 tablespoon of olive oil to the frying pan along with the onions. Reduce the heat to medium and fry for about 8 minutes, stirring frequently, until softened.

5. Add the carrots, 3 garlic cloves and the bacon or pancetta and continue to cook, stirring frequently for 5 minutes, until the onions and bacon are just starting to caramelise at the edges. Add the tomato purée, stir well and cook for another 1 minute.

6. Pour the ale and stock into the pan, stir it well and bring it to the boil. Pour the contents of the frying pan into the casserole with the beef, add the Worcestershire sauce, season well with salt and pepper and tuck in the bay leaves and thyme sprig. Cover the casserole with a lid, transfer it to the oven and braise the filling for 2 hours, then stir it and return it to the oven for a further 2 hours, until the meat is really tender, starts to fall apart and the sauce thickens and reduces.

7. Meanwhile, cook the potatoes in boiling salted water until just tender when tested with the point of a knife. Drain and leave to cool.

8. Add the potatoes to the beef and gently mix them together. Discard the bay and thyme and leave the filling to cool. Once cold, cover it and chill it until you are ready to assemble the pies.

Continues overleaf

9. To assemble, first melt the butter in a large frying pan over a medium heat. Add the mushrooms and the remaining garlic and cook, stirring frequently, for 3–4 minutes, until tender and browned. Season well, remove from the heat and leave to cool.

10. Make the hot water pastry. Combine both flours in a large mixing bowl, season well with salt and pepper and make a well in the centre.

11. Pour 150ml of water into a small pan, add the butter and lard and place it over a low heat to melt the fats. Bring the liquid to the boil and pour it into the mixing bowl. Using a wooden spoon or rubber spatula, mix the flour into the liquid, add all but 2 teaspoons of the beaten egg and continue to mix until the pastry is nearly smooth.

12. Turn out the pastry onto your work surface and gently knead it with your hands, taking care not to overwork it, until smooth.

13. Cut the pastry into six equal portions. Take one portion and cut off one third – this will be the pie lid. Lightly flour the work surface and roll out the larger piece to a circle 2cm larger all round than the top of the pie dish and 3mm thick. Use this to neatly line the pie dish, pressing the pastry into the corners and up the side with your fingers. Spoon one sixth of the chilled beef filling into the pie and top with the garlicky mushrooms.

14. Roll out the pastry for the lid until about 3mm thick. Brush the edges with water and place the lid on top of the pie, pressing the edges together to seal. Using a sharp knife, trim off any excess pastry (set the trimmings aside), then crimp the edges between your fingers.

15. Repeat with the remaining pastry and pie filling to make six pies in total.

16. Gather the pastry trimmings together into a ball, re-roll the pastry and cut out 18 little leaf shapes. Brush the leaves with water and stick three of them to the top of each pie. Make a small hole in the centre of each pastry lid to let out any steam and brush the pies with the remaining beaten egg. Chill the pies for 30 minutes while you heat the oven to 180°C/160°C fan/Gas 4.

17. Place the pies on baking trays and bake them for 40 minutes, until the filling is piping hot and the pastry is crisp and golden.

ST CLEMENT'S SQUARES

Making the most of an abundance of citrus at this time of year, St Clement's squares are a traybake of sharp curd on top of a shortbread base. Decorated simply with a dusting of icing sugar, think of them as zesty pick-me-ups on a sluggish, chilly day.

For the shortbread base
175g plain flour, sifted
150g unsalted butter,
    cubed and chilled
50g icing sugar, sifted,
    plus extra for dusting
pinch of salt

For the topping
juice and finely
    grated zest of
    2 unwaxed lemons
juice and finely grated
    zest of 2 unwaxed limes
juice and finely grated
    zest of 1 large
    unwaxed orange
5 eggs
375g caster sugar
2 tbsp plain flour

You will need
20cm square tin,
    greased, then lined
    (base and sides)
    with baking paper

1. Heat the oven to 170°C/150°C fan/Gas 3.

2. Make the shortbread base. Tip the flour, butter, icing sugar and salt into a food processor and blitz until the butter is rubbed into the flour. Continue blitzing for about 30 seconds, until the mixture starts to clump together. Tip the mixture into the lined tin and, with your hands, press it evenly over the base, then use the back of a spoon to create a compact, level layer. Bake the base on the middle shelf for about 25 minutes, until golden and firm.

3. Meanwhile, prepare the topping. Put the lemon, lime and orange zests into a large mixing bowl. Add the eggs and sugar and whisk until combined, but not do not over-mix as you don't want to incorporate air into the eggs.

4. Combine the lemon, lime and orange juices and measure out 250ml into a jug (drink any leftover, if there is any). Then, slowly pour the juices into the egg mixture, stirring continuously. Add the flour and mix to combine. Leave the mixture to one side for 5 minutes to allow any bubbles to burst.

5. When the shortbread is ready, remove it from the oven and reduce the oven temperature to 150°C/130°C fan/Gas 2.

6. Carefully pour the citrus mixture over the shortbread base and return the tin to the oven. Bake for 25 minutes, until the top sets.

7. Remove the St Clement's traybake from the oven and cool it to room temperature, then cover it and chill it for at least 2 hours to firm up. Cut the traybake into 5cm squares (to give 16 squares altogether) and dust them with icing sugar to serve.

PRUE'S MALT LOAF

Prunes, treacle and the aromatic spiciness of ginger – this malt loaf exudes winter baking in spades. The key to a great malt loaf is in the fruit-soaking – either in the microwave if you're short of time, or overnight at room temperature. For maximum squidgy texture, wrap the finished loaf and leave it for a few days before eating.

1 strong black tea bag
150ml just-boiled water
200g flame raisins
100g soft, pitted prunes,
   finely chopped
½ tsp bicarbonate
   of soda
150g malt extract,
   plus extra for glazing
40g black treacle
100g dark muscovado
   sugar
250g plain flour
1 tsp baking powder
2 eggs, lightly beaten
unsalted butter,
   to serve (optional)

You will need
900g loaf tin, oiled, then
   lined (base and sides)
   with baking paper

1. Heat the oven to 170°C/150°C fan/Gas 3.

2. Make the malt loaf. Place the tea bag in a jug and add the just-boiled water. Leave to brew for 5 minutes, then discard the bag.

3. Tip the raisins and prunes into a microwave-safe bowl, then pour the tea over. Cover with cling film and pierce a few holes in the top. Microwave on full power for 4 minutes. Carefully remove the bowl from the microwave and remove the cling film. (Alternatively, soak the fruit overnight in a covered bowl.) Stir in the bicarbonate of soda, then leave the fruit to stand for 10 minutes.

4. Pour the malt extract into a small pan with the treacle and sugar and cook, stirring continuously, over a low heat for 2–3 minutes, until the sugar dissolves. Remove from the heat and cool for 5 minutes.

5. Sift the flour and baking powder into a mixing bowl and make a well in the centre. Add the warm malt mixture and the tea-soaked fruit and any soaking liquid. Fold everything gently together, then add the beaten eggs and mix well. Pour the mixture into the lined tin and bake it for 1–1¼ hours, until a skewer inserted into the centre comes out clean. Remove the loaf from the oven, brush the top with malt extract, then leave the malt loaf to cool completely in the tin.

6. If you can bear to wait before tucking in, once the malt loaf is cool, wrap it tightly in baking paper and leave it to really develop its flavour and texture for 1–2 days. Then, turn it out and set it the right way up on a serving plate. Serve in slices (spread with butter, if you wish).

SPICED APPLE BRANDY SNAP BASKETS

These cute little mouthfuls are not difficult to make, but you'll need to mould them while they're still hot, so bank on creating just three at a time. They are neatly bitesized, making them a great option for a sweet treat at a seasonal party – with a glass of something fizzy in the other hand.

For the brandy snap baskets
90g unsalted butter
90g demerara sugar
90g runny honey
2 tsp apple juice
2 tsp brandy
90g plain flour, sifted
1 tsp ground cinnamon

For the crème diplomat
125ml whole milk
1 vanilla pod, split
   lengthways and
   seeds scraped out
25g caster sugar
2 egg yolks
2 tsp cornflour
2 tsp vanilla sugar
25g unsalted butter
85ml double cream
25g icing sugar, sifted

For the caramelised apples
65g dark brown soft sugar
50g unsalted butter
pinch of salt
½ tsp vanilla extract
½ tsp ground cinnamon
¼ tsp ground mixed
   spice
10g cornflour
1 tbsp brandy
1 Bramley apple,
   peeled, cored and
   cut into 5mm dice

Continues overleaf

1. Start the brandy snap baskets. Warm the butter, demerara sugar and honey in a medium pan over a very low heat, stirring occasionally, for about 10 minutes, until the sugar dissolves. Set aside.

2. Meanwhile, make the crème diplomat. Pour the milk into a medium saucepan, add the vanilla seeds and caster sugar and simmer over a low heat for 5 minutes, until warmed.

3. Whisk the egg yolks, cornflour and vanilla sugar in a mixing bowl with a balloon whisk until smooth. Gradually whisk in the warm milk, then pour it back into the pan and cook it over a medium heat, stirring continuously for 1–2 minutes, until smooth and thickened. Whisk in the butter until melted and smooth. Pour the crème diplomat into a shallow dish, cover the surface with cling film to prevent a skin forming and leave it to cool for 30 minutes, then transfer it to the fridge to chill until needed.

4. Make the caramelised apples. Place the dark brown soft sugar, butter, salt, vanilla, cinnamon and mixed spice into a medium, heavy-based pan over a low heat and cook, stirring, until the sugar dissolves and the buttery mixture is smooth. In a small bowl, mix the cornflour with the brandy until combined, then add this to the brown sugar mixture and stir over a low heat for 1–2 minutes, until thickened to a syrupy consistency. Remove the pan from the heat and stir in the diced apple until it is coated in the caramel. Leave to cool.

5. Heat the oven to 200°C/180°C fan/Gas 4.

6. Continue making the brandy snaps. When the sugar has dissolved in the pan, take the pan off the heat and stir in the apple juice and brandy. Leave the mixture to cool for 10 minutes, then, using a wooden spoon, beat in the flour and cinnamon until smooth.

Continues overleaf

You will need
2 baking trays, lined
  with baking paper
6cm round cutter
7cm-diameter fluted
  brioche moulds x 6
large piping bag

7. Place a level teaspoon of the brandy snap mixture on one of the lined baking trays, it will form a small circle. Place only three circles on each tray, allowing plenty of space for the mixture to spread, then bake the brandy snaps for 7–8 minutes, until lacy and a dark golden colour.

8. Using the round cutter, immediately cut the brandy snaps into neat circles, removing the excess mixture on the outside of the cutter with a knife. Lifting one at a time with a palette knife, press the brandy snaps into the brioche moulds, then leave them to cool and set – this will only take a minute or so. Once the brandy snap baskets are cool, carefully remove them to a wire rack. Repeat to bake 30 brandy snap baskets in total.

9. To assemble, by hand using a balloon whisk, whisk the double cream and icing sugar together in a mixing bowl until the mixture holds soft peaks. Then, fold in the chilled crème diplomat until combined and smooth.

10. Spoon the mixture into the large piping bag and snip the end to make a 2cm hole. Pipe the mixture into the brandy snap baskets to three quarters fill them, then top each with a small spoonful of the caramelised apples. Serve the filled brandy snap baskets within the hour, before they start to soften.

BAKER'S RECIPE

GEORGE'S KOURABIETHES

Traditional Christmas biscuits in my family are always buttery, crumbly kourabiethes, from Cyprus and Greece. As it goes, though, I make them all year round, because I couldn't possibly wait a whole year to sink my teeth into them.

65g blanched almonds, finely chopped
40g pistachios
250g unsalted butter, softened
200g caster sugar
1 egg, lightly beaten
pinch of salt
1 tsp vanilla paste
2 tbsp rosewater
1 tbsp brandy
525g plain flour
1 tbsp baking powder

To decorate
200ml rosewater
500g icing sugar, sifted

You will need
2 large baking trays, lined with baking paper
food-quality spray bottle

1. Heat the oven to 180°C/160°C fan/Gas 4.

2. Spread the almonds over one of the lined baking trays, sprinkle them with a little water and roast them in the oven for 4–5 minutes, until light golden. Leave the almonds to cool to room temperature, then transfer them to a plate and re-line the baking tray.

3. Blitz the pistachios in a food processor to the texture of fine breadcrumbs.

4. Beat the butter and sugar in a stand mixer fitted with the beater, on medium speed for about 3–5 minutes, until pale and creamy, scraping down the inside of the bowl from time to time. Add the egg and mix until thoroughly combined. Add the pistachios, almonds, salt, vanilla, rosewater and brandy and mix again to combine.

5. Sift the flour and baking powder into the bowl and mix everything together with a wooden spoon. As the mixture stiffens, use your hands to combine the mixture into a dough.

6. Roll the almond mixture into 40 walnut-sized balls and shape each ball into a crescent.

7. Place the biscuits on the lined baking trays, making sure there is enough space between them to spread slightly. Bake for about 20 minutes, until light golden brown. Leave the biscuits to cool completely on the baking trays on wire racks.

8. To decorate, fill a spray bottle with rosewater and place the icing sugar in a bowl. Once the biscuits have cooled, spray both sides of each one with rosewater, then dunk the biscuits in the bowl of icing sugar, making sure each is evenly coated. Repeat until all the biscuits are sprayed with rosewater and coated in icing sugar, ready to serve.

WINTER NO-KNEAD LOAF

The small quantity of yeast in this bread dough calls for a longer fermentation, which removes the need to knead. The result is a really flavourful loaf that is just the thing to enjoy in slices slathered with honey or in hunks dunked into a bowl of restorative and warming soup.

400g strong white
   bread flour
100g wholemeal
   spelt flour
2 tbsp medium oatmeal
2 tsp fine sea salt
1 tsp caster sugar
2g fast-action dried yeast
350ml lukewarm water

You will need
baking sheet, lined
   with baking paper
lidded cast-iron
   casserole, Dutch
   oven or baker's cloche
long, sharp knife,
   razor blade or lame

1. Start to make the loaf the evening of the day before you plan to bake it. In a large mixing bowl, thoroughly combine both flours, and the oatmeal, salt, sugar and yeast.

2. Make a well in the centre of the dry ingredients and add the lukewarm water. Mix well using a wet hand for about 2 minutes, until the dough is smooth – you are not kneading the dough, just mixing it. Shape the dough into a ball, cover it and set it aside in a cool part of the kitchen for 12 hours, until at least doubled in size and the top is covered in air bubbles.

3. Lightly flour the work surface and lightly knead the dough for 20 seconds, then shape it into a tight ball. Place the ball of dough on the lined baking sheet and dust it with flour. Loosely cover the dough and leave it to prove at room temperature for a further 1 hour.

4. Heat the oven to 220°C/200°C fan/Gas 7. Place a cast-iron casserole, Dutch oven or baker's cloche in the oven at the same time to heat up (it will need 30 minutes).

5. When the oven is hot and the dough is well risen, dust the dough with flour. Using a long, sharp knife, razor blade or lame, cut three or four slashes in the top of the dough and carefully transfer it to the hot baking pot. Cover the pot with the lid and bake the loaf for 40 minutes, until the bread is well risen, crisp and golden brown.

6. Remove the lid from the pot and continue to bake the loaf for a further 5 minutes to darken the crust. Carefully tip out the loaf and transfer it to a wire rack to cool before slicing.

JUDGE'S RECIPE

PAUL'S BAKLAVA

This baklava recipe uses a much quicker laminating technique for making flaky filo than the traditional roll and stretch method. There's also no pastry wastage, as all the trimmings are sprinkled back into the layers as you go. The filling is a classic – aromatic rosewater and nuts.

For the filo pastry
500g plain flour
2 tsp baking powder
¼ tsp salt
2 eggs
170g full-fat Greek yogurt
90ml vegetable oil
50g unsalted butter,
    melted, plus extra
    for greasing
1 tbsp white wine vinegar
200g cornflour,
    for sprinkling

For the syrup
135g caster sugar
300g runny honey
1 large unwaxed
    lemon, sliced
1 tbsp rosewater

For the filling
350g walnuts,
    finely chopped
350g pistachios,
    finely chopped
50g caster sugar
1 tbsp ground cinnamon
1 tbsp ground cardamom

To assemble
400g salted
    butter, melted

Continues overleaf

1. Make the filo pastry. Sift the flour, baking powder and salt into a mixing bowl and make a well in the centre. In a separate bowl, whisk the eggs, yogurt, vegetable oil, melted butter and vinegar together until smooth. Pour the egg mixture into the flour and bring everything together to form a dough.

2. Tip out the dough onto a lightly floured work surface and knead it for 10 minutes, until smooth, then divide it into six pieces. Shape each piece into a ball, then place the balls on a plate or baking tray, cover them with a clean tea towel and leave them to rest for 15 minutes.

3. Meanwhile, make the syrup. Place the sugar, honey and lemon slices in a pan with 200ml of water. Bring to the boil over a medium heat, stirring until the sugar dissolves. Reduce the heat and simmer for 5 minutes to infuse. Remove the syrup from the heat, pour into a heatproof jug, stir in the rosewater and leave to cool.

4. Lightly dust the work surface with cornflour. Roll out one of the balls of dough to a circle about 30cm diameter. Dust the top with cornflour, then fold the right-hand edge to the centre and the left-hand edge to the centre, so that they meet.

5. Dust again with cornflour, then fold the top down to the centre and the bottom up to the centre, to give a rough square.

6. Dust again with cornflour. Take each corner and fold them inwards so they meet in the middle to make a smaller square.

7. Dust again with cornflour, then repeat Step 6, folding the corners into the middle again to give an even smaller square. Turn the dough over (joins underneath), cover it and leave it to rest for 15 minutes.

Continues overleaf

To decorate
75g pistachios,
    finely ground
2 tsp edible dried
    rose petals

You will need
30cm sandwich tin,
    greased, then
    base-lined with
    baking paper

8. Repeat with the remaining five balls of dough until you have six small squares.

9. Make the filling. Mix the walnuts, pistachios, sugar, cinnamon and cardamom together in a bowl.

10. To assemble, roll out one of the squares of dough to a rough 30cm-diameter circle. Using the sandwich tin as a guide, cut a neat 30cm circle, and place this in the base of the tin. Lay any trimmings evenly on top.

11. Repeat with a second square of dough, placing the pastry circle on top of the first circle and again laying any trimmings on top. Repeat once more with another square of dough and trimmings. Spoon the nut mixture evenly on top of the three layers.

12. Repeat this layering process with the remaining squares of dough to make three more layers of filo, placing the trimmings from the top layer of filo on top of the fifth layer, so the top of the baklava is flat without any trimmings.

13. Cut the baklava into a star design (as in the photograph), slicing all the way through the layers to the base. Pour the melted butter over the top, then leave the baklava to stand for 10 minutes while the pastry absorbs the butter. Meanwhile, heat the oven to 170°C/150°C fan/Gas 3.

14. Bake the baklava for 1 hour, until the top is crisp and golden. Remove the baklava from the oven. Strain the cooled syrup through a sieve, then pour the syrup over the warm baklava. Leave it to soak in for 15 minutes before removing the baklava pieces from the tin.

15. To decorate, sprinkle the ground pistachios over the baklava (in a pattern, if you wish), and finish with the rose petals.

PRAWN & PORK POTSTICKERS

Linked to the cycle of the moon, Chinese New Year occurs within the months of January and February. These potsticker dumplings (or jiaozi to give them their Chinese name) are a delicious way to mark the occasion and a good introduction to making dumpling dough. Serve them with a ginger-infused sauce for dipping.

For the filling
15g dried shiitake
    mushrooms
just-boiled water
1 large garlic clove,
    roughly chopped
4cm piece of fresh
    ginger, peeled and
    roughly chopped
1 red chilli, deseeded
    and roughly chopped
150g raw peeled king
    prawns, de-veined,
    roughly chopped
175g minced pork
small handful of
    coriander, leaves
    picked and finely
    chopped
2 tbsp sliced water
    chestnuts, drained
    and finely chopped
3–4 spring onions,
    trimmed and
    thinly sliced
1 tbsp soy sauce
2 tsp cornflour
dash of sesame oil
pinch of ground
    white pepper

Continues overleaf

1. Make the filling. Place the dried mushrooms in a small, heatproof bowl, pour over enough just-boiled water to cover and leave them for 10 minutes, until rehydrated. Drain, discarding the soaking water, then pat the mushrooms dry and finely chop them.

2. Meanwhile, tip the garlic, ginger and chilli into a food processor and pulse them until finely chopped. Add the prawns and pulse briefly again. Add the minced pork and pulse again to combine, then scoop the mixture into a bowl.

3. Add the coriander, water chestnuts, spring onions and chopped rehydrated mushrooms to the pork and prawn mixture. Stir in the soy sauce, cornflour and sesame oil. Season with pepper and mix until thoroughly combined. Cover and chill while you prepare the dumpling wrappers.

4. Combine the flour and salt in a bowl. Gradually add the just-boiled water, mixing continuously until the dough is smooth and no longer sticky. Add a little more flour if the dough is too wet, or water if it's too dry. Knead the dough in your hands for 2–3 minutes, until smooth, then return it to the bowl, cover it and leave it to rest for 15 minutes. Knead again for 3 minutes, then cover and leave for 1 hour.

5. Meanwhile, make the dipping sauce. Place the ginger in a bowl with the chilli oil, soy sauce and both vinegars, and mix to combine. Cover and set aside.

6. Turn out the dough onto a lightly floured work surface and knead it for 30 seconds. Divide the dough in half and, using your hands, roll each half into a sausage, about 2cm thick. Cut each sausage into 12 equal pieces.

Continues overleaf

For the dumpling wrappers
200g plain flour,
    plus extra if needed
good pinch of salt
100ml just-boiled water
1–2 tbsp sunflower oil

For the dipping sauce
4cm piece of fresh
    ginger, peeled and
    cut into fine strips
2 tsp chilli oil
2 tbsp soy sauce
2 tbsp black rice vinegar
2 tsp rice vinegar

7. Keep the work surface dusted with flour to prevent the dough sticking, then roll out each piece into a neat disc, about 1–2mm thick and 12cm in diameter. Keep the remaining dough covered with a clean tea towel until needed. Flip and turn the dough as you roll it to prevent it sticking and dust it with more flour as needed. Place each dough disc on a lightly floured tray (or trays), covering it with a clean tea towel while you roll out the remaining dough pieces, one by one.

8. Working in batches, lay six dumpling wrappers on the work surface and place a neat dessertspoonful of filling in the middle of each. Brush the edges of the wrappers with cold water, fold them over and pinch the dough together to seal the filling into a half-moon-shaped dumpling. Place the filled dumplings on a lightly floured tray, cover and fill the remaining wrappers in the same way.

9. Heat 1 tablespoon of sunflower oil in a large frying pan. Add half the dumplings and cook them over a medium heat for about 2 minutes, until the underside of each is golden brown. Add 3–4 tablespoons of water to the pan, immediately cover it with a lid and continue to cook for a further 2 minutes, or until the dumplings are cooked through.

10. Remove the cooked dumplings from the pan to a plate and keep them warm while you heat the remaining sunflower oil in the frying pan and cook the remaining dumplings in the same way. Serve the dumplings warm with the dipping sauce.

MINCEMEAT & MARZIPAN COURONNE

Does anything say winter baking more than mincemeat and marzipan?
Here, the two of them escape the festive pies and cake and are reinvented together
in a showstopping couronne that sits somewhere between a babka and a stollen.

450g strong white
    bread flour
75g light brown
    soft sugar or light
    muscovado sugar
10g fast-action
    dried yeast
1 tsp ground mixed spice
½ tsp salt
125ml whole milk
125g unsalted
    butter, softened
2 large eggs, beaten,
    plus extra for glazing
1 tsp vanilla paste

For the filling
50g marzipan, crumbled
450g mincemeat
50g flaked almonds,
    toasted
40g nibbed pistachios,
    roughly chopped
1 tbsp pearl sugar

To decorate
100g icing sugar, sifted
juice of ½ lemon
    or ¼ orange
50g glacé cherries,
    quartered
50g nibbed pistachios
1 tbsp edible silver balls

You will need
small piping bag

1. Tip the flour into the bowl of a stand mixer fitted with the dough hook. Add the sugar, yeast, mixed spice and salt and mix to combine. Make a well in the centre.

2. Warm the milk until lukewarm, add the butter and pour the mixture into the well along with the eggs and vanilla. Mix on low–medium speed until combined, scraping down the inside of the bowl from time to time. Continue to mix for about 5 minutes, until the dough is smooth and elastic and starts to cleanly leave the side of the bowl. Shape the dough into a ball, place it in an oiled bowl, cover it and leave it at room temperature for 1–1½ hours, until doubled in size.

3. Meanwhile, make the filling. Tip the crumbled marzipan into a bowl, add the mincemeat, almonds and pistachios and mix well.

4. Turn out the dough onto a lightly floured work surface and roll it into a neat 50 x 30cm rectangle with one of the long sides nearest you. Spread the mincemeat mixture evenly over the top. Starting at a long side, roll the dough into a Swiss roll encasing the filling.

5. Transfer the roll to a sheet of baking paper and slice it in half lengthways. With the cut sides facing upwards, twist the halves around each other, shaping them into a ring at the same time. Seal the ends together. Slide the ring (on the baking paper) onto a baking sheet, cover it and leave it at room temperature for 1 hour, until the dough is puffy. Meanwhile, heat the oven to 180°C/160°C fan/Gas 4.

6. Brush the couronne with beaten egg to glaze and scatter it with pearl sugar. Bake it for 25 minutes, then reduce the oven temperature to 170°C/150°C fan/Gas 3 and bake it for a further 10–15 minutes, until golden brown (cover it loosely with foil to prevent it burning, if needed). Cool it on the baking tray, then transfer it to a serving plate.

7. To decorate, mix the icing sugar with the juice to a drizzly icing. Spoon this into the small piping bag, snip the end and pipe zig-zag lines across the wreath. Scatter with cherries, pistachios and silver balls and leave the icing to set for 30 minutes before serving.

MAGGIE'S ORANGE & LEMON CAKE

This is my great nieces and nephews' favourite birthday cake, so much so that they are incredulous that every year I still ask them what they'd like – I should know it will be this one! They call it 'the-lemon-curd-in-the-middle cake'.

For the sugar-paste flowers
100g yellow sugar paste
100g orange sugar paste

For the lemon sponge
75g unsalted
  butter, softened
125g caster sugar
2 eggs, lightly beaten
1 tbsp homemade/good-
  quality lemon curd
finely grated zest of
  ½ unwaxed lemon
1 tsp lemon essence
150g self-raising flour
1 tsp baking powder
2½ tbsp whole milk

For the orange sponges
150g unsalted
  butter, softened
250g caster sugar
4 eggs, lightly beaten
2 tbsp homemade/
  good-quality
  lemon curd
finely grated zest of
  1 unwaxed orange
2 tsp orange essence
300g self-raising flour
2 tsp baking powder
5 tbsp whole milk
⅛ tsp orange food-
  colouring paste

Continues overleaf

1. Make the sugar-paste flowers. Roll the yellow sugar paste out between two sheets of baking paper, until the paste is about 3mm thick. Using the flower cutters, stamp out flower shapes, then place the shapes on a fresh sheet of baking paper to dry. Repeat with the orange sugar paste. Stamp out rounds for the centres, too. Leave all the flowers and rounds to dry for at least 4 hours, ideally overnight.

2. Heat the oven to 170°C/150°C fan/Gas 3.

3. Make the lemon sponge. Beat the butter and caster sugar in a stand mixer fitted with the beater, on medium speed for about 3–5 minutes, until pale and creamy. Add the eggs, a little at a time, mixing well between each addition and scraping down the inside of the bowl from time to time.

4. Add the lemon curd, lemon zest and lemon essence and mix again to combine. Sift the flour and baking powder into the bowl, add the milk and mix again until smooth and combined. Spoon the mixture into one of the lined cake tins and spread it level. Bake it on the middle shelf for about 25 minutes, until well risen, golden and a skewer inserted into the centre comes out clean.

5. Leave the sponge in the tin for 2–3 minutes, then turn it out onto a wire rack to cool completely while you make the orange sponges. Grease and line the cake tin again as you will need two tins this time.

6. Prepare the orange sponges using the same method above, but adding orange zest instead of lemon, and orange essence and orange food colouring when you add the milk. Divide the mixture equally between the tins and spread it level. Bake the sponges for about 25 minutes, until well risen, golden and a skewer inserted into the centre of each comes out clean.

Continues overleaf

For the meringues
2 egg whites
pinch of salt
125g caster sugar
⅛ tsp yellow food-
    colouring paste
⅛ tsp orange food-
    colouring paste

For the buttercream
300g unsalted
    butter, softened
600g icing sugar, sifted
3 tsp vanilla paste
4 tbsp homemade or
    good-quality, shop-
    bought lemon curd,
    plus 4 tbsp for filling
4 tbsp whole milk

You will need
assorted flower cutters
20cm round cake tins x 2,
    greased, then base-lined
    with baking paper
medium piping bag
    fitted with a medium
    open star nozzle
cake-decorating
    paint brush
2 large baking sheets,
    lined with baking paper
medium piping bag
    fitted with a medium
    closed star nozzle
medium piping bag
    fitted with a medium
    plain nozzle
ridged decorating comb

7. Leave the sponges in the tins for 2–3 minutes, then turn them out onto another wire rack to cool completely.

8. Meanwhile, make the meringues. Reduce the oven to 120°C/100°C fan/Gas ½. Whisk the egg whites and salt in a stand mixer fitted with the whisk, on medium speed until the egg whites almost hold firm peaks. Add the sugar, 1 tablespoon at time, and whisk until the meringue is bright white, silky smooth and very firm.

9. Take the piping bag fitted with a medium open star nozzle and, using the paint brush, paint three stripes of yellow food colouring equally spaced around the inside of the piping bag, starting from the open end of the nozzle to halfway up the bag. Spoon half of the meringue mixture into the bag and twist the end to seal. Pipe small, stripy meringue kisses, about 2–4cm in diameter on a lined baking sheet.

10. When you've used up the stripy yellow meringue, repeat with the second piping bag fitted with the medium closed star nozzle, orange food colouring and the remaining meringue mixture. Bake the meringues for 1 hour, until crisp and dry. Turn off the oven and leave the meringues inside to cool completely (about 1 hour).

11. Meanwhile, make the buttercream. Beat the butter in a stand mixer fitted with the beater, on low speed for about 3–5 minutes, until pale and creamy. Add half the icing sugar and mix to combine. Add the remaining icing sugar, along with the vanilla, lemon curd and milk and beat again for about 2 minutes, until smooth, soft and pale.

12. To assemble, place one orange sponge on a serving plate or board and spread over about 3 tablespoons of buttercream in an even layer. Top with the lemon sponge. Spoon 6 tablespoons of buttercream into the piping bag fitted with a medium plain nozzle and pipe a ring of buttercream around the edge of the cake. Fill the middle with the 4 tablespoons of lemon curd and top with the second orange sponge.

13. Using a palette knife, cover the cake in a smooth, very thin layer of buttercream to crumb coat and chill it for 30 minutes, until firm. Spread the remaining buttercream over the top and side of the cake. For the semi-naked look, run a ridged decorating comb around the side of the cake with a firm pressure so that parts of the cake appear through the buttercream. Arrange the meringue kisses and sugar-paste flowers on top of the cake to serve.

CONVERSION TABLES

WEIGHT

METRIC	IMPERIAL	METRIC	IMPERIAL	METRIC	IMPERIAL	METRIC	IMPERIAL
25g	1oz	200g	7oz	425g	15oz	800g	1lb 12oz
50g	2oz	225g	8oz	450g	1lb	850g	1lb 14oz
75g	2½oz	250g	9oz	500g	1lb 2oz	900g	2lb
85g	3oz	280g	10oz	550g	1lb 4oz	950g	2lb 2oz
100g	4oz	300g	11oz	600g	1lb 5oz	1kg	2lb 4oz
125g	4½oz	350g	12oz	650g	1lb 7oz		
140g	5oz	375g	13oz	700g	1lb 9oz		
175g	6oz	400g	14oz	750g	1lb 10oz		

VOLUME

METRIC	IMPERIAL	METRIC	IMPERIAL	METRIC	IMPERIAL	METRIC	IMPERIAL
30ml	1fl oz	150ml	¼ pint	300ml	½ pint	500ml	18fl oz
50ml	2fl oz	175ml	6fl oz	350ml	12fl oz	600ml	1 pint
75ml	2½fl oz	200ml	7fl oz	400ml	14fl oz	700ml	1¼ pints
100ml	3½fl oz	225ml	8fl oz	425ml	⅔ pint	850ml	1½ pints
125ml	4fl oz	250ml	9fl oz	450ml	16fl oz	1 litre	1¾ pints

US CUP

INGREDIENTS	1 CUP	3/4 CUP	2/3 CUP	1/2 CUP	1/3 CUP	1/4 CUP	2 TBSP
Brown sugar	180g	135g	120g	90g	60g	45g	23g
Butter	240g	180g	160g	120g	80g	60g	30g
Cornflour (cornstarch)	120g	90g	80g	60g	40g	30g	15g
Flour	120g	90g	80g	60g	40g	30g	15g
Icing sugar (powdered/confectioners')	100g	75g	70g	50g	35g	25g	13g
Nuts (chopped)	150g	110g	100g	75g	50g	40g	20g
Nuts (ground)	120g	90g	80g	60g	40g	30g	15g
Oats	90g	65g	60g	45g	30g	22g	11g
Raspberries	120g	90g	80g	60g	40g	30g	--
Salt	300g	230g	200g	150g	100g	75g	40g
Sugar (caster/superfine)	225g	170g	150g	115g	75g	55g	30g
Sugar (granulated)	200g	150g	130g	100g	65g	50g	25g
Sultanas/raisins	200g	150g	130g	100g	65g	50g	22g
Water/milk	250ml	180ml	150ml	120ml	75ml	60ml	30ml

LINEAR

METRIC	IMPERIAL		METRIC	IMPERIAL		METRIC	IMPERIAL		METRIC	IMPERIAL
2.5cm	1 in		7.5cm	3 in		13cm	5 in		20cm	8 in
3cm	1¼ in		8cm	3¼ in		14cm	5½ in		21cm	8¼ in
4cm	1½ in		9cm	3½ in		15cm	6 in		22cm	8½ in
5cm	2 in		9.5cm	3¾ in		16cm	6¼ in		23cm	9 in
5.5cm	2¼ in		10cm	4 in		17cm	6½ in		24cm	9½ in
6cm	2½ in		11cm	4¼ in		18cm	7 in		25cm	10 in
7cm	2¾ in		12cm	4½ in		19cm	7½ in			

SPOON MEASURES

METRIC	IMPERIAL
5ml	1 tsp
10ml	2 tsp
15ml	1 tbsp
30ml	2 tbsp
45ml	3 tbsp
60ml	4 tbsp
75ml	5 tbsp

COOK'S NOTES

Oven temperatures: Ovens vary – not only from brand to brand, but from the front to the back of the oven, as well as (in a non-fan oven) between the top and bottom shelves. Invest in an oven thermometer if you can. Always preheat, and use dry oven gloves.

Eggs: Eggs are medium and should be at room temperature, unless specified. Some recipes may contain raw or partially cooked eggs. Pregnant women, the elderly, babies and toddlers, and people who are unwell should be aware of these recipes.

Butter: In the recipes, 'softened butter' means to soften to room temperature, unless otherwise specified. You should be able to leave an indentation with your fingertip when you press down.

Herbs, vegetables and fruit: Use fresh herbs and fresh, ripe medium-sized vegetables and fruit unless the recipe specifies otherwise.

Spoon measures: All teaspoons and tablespoons are level unless otherwise stated.

Waxed citrus: When a recipe calls for citrus zest, it's preferable to use unwaxed fruit. However, some citrus, such as grapefruits and blood oranges, are hard to find unwaxed. In this case, place the fruit in a colander, pour over boiling water, then dry the fruit thoroughly to remove the waxy residue before zesting.

Allergies or special diets: We want you to share these recipes with your loved ones and your community as often as possible. Please be aware, though, that some recipes contain allergens. If you are baking for others, do check before you share.

BAKING TIPS & TECHNIQUES

Use these tips and techniques to help you get the best results from your bakes.

―――――

FOLDING IN

This is a way to combine two (or more) ingredients as delicately as possible so you don't knock out all the air. A large metal spoon or a rubber spatula is best for folding.

Cut down through the mixture to the bottom of the bowl, turn the spoon or spatula upwards and draw it up, then flip it over so the mixture flops onto the surface. Give the bowl a quarter turn and repeat to combine.

RUBBING IN

This is a way to combine butter and flour and add air when making pastry and simple cake mixtures. Use only your fingertips and thumbs (which are cooler than your palms).

Pick up a little of the butter and flour mixture, lift your hands and gently rub your fingers and thumbs together to combine the mixture as it falls. Keep doing this until the mixture has a crumb-like consistency.

MELTING CHOCOLATE

Put the chopped chocolate into a heatproof bowl and set this over a pan of steaming hot, simmering, but not boiling water. As the chocolate softens, stir it gently. It is ready to use as soon as it is liquid and smooth, around 30°C (if you have a cooking thermometer). Alternatively, microwave in 10-second bursts, checking and stirring each time.

RIBBON STAGE

Whisking eggs and sugar thoroughly builds up a thick mass of tiny air bubbles that forms the structure of a cake. Use a large bowl – after 4–5 minutes of whisking on high speed, the initial volume of eggs and sugar will increase five-fold. The ribbon stage occurs when you lift the whisk out of the bowl and the mixture on it falls back onto the surface to make a distinct, thick, ribbon-like trail.

BLIND BAKING

This means to bake an unfilled tart so the pastry is cooked before adding the filling. Line the pastry case with the baking paper (cut to size and crumpled up to make it more flexible) and fill with ceramic baking beans, rice or dried beans. Bake as stated in the recipe (or for about 12–15 minutes, until set and firm). Remove the paper and beans, then return the pastry case to the oven and bake for a further 5–10 minutes, until the pastry is thoroughly cooked and starting to colour.

FROSTING FRUIT

This simple technique is a beautiful way to create edible berry and herb decorations – it works for small berries, such as cranberries and redcurrants, and grapes, blackcurrants, blackberries and physallis, as well as herbs such as rosemary sprigs and sage leaves. Simply whisk an egg white in a bowl to loosen it. Use a pastry brush to coat the fruit or herbs in the egg white, then dip them into a bowl of caster sugar (or sprinkle them using a sugar shaker, if you have one). Leave them to dry on a lined baking sheet for 1 hour before using to decorate your bakes.

KNEADING BREAD DOUGH

Kneading a dough develops the gluten in the flour to create a structure that stretches around the bubbles of carbon dioxide, released as the yeast (or other raising agent) activates in the heat of the oven.

To knead by hand, turn out the dough onto a lightly flour-dusted or oiled worktop. Hold down one end with your hand and use the other hand to pull and stretch out the dough away from you. Gather the dough back into a ball again, give it a quarter turn, then repeat the stretching and gathering. As you knead you'll notice the dough starts to feel pliable, then stretchy, then very elastic and silky smooth. Nearly all doughs need 10 minutes of thorough kneading.

To knead in a stand mixer, use a dough hook on the lowest speed and knead for about 5 minutes. While it's almost impossible to over-knead by hand (your arms will give out first), you can stretch the gluten beyond repair in a mixer, which can hamper the rise.

To test if the dough has been kneaded enough, stretch a small piece between your fingers to a thin, translucent sheet. If it won't stretch or it tears easily, knead it for longer.

RISING AND PROVING

Place the dough in a moist, warm spot. A room temperature of 20–24°C is ideal – if the room is too hot, the yeast will grow too rapidly and the dough will become distorted (and maybe develop a slight aftertaste); too cool and the yeast develops more slowly (although this can give a richer flavour and chewier crumb). Proving is the last period of rising prior to baking, after shaping a bread dough. The time this takes depends on the temperature of the dough, and how lively your yeast is. To test whether the dough is well proved, gently prod it: if it springs back, it's not ready; if it returns to its original state fairly slowly, or if there's a very slight dent left, it's ready.

KNOCKING BACK BREAD DOUGH

Knocking back or punching down risen dough usually happens after rising and before shaping and proving. It breaks up the large gas bubbles that have formed within it to make smaller, finer bubbles that expand more evenly during baking, causing a more even rise. Use your knuckles to punch down the dough. Some bakers fold or flop the dough over on itself a few times.

PERFECTING A BREAD CRUST

First, make sure the oven is thoroughly heated, so the dough quickly puffs (called 'oven-spring') and then sets evenly.

For a crisp upper crust, create a burst of steam to keep the surface of the bread moist, helping the bread to rise easily. Once the surface has set, the moisture evaporates, leaving a crisp finish. To create the steam, put an empty roasting tin on the floor of the oven as it heats up. Then, immediately as you put in the unbaked loaf, pour cold water or throw a handful of ice cubes into the hot tin. Close the door to trap in the steam.

For a crisp base, put a baking sheet or baking stone in the oven to heat up. Then carefully transfer your loaf onto the hot baking sheet or stone for baking.

INSPIRE ME...

Use this visual index when you need inspiration for a bake by type or special diet, or when you specifically want a judge's recipe to impress. Note that, unless they contain gelatine leaves, sweet bakes tend anyway to be vegetarian, so we've separated out savoury vegetarian recipes only into a category of their own.

BISCUITS

Cherry Blossom Shortbreads (p.59)

Dairy-free Mango Ice-cream Sandwiches (p.115)

George's Kourabiethes (p.252)

Hamantaschen (p.84)

Paul's Caramel Biscuit Bars (p.219)

Paul's Jammy Biscuits (p.93)

St Clement's Squares (p.245)

BREADS

Brunch Pikelets (p.52)

Feta, Grape & Fennel Focaccia (p.185)

Feta, Oregano & Sundried Tomato Knots (p.141)

Mincemeat & Marzipan Couronne (p.263)

BREADS *CONTINUED*

Panettone (p.239)

Paul's Ciabatta Breadsticks (p.199)

Pumpkin Rolls (p.167)

Semlor (p.37)

Super-seeded Soda Bread (p.70)

Wild Garlic Flatbreads (p.81)

Winter No-knead Loaf (p.255)

CAKES (LARGE)

Amanda's Lemon & Elderflower Palette Cake (p.151)

Banana, Tahini & Caramel Loaf (p.158)

Blackberry & Pear Crumble Cake (p.200)

Blackcurrant & Almond Cake (p.143)

Chigs's Mango & Coconut Upside Down Cake (p.74)

Chocolate & Raspberry Ruffle Wedding Cake (p.123)

Chocolate Hazelnut Torte (p.193)

Crystelle's Chai & Jaggery Cake (p.63)

CAKES (LARGE) *CONTINUED*

Dark Masala & Stout Christmas Cake (p.225)

Double Chocolate Beetroot Devil's Food Cake (p.170)

Fig, Honey & Almond Cake (p.175)

Giuseppe's Celebration Cake (p.165)

Jairzeno's Chocolate Mint Cake (p.79)

Jürgen's Pear & Chocolate Charlotte (p.187)

Maggie's Orange & Lemon Cake (p.265)

Parsnip, Maple & Pecan Cake (p.216)

Peach Bellini Cake (p.90)

Pear & Walnut Cake (p.161)

Persian Love Cake (p.232)

Plum & Ginger Cake (p.195)

Primrose & Lemon Cake (p.34)

Prue's Malt Loaf (p.246)

Prue's Prinzregententorte (p.49)

Rochica's Strawberry-topped Cookies & Cream Cake (p.131)

CAKES (LARGE) *CONTINUED*

Ruby Grapefruit Bundt (p.54)

Strawberry & Clotted Cream Cake (p.120)

Toffee Apple Cake (p.179)

Tom's Blackberry & Apple Cake with Chai Buttercream (p.207)

CAKES (SMALL/INDIVIDUAL)

Cherry & Almond Friands (p.95)

Mini Hummingbird Cakes (p.68)

Mini Rolls (p.57)

Seville Orange Lamingtons (p.221)

GLUTEN-FREE BAKES

Fig, Honey & Almond Cake (p.175)

Parsnip, Maple & Pecan Cake (p.216)

Peach Bellini Cake (p.90)

Primrose & Lemon Cake (p.34)

JUDGES' RECIPES

Paul's Baklava (p.257)

Paul's Caramel Biscuit Bars (p.219)

Paul's Ciabatta Breadsticks (p.199)

Paul's Jammy Biscuits (p.93)

Prue's Malt Loaf (p.246)

Prue's Prinzregententorte (p.49)

Prue's Sablé Breton (p.137)

Prue's Vegan Sausage Rolls (p.173)

PUDS & DESSERTS

Apple & Quince Chaussons (p.203)

Apple, Pecan & Miso Caramel Tart (p.209)

Apricot Frangipane Traybake (p.117)

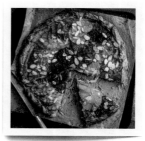

Blood Orange Galette (p.227)

Chocolate & Raspberry Ripple Cheesecake Brownies (p.100)

Chouxnuts (p.109)

Dairy-free Mango Ice-cream Sandwiches (p.115)

Date & Walnut M'Hanncha (p.235)

Freya's Piña Colada Custard Slice (p.103)

Gooseberry Roulade (p.98)

Jürgen's Pear & Chocolate Charlotte (p.187)

New York Cheesecake with Cranberries (p.236)

PUDS & DESSERTS *CONTINUED*

Passionfruit Soufflés (p.72)

Pecan Pie (p.190)

Prue's Prinzregententorte (p.49)

Prue's Sablé Breton (p.137)

Rhubarb & Custard Tart (p.41)

Spiced Apple Brandy Snap Baskets (p.249)

Tropical Pavlova (p.133)

SAVOURY

Asparagus, Ham & Cheese Danish Pastries (p.45)

Asparagus, Pea & Mint Quiche (p.111)

Beef & Potato Pies (p.241)

Brunch Pikelets (p.52)

Cheese, Ham & Piccalilli Pasties (p.127)

Feta, Grape & Fennel Focaccia (p.185)

Feta, Oregano & Sundried Tomato Knots (p.141)

Free-form Tomato Tart (p.105)

INSPIRE ME...

Lizzie's Sprout & Chestnut Tarts (p.231)

Paul's Ciabatta Breadsticks (p.199)

Pizza Bianca di Primavera (p.65)

Prawn & Pork Potstickers (p.259)

Prue's Vegan Sausage Rolls (p.173)

Pumpkin Rolls (p.167)

Spiced Lamb & Spinach Filo Pie (p.76)

Super-seeded Soda Bread (p.70)

Vegetable Samosas (p.181)

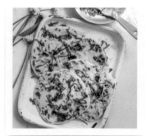

Wild Garlic Flatbreads (p.81)

Winter No-knead Loaf (p.255)

SWEET PASTRY & PÂTISSERIE

Apple & Quince Chaussons (p.203)

Apple, Pecan & Miso Caramel Tart (p.209)

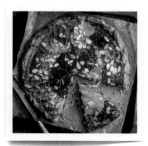

Blood Orange Galette (p.227)

Chouxnuts (p.109)

SWEET PASTRY & PÂTISSERIE *CONTINUED*

Cruffins (p.147)

Date & Walnut M'Hanncha (p.235)

Freya's Piña Colada Custard Slice (p.103)

Paul's Baklava (p.257)

Prue's Sablé Breton (p.137)

Rhubarb & Custard Tart (p.41)

Spiced Apple Brandy Snap Baskets (p.249)

TRAYBAKES

Apricot Frangipane Traybake (p.117)

Chocolate & Raspberry Ripple Cheesecake Brownies (p.100)

St Clement's Squares (p.245)

VEGAN

Chocolate & Raspberry Ruffle Wedding Cake (p.123)

Dark Masala & Stout Christmas Cake (p.225)

Double Chocolate Beetroot Devil's Food Cake (p.170)

Freya's Piña Colada Custard Slice (p.103)

INSPIRE ME...

VEGAN *CONTINUED*

Prue's Vegan Sausage Rolls
(p.173)

Wild Garlic Flatbreads (p.81)

VEGETARIAN SAVOURY

Prue's Vegan Sausage Rolls
(p.173)

Pumpkin Rolls (p.167)

Super-seeded Soda Bread
(p.70)

Vegetable Samosas (p.181)

Wild Garlic Flatbreads (p.81)

Winter No-knead Loaf (p.255)

INDEX

A

almond extract 25
almond paste see marzipan
almonds 27
  apricot frangipane
    traybake 117
  blackcurrant & almond
    cake 143–4
  cherry & almond friands 95
  fig, honey & almond cake 175
  George's kourabiethes 252
  mincemeat & marzipan
    couronne 263
  mini rolls 57–8
  parsnip, maple & pecan
    cake 216
  peach Bellini cake 90
  Persian love cake 232
  primrose & lemon cake 34–6
  ruby grapefruit bundt 54
  vegan marzipan 225–6
Amanda's lemon & elderflower
  palette cake 151–2
apples: apple & quince
  chaussons 203–4
  apple, pecan & miso caramel
    tart 209–10
  caramelised apples 249
  crisps 170
  dark masala & stout
    Christmas cake 225–6
  toffee apple cake 179–80
  Tom's blackberry & apple
    cake 207–8
apricots (dried): dark masala &
  stout Christmas cake 225–6
  spiced lamb & spinach
    filo pie 76
apricots (fresh): apricot
  frangipane traybake 117
aquafaba: vegan royal icing 226

asparagus: asparagus,
  ham & cheese Danish
    pastries 45–7
  asparagus, pea & mint
    quiche 111–12

B

bacon: beef & potato pies 241–2
  Lizzie's sprout & chestnut
    tarts 231
baking beans 18
baking tins 18–19
baking tips & techniques
  270–71
baklava 257–8
bananas: banana, tahini
  & caramel loaf 158
  mini hummingbird cakes 68
bavarois: chocolate 187–8
  pear 188
beef & potato pies 241–2
beer: beef & potato pies 241–2
  dark masala & stout
    Christmas cake 225–6
beetroot: double chocolate
  beetroot devil's food
    cake 170
bicarbonate of soda 23
biscuit sponge 131–2
biscuits 272
  cherry blossom
    shortbreads 59–60
  dairy-free mango ice-cream
    sandwiches 115–16
  George's kourabiethes 252
  Paul's caramel biscuit
    bars 219–20
  Paul's jammy biscuits 93–4
blackberries: blackberry &
  pear crumble cake 200
  buttercream 161–2

Tom's blackberry & apple
  cake 207–8
blackcurrant & almond
  cake 143–4
blenders 20
blind baking 270
blood orange galette 227
blueberries: tropical
  pavlova 133–4
bowls 19
brandy snap baskets 249–50
bread 272–3
  feta, grape & fennel
    focaccia 185
  pumpkin rolls 167
  super-seeded soda bread 70
  techniques 271
  wild garlic flatbreads 81
  winter no-knead loaf 255
breadsticks, Paul's ciabatta 199
broccoli: pizza bianca di
  primavera 65–6
brownies: chocolate &
  raspberry ripple
    cheesecake brownies 100
  chocolate & raspberry ruffle
    wedding cake 123–4
brunch pikelets 52
brushes, pastry 21
bundt, ruby grapefruit 54
buns: feta, oregano & sundried
  tomato knots 141–2
  semlor 37–8
butter 23
  rubbing in 270
buttercream 64, 132,
  143–4, 151–2
  blackberry 161–2
  chai-custard 207–8
  lemon 266
  see also icing

buttermilk 24
  brunch pikelets 52
  Chrystelle's chai & jaggery
    cake 63–4
  peach Bellini cake 90
  super-seeded soda bread 70

C

cakes 273–5
  Amanda's lemon &
    elderflower palette
    cake 151–2
  banana, tahini & caramel
    loaf 158
  blackberry & pear crumble
    cake 200
  blackcurrant & almond
    cake 143–4
  Chigs's mango & coconut
    upside down cake 74
  chocolate & raspberry ruffle
    wedding cake 123–4
  Chrystelle's chai & jaggery
    cake 63–4
  dark masala & stout
    Christmas cake 225–6
  double chocolate beetroot
    devil's food cake 170
  fig, honey & almond cake 175
  Giuseppe's celebration cake
    165–6
  Jairzeno's chocolate mint
    cake 79–80
  Maggie's orange & lemon
    cake 265–6
  panettone 239–40
  parsnip, maple & pecan
    cake 216
  peach Bellini cake 90
  pear & walnut cake 161–3
  Persian love cake 232
  plum & ginger cake 195
  primrose & lemon cake 34–6
  Prue's Prinzregententorte
    49–51
  Rochica's strawberry-topped
    cookies & cream cake 131–2

ruby grapefruit bundt 54
strawberry & clotted cream
  cake 120
toffee apple cake 179–80
Tom's blackberry & apple
  cake 207–8
see also small cakes;
  traybakes
candied peel & grapefruit
  syrup 54
caramel: apple, pecan & miso
  caramel tart 209–10
  banana, tahini & caramel
    loaf 158
  caramel filling 219–20
  caramelised apples 249
  caramelised pecans 209–10
  Chigs's mango & coconut
    upside down cake 74
  Paul's caramel biscuit
    bars 219–20
  praline 133–4, 193–4
  salted toffee frosting 180
  toffee apple cake 179–80
caramelised red onion
  chutney 174
cardamom: semlor 37–8
caster sugar 27–8
chai tea: chai-custard
  buttercream 207–8
  Chrystelle's chai & jaggery
    cake 63–4
  dark masala & stout
    Christmas cake 225–6
Chantilly cream 109–10,
  133–4, 166
  honey vanilla Chantilly
    cream 90
charlotte, Jürgen's pear
  & chocolate 187–8
chaussons, apple & quince
  203–4
cheese: asparagus, ham
  & cheese Danish
  pastries 45–7
  asparagus, pea & mint
    quiche 111–12

cheese, ham & piccalilli
  pasties 127
feta, grape & fennel
  focaccia 185
feta, oregano & sundried
  tomato knots 141–2
free-form tomato tart 105
Lizzie's sprout & chestnut
  tarts 231
Paul's ciabatta breadsticks
  199
pizza bianca di primavera 65–6
see also individual
  cheese names
cheesecakes: chocolate
  & raspberry ripple
  cheesecake brownies 100
New York cheesecake
  with cranberries 236
cherry & almond friands 95
cherry blossom
  shortbreads 59–60
chestnuts: Lizzie's sprout
  & chestnut tarts 231
chickpeas: spiced lamb
  & spinach filo pie 76
Chigs's mango & coconut
  upside down cake 74
chocolate 24
  chocolate & raspberry ripple
    cheesecake brownies 100
  chocolate & raspberry ruffle
    wedding cake 123–4
  chocolate bavarois 187–8
  chocolate drip 132
  chocolate ganache 50–51
  chocolate glaze 193–4
  chocolate hazelnut
    torte 193–4
  double chocolate beetroot
    devil's food cake 170
  ganache 170
  Giuseppe's celebration
    cake 165–6
  glaze 79–80
  Jairzeno's chocolate
    mint cake 79–80

Jürgen's pear & chocolate
  charlotte 187–8
melting 270
mini rolls 57–8
Paul's caramel biscuit
  bars 219–20
pecan pie 190
Prue's Prinzregententorte 49–51
Rochica's strawberry-topped
  cookies & cream cake 131–2
Seville orange
  lamingtons 221–2
tropical pavlova 133–4
choux pastry: chouxnuts
  109–10
Christmas cake, dark masala
  & stout 225–6
Chrystelle's chai & jaggery
  cake 63–4
chutney, caramelised red
  onion 174
ciabatta breadsticks 199
clotted cream: strawberry &
  clotted cream cake 120
cocoa powder 24
coconut: coconut & jaggery
  filling 63–4
  mini hummingbird cakes 68
  Seville orange lamingtons
    221–2
coconut cream: Chigs's mango
  & coconut upside down
  cake 74
  coconut & jaggery filling 63–4
  coconut vanilla frosting 123–4
  dairy-free mango ice-cream
    sandwiches 115–16
coconut milk: chocolate &
  raspberry ruffle wedding
  cake 123–4
  custard 103–4
coconut oil 24
conversion tables 268–9
cooling racks 19
cornflour 26
couronne, mincemeat
  & marzipan 263

cranberries: New York
  cheesecake with
  cranberries 236
  panettone 239–40
cream 24–5
  apple, pecan & miso
    caramel tart 209–10
  Chantilly cream 109–10,
    133–4, 166
  chocolate bavarois 187–8
  chocolate drip 132
  chocolate ganache 50–51
  chocolate glaze 193–4
  custard 41–2
  glaze 79–80
  gooseberry roulade 98
  honey vanilla Chantilly
    cream 90
  pear bavarois 188
  semlor 37–8
  strawberry & clotted cream
    cake 120
cream cheese: apple, pecan
  & miso caramel tart 209–10
  cream-cheese filling 216
  frosting 68, 79–80
  see also cheesecakes
cream of tartar 23
crème diplomat 249
crème fraîche 24
crème mousseline 138–9
crème pâtissière 165–6
crisps, apple & beetroot 170
croissants: cruffins 147–8
cruffins 147–8
crust, bread 271
cucumber: tzatziki 199
curd: lemon curd 151
  orange curd 221–2
  primrose & lemon curd
    34–6
custard: chai-custard
  buttercream 207–8
  Freya's piña colada custard
    slice 103–4
  rhubarb & custard tart 41–2
cutters, pastry 21

D
dairy-free mango ice-cream
  sandwiches 115–16
dairy-free spreads 23
Danish pastries: asparagus,
  ham & cheese 45–7
dark chocolate 24
dates: dark masala & stout
  Christmas cake 225–6
  date & walnut m'hanncha 235
decorations: apple & beetroot
  crisps 170
  chocolate 137–8
  chocolate crowns 49–51
  equipment 19
  sugar-paste flowers 265
devil's food cake, double
  chocolate beetroot 170
digital scales 20
dips: dipping sauce 259–60
  tzatziki 199
double chocolate beetroot
  devil's food cake 170
double cream 24
dough scrapers 19
dried fruit 25
  see also individual dried
    fruit names
dumplings: prawn & pork
  potstickers 259–60

E
egg whites 25
eggs 25
  brunch pikelets 52
  custard 41–2
elderflower syrup: Amanda's
  lemon & elderflower
  palette cake 151–2
equipment 18–22

F
fats 23–4
fennel: feta, grape &
  fennel focaccia 185
feta, grape & fennel
  focaccia 185

feta, oregano & sundried
    tomato knots 141–2
fig, honey & almond cake 175
fillings: caramel filling 219–20
    coconut & jaggery filling 63–4
    cream-cheese filling 216
    see also buttercream;
        ganache; icing
filo pastry: date & walnut
    m'hanncha 235
    Paul's baklava 257–8
    spiced lamb & spinach
        filo pie 76
flaky pastry 105
flatbreads, wild garlic 81
flour 26–7
    rubbing in 270
flowers, sugar-paste 265
focaccia: feta, grape
    & fennel 185
folding in 270
fondant icing sugar 28
food processors 20
frangipane: apricot frangipane
    traybake 117
free-form tomato tart 105
Freya's piña colada custard
    slice 103–4
friands, cherry & almond 95
frosted rosemary &
    redcurrants 226
frosting 68, 79–80
    coconut vanilla 123–4
    salted toffee 180
    see also icing
frosting fruit 270
fruit: frosting 270
    seasonal harvests 13
    see also individual
        fruit names

G
galette, blood orange 227
ganache 50–51, 170
garlic see wild garlic
génoise sponge 187
George's kourabiethes 252

ginger: plum & ginger
    cake 195
Giuseppe's celebration
    cake 165–6
glaze 79–80, 188, 193–4
gluten-free bakes 275
gluten-free flours 26
gooseberry roulade 98
granulated sugar 28
grapefruit: ruby grapefruit
    bundt 54
grapes: feta, grape &
    fennel focaccia 185

H
ham: asparagus, ham & cheese
    Danish pastries 45–7
    cheese, ham & piccalilli
        pasties 127
hamantaschen 84
hazelnuts 27
    chocolate hazelnut
        torte 193–4
    Giuseppe's celebration
        cake 165–6
    plum & ginger cake 195
honey: fig, honey & almond
    cake 175
    honey vanilla Chantilly
        cream 90
    Paul's baklava 257–8
hot water pastry 241–2
hummingbird cakes 68

I
ice-cream sandwiches,
    dairy-free mango
    115–16
icing 103–4, 109–10
    glaze 79–80, 188
    vegan royal icing 226
    see also buttercream;
        frosting
icing sugar 28
ingredients 23–8
Irish cream liqueur:
    buttercream 132

J
jaggery: Chrystelle's chai
    & jaggery cake 63–4
Jairzeno's chocolate mint
    cake 79–80
jam: cruffins 147–8
    hamantaschen 84
    Paul's jammy biscuits 93–4
    pineapple jam 103–4
    quick & easy berry jam 149
    raspberry jam 93, 109, 137–8
jam sugar 28
joconde sponge 57–8
jugs, measuring 20
Jürgen's pear & chocolate
    charlotte 187–8

K
kale: pizza bianca di
    primavera 65–6
kneading bread dough 271
knocking back, bread-
    making 271
kourabiethes 252

L
lactose-free cream 25
lamb: spiced lamb &
    spinach filo pie 76
lamingtons, Seville
    orange 221–2
lemon: Amanda's lemon
    & elderflower palette
    cake 151–2
    buttercream 266
    Maggie's orange & lemon
        cake 265–6
    primrose & lemon cake 34–6
    St Clement's squares 245
lentils: Prue's vegan sausage
    rolls 173–4
limes: Dairy-free mango
    ice-cream sandwiches 115–16
    tropical pavlova 133–4
    St Clement's squares 245
Lizzie's sprout & chestnut
    tarts 231

M

Maggie's orange & lemon cake 265–6
malt loaf 246
mangoes: Chigs's mango & coconut upside down cake 74
  dairy-free mango ice-cream sandwiches 115–16
  tropical pavlova 133–4
maple syrup: dark masala & stout Christmas cake 225–6
  parsnip, maple & pecan cake 216
  pecan pie 190
marzipan (almond paste): mincemeat & marzipan couronne 263
  semlor 37–8
  vegan marzipan 225–6
mascarpone cheese: mini rolls 57–8
  pizza bianca di primavera 65–6
melting chocolate 270
meringue: gooseberry roulade 98
  Maggie's orange & lemon cake 265–6
  meringue kisses 137
  tropical pavlova 133–4
m'hanncha, date & walnut 235
milk: chai-custard buttercream 207–8
  chocolate bavarois 187–8
  crème diplomat 249
  crème mousseline 138–9
  crème pâtissière 165–6
  custard 41–2
  pear bavarois 188
milk chocolate 24
mincemeat & marzipan couronne 263
mini hummingbird cakes 68
mini rolls 57–8
mint: asparagus, pea & mint quiche 111–12

Jairzeno's chocolate mint cake 79–80
miso: apple, pecan & miso caramel tart 209–10
mixers, electric 19–20
muffin tins 19
muscovado sugars 28
mushrooms: beef & potato pies 241–2
  Prue's vegan sausage rolls 173–4

N

New York cheesecake 236
nozzles, piping 21
nuts 27
  dark masala & stout Christmas cake 225–6
  see also individual nut names

O

olives: free-form tomato tart 105
  Paul's ciabatta breadsticks 199
onions: caramelised red onion chutney 174
oranges: blood orange galette 227
  St Clement's squares 245
  Maggie's orange & lemon cake 265–6
  rhubarb & custard tart 41–2
  Seville orange lamingtons 221–2

P

palette knives 21
panettone 239–40
parsnips: parsnip, maple & pecan cake 216
  vegetable samosas 181–2
passionfruits: passionfruit soufflés 72
  tropical pavlova 133–4
pastries 279
  apple & quince chaussons 203–4

asparagus, ham & cheese Danish pastries 45–7
  cheese, ham & piccalilli pasties 127
  cruffins 147–8
  date & walnut m'hanncha 235
  Freya's piña colada custard slice 103–4
  hamantaschen 84
  Paul's baklava 257–8
  Prue's vegan sausage rolls 173–4
  vegetable samosas 181–2
  see also pies; tarts
pastry 41–2, 111, 127, 190, 227, 231
  filo pastry 76, 235, 257–8
  flaky pastry 105
  hot water pastry 241–2
  pâte sucrée 209–10
  puff pastry 203
  rough puff pastry 103–4, 173
  sablé dough 137–8
  samosas 181–2
pastry cutters 21
pâte sucrée 209–10
Paul's baklava 257–8
Paul's caramel biscuit bars 219–20
Paul's ciabatta breadsticks 199
Paul's jammy biscuits 93–4
pavlova, tropical 133–4
peaches: peach & prosecco compôte 90
  peach Bellini cake 90
pears: blackberry & pear crumble cake 200
  date & walnut m'hanncha 235
  Jürgen's pear & chocolate charlotte 187–8
  pear & walnut cake 161–3
peas: asparagus, pea & mint quiche 111–12
pecan nuts 27
  apple, pecan & miso caramel tart 209–10
  caramelised pecans 209–10
  mini hummingbird cakes 68

parsnip, maple & pecan
cake 216
pecan pie 190
Persian love cake 232
piccalilli 128
cheese, ham & piccalilli
pasties 127
pies: beef & potato pies 241–2
spiced lamb & spinach
filo pie 76
pikelets, brunch 52
pineapple: mini hummingbird
cakes 68
pineapple jam 103–4
piping bags and nozzles 21
pistachios 27
dairy-free mango ice-cream
sandwiches 115–16
George's kourabiethes 252
mincemeat & marzipan
couronne 263
panettone 239–40
Paul's baklava 257–8
Persian love cake 232
pistachio paste 137–8
tropical pavlova 133–4
pizza bianca di primavera 65–6
plain flour 26
plum & ginger cake 195
pork: prawn & pork
potstickers 259–60
potatoes: beef & potato
pies 241–2
pizza bianca di
primavera 65–6
vegetable samosas 181–2
potstickers, prawn
& pork 259–60
praline: chocolate hazelnut
torte 193–4
pistachio praline 133–4
prawn & pork potstickers
259–60
primrose & lemon cake 34–6
Prinzregententorte 49–51
prosecco: peach & prosecco
compôte 90

prosecco syrup 90
Prue's malt loaf 246
Prue's Prinzregententorte
49–51
Prue's sablé Breton 137–9
Prue's vegan sausage
rolls 173–4
prunes: Prue's malt loaf
246
puff pastry 203
pumpkin rolls 167

Q
quiche: asparagus,
pea & mint 111–12
quince: apple & quince
chaussons 203–4

R
raisins: dark masala & stout
Christmas cake 225–6
panettone 239–40
Prue's malt loaf 246
raspberries: chocolate &
raspberry ripple
cheesecake brownies 100
chocolate & raspberry ruffle
wedding cake 123–4
jam 93, 109, 137–8, 149
redcurrants, candied 226
rhubarb & custard tart 41–2
ribbon stage 270
ricotta cheese: mini
rolls 57–8
rising, bread-making 271
Rochica's strawberry-
topped cookies &
cream cake 131–2
rolling pins 21
rolls, pumpkin 167
rosemary, frosted 226
rosewater: George's
kourabiethes 252
rough puff pastry 103–4, 173
roulade, gooseberry 98
royal icing, vegan 226
rubbing in 270

ruby grapefruit bundt 54
rum: dark masala & stout
Christmas cake 225–6
rye flour 26

S
sablé dough 137–8
St Clement's squares 245
salted toffee frosting 180
samosas, vegetable 181–2
sandwich tins 19
sausage rolls, Prue's
vegan 173–4
scales, digital 20
seasonal harvests 13
seeds: super-seeded
soda bread 70
self-raising flour 26
semlor 37–8
semolina flour 26
sesame caramel 158
Seville orange
lamingtons 221–2
shortbread: apricot
frangipane traybake 117
cherry blossom
shortbreads 59–60
Paul's caramel biscuit
bars 219–20
St Clement's squares 245
sieves 21–2
single cream 25
small cakes 275
cherry & almond friands 95
mini hummingbird cakes 68
mini rolls 57
Seville orange
lamingtons 221–2
see also cakes; traybakes
smoked salmon: brunch
pikelets 52
soda bread, super-seeded 70
soufflés, passionfruit 72
soured cream 25
blackberry & pear
crumble cake 200
caramel sauce 162–3

chocolate & raspberry
   ripple cheesecake
   brownies 100
New York cheesecake 236
salted toffee frosting 180
soya-based creams 25
soya milk: custard 103–4
spices, ground 25
spinach: spiced lamb &
   spinach filo pie 76
sponge: génoise sponge 187
   joconde sponge 57–8
   sponge fingers 187
sponge tins 19
sprouts: Lizzie's sprout
   & chestnut tarts 231
squash: vegetable
   samosas 181–2
stand mixers 20
stoneground flour 26
stout: dark masala & stout
   Christmas cake 225–6
strawberries: quick & easy
   berry jam 149
   Rochica's strawberry-topped
   cookies & cream cake
   131–2
   strawberry & clotted
   cream cake 120
streusel topping: apricot
   frangipane traybake 117
strong bread flour 26–7
sugar-paste flowers 265
sugar thermometers 22
sultanas: panettone 239–40
super-seeded soda bread 70
Swiss roll tins 19
syrup 28
   candied peel &
   grapefruit 54
   primrose & lemon 34–6
   prosecco 90
   vanilla 166

T
tahini: banana, tahini
   & caramel loaf 158

tart tins 19
tarts: apple, pecan & miso
   caramel tart 209–10
   asparagus, pea & mint
   quiche 111–12
   blind baking 270
   blood orange galette 227
   free-form tomato tart 105
   Lizzie's sprout & chestnut
   tarts 231
   pecan pie 190
   Prue's sablé Breton 137–9
   rhubarb & custard
   tart 41–2
   see also pastries; pies
toffee apple cake 179–80
tomatoes: feta, oregano
   & sundried tomato
   knots 141–2
   free-form tomato tart 105
   spiced lamb & spinach
   filo pie 76
Tom's blackberry & apple
   cake 207–8
torte, chocolate
   hazelnut 193–4
traybakes 280
   apricot frangipane
   traybake 117
   chocolate & raspberry ripple
   cheesecake brownies 100
   St Clement's squares 245
tropical pavlova 133–4
turntables, cake-decorating 19
tzatziki 199

U
upside down cake, Chigs's
   mango & coconut 74

V
vanilla 25
   coconut vanilla
   frosting 123–4
   custard 41–2
   honey vanilla Chantilly
   cream 90

Rochica's strawberry-
   topped cookies &
   cream cake 131–2
vanilla syrup 166
vegan marzipan 225–6
vegan recipes 280
vegan royal icing 226
vegan sausage rolls 173–4
vegetable samosas 181–2
vegetables: piccalilli 128
   seasonal harvests 13
   see also individual
   vegetable names
vegetarian recipes
   (savoury) 280

W
walnuts 27
   date & walnut
   m'hanncha 235
   Paul's baklava 257–8
   pear & walnut cake 161–3
   Prue's vegan sausage
   rolls 173–4
wedding cake, chocolate
   & raspberry ruffle 123–4
whipping cream 25
whisks 20
white chocolate 24
wholemeal flour 27
wild garlic flatbreads 81
wine: peach & prosecco
   compôte 90
   prosecco syrup 90
winter no-knead loaf 255

Y
yeast 28
yogurt: fig, honey &
   almond cake 175
   gooseberry roulade 98
   parsnip, maple & pecan
   cake 216
   primrose & lemon cake 34–6
tzatziki 199

This book is published to accompany the television series entitled *The Great British Baking Show*, broadcast on Channel 4 in 2021

The Great British Baking Show® is a registered trademark of Love Productions Ltd

Series produced for Channel 4 Television by Love Productions

The Great British Bake Off: A Bake for All Seasons

First published in The United States in 2021 by Sphere

10 9 8 7 6 5 4 3 2 1

ISBN 978-07515-8417-2

New recipes developed and written by:
Annie Rigg and Lisa Sallis
Commissioning Editor: Fiona Rose
Design & Art Direction: Smith & Gilmour
Project Editor: Judy Barratt
Copyeditor: Nicola Graimes
Editorial Assistant: Ruth Jones
Recipe Tester: Mitzie Wilson
Food Photographer: Ant Duncan
On-set GBBO Photography: Mark Bourdillon and Jack Stoneman
Food Stylist: Annie Rigg
Assistant Food Stylist: Lola Milne
Props Stylist: Hannah Wilkinson
Production Manager: Abby Marshall
Cover Design: Smith & Gilmour

Publisher's thanks to: Lochie Armstrong, Hilary Bird, Hugh Dowdall, Isabella Duncan, Jasper Duncan, Jon Leigh, Maddocks Farm Organics, Nordicware, Julia Parker, Anne Sheasby and Johnny and Sarah Stevenson.

Typeset in ITC Caslon and Neutraface
Colour origination by Born Group
Printed and bound in Canada

Papers used by Sphere are from well-managed forest and other responsible sources.

Sphere
An imprint of Little, Brown Book Group, Carmelite House, 50 Victoria Embankment, London EC4Y 0DZ
An Hachette UK Company
www.hachette.co.uk www.littlebrown.co.uk
Hachette Ireland
8 Castlecourt Centre, Castleknock, Dublin 15

WITH THANKS

Love Productions would like to thank the following people:
Executive Producer: Jenna Mansfield
Food & Challenge Producer: Katy Bigley
Home Economist: Becca Watson
Love Executives: Letty Kavanagh, Rupert Frisby, Kieran Smith, Joe Bartley
Publicists: Amanda Console, Shelagh Pymm
Comissioning Editor: Vivienne Molokwu

Thank you also to: Paul, Prue, Noel and Matt. *And to the bakers for their recipes:* Amanda, Chigs, Crystelle, Freya, George, Giuseppe, Jairzeno, Jürgen, Lizzie, Maggie, Rochica and Tom.